# Jesuit Studies

*Contributions to the arts and sciences*

*by members of the Society of Jesus*

# Jesuit Studies

---

The Churches and the Schools
FRANCIS X. CURRAN

Deception in Elizabethan Comedy
JOHN V. CURRY

Bishop Lancelot Andrewes
MAURICE F. REIDY

Master Alcuin, Liturgist
GERALD ELLARD

Theodore Dwight Woolsey
GEORGE A. KING

The Praise of Wisdom
EDWARD L. SURTZ

The Wagner Housing Act
TIMOTHY L. MCDONNELL

The Honor of Being a Man
EDWARD GANNON

The Presidential Election of 1880
HERBERT J. CLANCY

Work and Education
JOHN W. DONOHUE

Northern Parish
JOSEPH B. SCHUYLER

The Frontier Wage
BERNARD W. DEMPSEY

St. Thomas Aquinas on Analogy
GEORGE P. KLUBERTANZ

King and Church
W. EUGENE SHIELS

Catholics and the American Revolution
CHARLES H. METZGER

Diplomatic Protest in Foreign Policy
JOSEPH C. McKENNA

The Political Theory of John Wyclif
L. J. DALY

Papist Pamphleteers
THOMAS H. CLANCY

JESUIT STUDIES

# Conscience, Obligation, and the Law

THE MORAL BINDING POWER OF THE CIVIL LAW

*David Cowan Bayne*, S.J.

LOYOLA UNIVERSITY PRESS

Chicago, 1966

*to* M. B.

Corporation law and jurisprudence are actually poles apart. Some justification, or at least explanation, therefore, should probably be advanced for the presence of a corporation lawyer in the jurisprudential field. Some explanation, that is, beyond some years of work in philosophy and theology.

The real explanation, and motivation, for this present work is far more compelling than any amount of formal study in the field of jurisprudence. This book was written out of a persistent compulsion. A ten-year vexation, almost an irritation, left no choice. The question of the moral binding force of the civil law —the central concern in the philosophy of the law—after four hundred years of controversy, was still as unresolved as ever, if not more so. What is even more so? Majority opinion embraced the *lex pure poenalis*—the purely penal law—which holds that substantial areas of the civil law do not bind in conscience at all, to the author an incredible and intolerable holding.

Unite this vexed attitude with the training and outlook of the lawyer, and you will have considerable insight into the approaches of this volume. Two distinct offspring were bred of this union.

First, it was determined, after considerable reflection, that the scholarship, techniques, and mechanics of research in the field of jurisprudence would be suitably adapted, under the circumstances, to the lawyer's approach. Nothing so formal as a brief was to be attempted, but somewhat of the adversary's stance was assumed. A firm stand was taken. Arguments were set for proof. The plan of attack was outlined in the early stages. Short of a formal complaint, an answer, and a replication, the reasoning, posture, and procedures of counsel for the plaintiff were employed.

Second, since the penal-law doctrine has been, and is, in such pronounced possession, the position of an adversary recommended itself as far more stimulating and exhilarating than otherwise. A completely dispassionate treatment would undoubtedly have been the traditional approach of the jurisprudent, the ethician, or the moralist. *Lex pure poenalis*, therefore, was named defendant. Its arguments were advanced and its replies to the rebuttals presented in due order.

It should be remarked strongly, however, that the use of this device of the negative proceeding was employed only in the firm conviction that an unprejudiced treatment of both sides would result. This was an apparatus designed to ferret out every single argument pro and con. Merely because counsel for the plaintiff feels so determined that the civil law does bind in conscience does not mean that the reader may not, perhaps should not, hand down the decision for the defendant. It is certainly hoped that this method has not detracted from the objectivity of the presentation or, more important, dimmed the impartial scholarship at the base of both positions. This has been a sincere search for the truth of the matter. But most important, this treatise is an attempt to formulate a positive philosophy of the civil law, in spite of the negative approach of an adversary.

One further point should be noted, lest the reader risk acute schizophrenia from an incessant jumping from the body of the text to the footnotes. Let the reader rest in the knowledge that the footnotes have only two, and no more, burdens to bear. First, there is a formal citation to every document or authority relied upon. There is no collateral comment whatsoever in any footnote. This will gratify any wish, therefore, to consult the source directly. Second, since this study is meant to be exacting and meticulous in its scholarship, every translation is accompanied by the original, verbatim text. This will permit personal discovery and reprobation of any biased or prejudicial renderings. Beyond these two purposes, resort to the footnotes is unnecessary.

The Reverend Leo C. Brown, S.J., and William Francis Clark, Esquire, Thomas William Watkins, Esquire, and John J. Slavin, Esquire, all of the Michigan Bar, not only read the manuscript but aided immeasurably in criticism and evaluation. Fellow Jesuits John J. Kinsella and William L. Wade supported the venture along the way. Finally, gratitude should be expressed to Clotilda Gassner, Elizabeth Anderson Sposato, and longtime secretary Rosemary Lahey Mervenne.

DAVID C. BAYNE, S.J.

THE SCHOOL OF LAW
SAINT LOUIS UNIVERSITY
The Feast of Robert Cardinal Bellarmine, S.J.

# CONTENTS

---

xiii

PART ONE

---

# The Theories of the Law

*From Aquinas to Holmes*

In relation to those laws which enjoin only *positive duties* . . .
here I apprehend conscience is no farther concerned, than by directing
a submission to the penalty. . . . the obligation of the law seems
chiefly to consist in the penalty . . .
*William Blackstone*[1]


Human laws, whether enacted by magistrate or by church,
are necessary to be observed (I speak of such as are just and good),
but do not therefore in themselves bind the conscience.
*John Calvin*[2]


The will of the sovereign is law, because he has power to compel obedience
or punish disobedience, and for no other reason.
*Oliver Wendell Holmes, Jr.*[3]


It would be absurd to say that the penal law theory is responsible for the axiom,
"It is all right if you don't get caught,"
but it has an unwholesome relation to it, . . .
the consequences can be very harmful for the commonwealth.
*Matthew Herron*[4]

## CHAPTER I

# Moral Obligation or No

## *What Impact on Society?*

Each age in the history of mankind, one would like to think, has been fervently jealous of its traditions for high moral standards, for justice and order in the nation, for love and respect for the law. This age is no different, and the signs of incipient national decadence appearing in the communication arts, entertainment, domestic relations, and government—visible like beacons in the events surrounding the assassination of President Kennedy—have perhaps given rise to the marked resurgence of interest by lawyers, jurists, and moral theologians in the question so fundamental to the right order of society: Does the civil law bind in conscience?

At the core of any analytical and systematic treatment of the binding force of the civil law lies the highly controverted doctrine of *lex pure poenalis*, "the purely penal law." From its genesis in the 1200s, through Aquinas, Suarez, Bellarmine, and Blackstone, to the numerous commentators of the present day, this doctrine has elicited treatise after treatise and commentary after commentary, and rightly so. Although it is true that the theory has been almost the exclusive concern of Roman Catholic theologians and jurists, others (for example, Calvin, Blackstone, and even Holmes in passing) have touched on the subject.

There is a tendency to exaggerate the practical implications of the doctrine. It would certainly not undermine all respect for law and right order. Yet it cannot be denied that its teachings could and should have a profound influence on the practical mores of a nation, possibly, in the long run, a seriously harmful one. It is irresistible to conjecture that the lamentable state of tax collection, at least among the educated, in the solidly Catholic countries of Italy and France is quite possibly referable to the doctrine.

By way of a tentative working description, with an exact definition and delineation later, it could be said that the doctrine of *lex pure poenalis* states in its simplest form: "A merely penal law is one that obliges subjects to do what is prescribed, not under pain of sin, but under penalty of having to submit to whatever punishment is inflicted for violation."[5] One does not commit a moral fault if he disobeys a merely penal law, but according to most moralists he would be bound in conscience not to resist the imposition of the penalty incurred. There is moral obligation, not to the law itself, but to the sanction only.

The case must not be overstated, however. The "purepenalists"[6] concede a moral obligation in most laws, place some obligation of some kind in all laws, and maintain that only the purely penal laws—as numerous as they may be—do not bind in conscience. These classifications are for later elaboration.

The term "civil law" is used in contradistinction primarily to the ecclesiastical. But it also excludes the divine and natural —not the common law or the criminal, both of which it encompasses. It obviously also includes the law of the "civil-law" countries of the Justinian Code and the Code Civil of Napoleon.

The standard penal-law examples are local police regulations, hunting and fishing laws, statutes and ordinances regulating the speed and conduct of motor vehicles, mendicancy, military conscription, laws restricting the import and sale of alcoholic beverages, those prohibiting consumption of liquor by minors, import duties, various forms of taxes (especially sales and luxury), and the like.

At the outset let it be understood that in a matter so controverted there could scarcely be unanimity. There is not only conflict between the advocates and opponents of the theory but also among the proponents themselves. When, therefore, a position or thesis is attributed to the "penal-law lawyers" *passim* throughout this treatise, it means only that a representative group so teaches—not that vehement opposition even within the school is totally absent or that qualifications and exceptions are not to be found. This is an important caution, but it will not be repeated *toties quoties.* Thus, the examples given would be accepted by a respectable majority of the penal-law lawyers, perhaps rejected by a very few. This is true of the tax examples to follow shortly.

This doctrine of *lex pure poenalis,* moreover, has been espoused by the overwhelming majority of moral theologians (not merely by Blackstone, Calvin, Holmes, and others) as a practical norm of daily conduct for the people. Twenty-five years ago, the respected moralist Güenechea said: "Among the recent writers there is scarcely a moralist or canonist of any name who rejects the doctrine of the purely penal law."[7] "The extrinsic evidence [the number of proponents] is overwhelming on the side of the penal law."[8]

## The Impact Illustrated

Perhaps the most cogent intimation of the far-reaching implications of the doctrine lies in a cursory analysis of the recent adjudications of the federal courts of the United States, as set off against the pronouncements of penal-law lawyers.

Among those areas of law where the theory is admittedly applicable, the most rewarding is the field of taxation. From the standpoints of clarity and relative certainty of applicability, and of freedom from qualification, mitigation, and exception, it is unequaled. For this reason, examples involving federal excise taxes will introduce this complex and delicate matter. It should be borne in mind that the introductory concepts of the purely penal law are tentative and at best broadly descriptive.

In all the cases to follow, the federal courts have handed down their decisions in favor of the Government. To the taxpayer in each of these fact situations, the penal-law lawyer would have counseled that the taxpayer had had, and would have in the future in similar cases, full in the face of federal opinions, no moral obligation to pay. Either as moralist or canonist, in treatises or commentaries, as confessor to penitent or adviser in personal guidance, the "merepenalist"[9] would say that one might not lie but nonetheless need not pay. Consistent with collateral honesty and integrity, there is no need to volunteer a declaration or refrain from taking any steps which would conceal the taxable event and its amount from the Government. Only remember, of course, that there is a conscience obligation to pay the tax, as well as any penalties attaching thereto, upon apprehension and conviction.

### THE MEREPENALISTS

A satisfactory conspectus of this teaching could be achieved by consulting three accepted treatises: those of Davis, Aertnys-Damen, and Genicot-Salsmans.

Henry Davis, S.J., one of the more prominent moralists of England, in speaking of the obligation of paying taxes, categorically states:

> In England it is certainly penal only, because the executive exercises considerable vigilance, inflicts heavy fines, and imposes heavy direct taxes to recoup losses. It appears unreasonable to expect good citizens, who certainly are in the minority [sic], to be obliged in conscience to pay taxes, whereas so many others openly repudiate

the moral obligation, if there is one. It seems unjust that good people should feel an obligation to be mulcted and to pay readily, in order to balance the evasions of so many.[10]

Davis adds an enlightening summary statement. "The opinions of other authors writing for their respective countries cannot be universally adopted for this country. Lehmkuhl and Marres take very strict views for Germany and Holland; and Gousset for France; while Genicot, Waffelaert, Bucceroni, Palmieri, Vermeersch, and Crolly consider the law penal."[11]

Aertnys-Damen writes: "Indeed according to some authors all tax laws could be said to be merely penal."[12] Of these Aertnys-Damen lists Genicot, Biederlack, Bucceroni, Palmieri, Sabetti, Berardi, and Crolly.

Genicot and Salsmans maintain that this is the rule. "More probably tax laws such as are today in effect in many countries are in essence merely penal. Wherefore they only oblige either to the payment of the tax in the beginning or to peaceful submission to the penalty or fine imposed on delinquents."[13]

Healy, whose instruction is almost universal in Catholic colleges across the United States, would presumably remove any moral binding force from such laws. Thus, in regard to customs duties, Healy counsels the college students:

> If asked by a customs official, "Anything to declare?" I may answer, "No," even though I have several thousand dollars' worth of taxable articles. [Healy here has resort to a second ethical principle, the broad mental reservation.] My answer means: "I have no dutiable goods that I wish to reveal for taxation. It may be that I actually have such goods on my person. I need not expose them to your view. It is your duty to discover them." In acting thus, however, one must beware of scandal.[14]

In this example Healy presupposes the penal-law nature of the customs tax, or the obligation to declare could not be avoided merely by a broad mental reservation. It should be of some interest that the author encountered an embarrassingly pertinent instance of what the opponents of the doctrine refer to as the scandal of the purely penal law. In a radio debate (KMOX, St. Louis, September 1960) with the Reverend Frank Kellogg, pastor of the Maplewood Baptist Church in St. Louis, on the subject of the religious issue in the 1960 presidential campaign, Mr. Kellogg, citing Healy, evinced sincere and justifiable shock. In the light of the contents of this study, the difficulty experienced in response can readily be imagined.

The editors of the *American Ecclesiastical Review* (a popular semilearned journal for day-to-day guidance of the parish priest) made two sweeping endorsements of penal law in a case of conscience submitted to them for solution. "The theologians of our country, Kenrick, Konings, Sabetti, hold that our civil laws may be regarded as penal only . . . civil law . . . granting it is just, cannot be said to bind under sin."[15]

Lest the picture appear completely one-sided, consult Land, a modern Jesuit moralist, who, treating specifically of the tax question, concludes firmly, "Tax laws do bind in conscience."[16]

### Evasion at the Club

*Vitter v. United States*

Albert L. Vitter, Jr., pursuant to his desire to become a regular member of the New Orleans Country Club, purchased on February 4, 1957, one share of the capital stock of the club at a cost of fifty-six hundred dollars plus brokerage. It was a requisite to regular membership that each member be a registered holder, although not necessarily an owner, of one share of stock in the club. It was somewhat unusual that N.O.C.C. was traded in the New Orleans over-the-counter market and could be owned by a nonmember. A second requisite to membership was payment of an initiation fee directly to the club. The stock was assessable and, in and of itself, offered no privileges whatsoever to the holder.

In the final event, Vitter was faced with paying an excise tax in the amount of twenty percent of any amount paid as an initiation fee to any social, athletic, or sporting club or organization,[17] irrespective of the organization or person to whom the fee was paid.[18]

In resisting the imposition of the excise tax, Taxpayer was unsuccessful in the district court.[19] On appeal the Fifth Circuit with one dissent affirmed the district court and concluded:

> The one thing in this case as obvious as a water hazard is that for Taxpayer to achieve the status of a regular member of NOCC, he had to hold a share of stock. . . . In a real sense, then, this, in the words of the statute, was "required as a condition precedent to membership." 22 U.S.C.A. § 4242(b).[20]

It has in fact been uniformly held that payments made to former owners of stock to comply with the club's requirement that a member be a stockholder are within the broad definition of "initiation fees."[21]

In a later case on similar but simpler facts, a member of the Brookhaven Country Club in Dallas was taxed on his initiation fee although it was denominated a "voluntary contribution."[22]

Thus, the federal courts both district and circuit are clear that persons who wish to enjoy the privileges of such athletic clubs are indebted to the Government in the amount of the twenty-percent excise tax. Yet the penal-law moralist would in future similar cases counsel that they are not morally bound to pay, may take all legitimate means to evade such a tax, and are held morally only to the payment upon apprehension. The word "evade" is used in contradistinction to legitimate avoidance within the justifiable interpretation of the Code.

### Down Town Ass'n. of the City of N.Y. v. United States

In the year 1860, a group of successful business and professional men formed the Down Town Association of the City of New York (concededly today the most exclusive) to furnish "to persons engaged in commercial and professional pursuits in the City of New York, facilities for social intercourse, and such accommodations as are required during the intervals of business while at a distance from their residences . . ."[23]

As the years passed, all other activities of the club gradually ceased until the noonday luncheon with an occasional cocktail was the only purpose served by the clubhouse at 62 Pine Street.

Membership in the club was obtained by application, election, and payment of an entrance fee of three hundred dollars (in the late fifties) and yearly dues. The sole restriction on membership was a limitation in number. The members, although predominantly lawyers, represented numerous occupations.

During the five-year period under observation, taxes were paid in the amount of $129,090.87. The membership contested this payment.

In affirming the district court's decision for the Government, the Second Circuit adverted to the fact that there was no doubt considerable business transacted during the luncheon hour at the club. The opinion countered, however, in the words of the lower court, with the conclusion that the club's "only reason for being is to afford those members a facility for enjoying lunch in convenient and pleasant surroundings and with company attractive to them. We call such a purpose altogether social. Plaintiff has no 'different or predominant' purpose required by the regulation."[24] The court in referring to a treasury regulation concluded that the social features were a material purpose of the organization and not subordinate and merely incidental to the active furtherance of a different and predominant purpose.[25]

That such a tax question is of frequent occurrence can readily be realized by some reflection on the multitude of similar organizations and the many instances that have gone as far as litigation. Nor has litigation been confined to the rank and file. Witness: The Yondotega Club, Detroit; Downtown Club, Dallas; Quinnipiack Club, New Haven; and the Detroit Club.[26]

## Is Gambling Taxable?

*Merou Grotto, Inc. v. United States*

The Merou Grotto, Incorporated, is a local subdivision of a Masonic group known as the Mystic Order of Veiled Prophets of the Enchanted Realm, located in Lafayette, Indiana. Membership in the Grotto is limited to Master Masons in good standing. It is an Indiana nonprofit corporation. In addition to its humanitarian activities, the Grotto sponsors a number of social functions. Among the latter was a weekly lottery under the name of M.G.I. Tickets for the lottery were a dollar each. The sales were made to the general public. Gross receipts for the three-year tax period totaled $348,400. Charitable donations for the period averaged 9.7 percent per year of the profits.

The commissioner of internal revenue made an assessment in September 1955 against the Grotto in the sum of $79,740.70 for wagering excise taxes[27] for the period of March 1, 1953, through August 31, 1954. This comprised taxes of $33,551.20, the hundred-percent penalty of $33,551.20 for willful failure to account for and pay over the tax, the twenty-five-percent penalty of $8,387.81 for failure to file a return, and interest of $4,250.49.

This assessment Merou Grotto contested, claiming an excise-tax exemption under statutory provisions which exempt any drawing conducted by an income-tax-exempt organization.

The district court in holding for the United States Government stated:

> It is evident . . . that the drawings, which were held among the general public and with nonmember soliciting agents, are not conducted to raise money for charitable or social welfare purposes. . . . Almost the entire proceedings of the drawing were used for the general operating expenses of the Grotto. . . . The entire lottery was carried on in the manner of an operation conducted for profit, rather than in a manner similar to a drawing occasionally conducted by a charitable, religious, or other nonprofit organization.[28]

The courts have consistently held that an organization is not exempt from the excise tax which engages in a lottery or pool for profit of such scope and duration that the purpose for which the income-tax exemption was granted becomes secondary in importance to the business of gambling.[29] The *Grotto* case is only one of several recent instances of a similar nature.[30]

### THE IMPACT PINPOINTED

These reflections and other tax samplings[31] should tell several things about the importance and timeliness of an intensive analysis of the question of the binding power of the civil law and of the concept of the purely penal law:

1 Among the various classes of laws regarded as penal, the field of taxation in its many forms is probably the most impressive, since there is apparently no middle ground between clear-cut denial of any moral obligation to pay on the part of the penal-law lawyer and the equally determined conviction of the federal courts and the Government that the taxes are due and owing according to the law. Whereas distinctions, mitigations, and qualifications might arise in other areas of the penal law, this is less true of taxation.

2 Although taxation is only one example and the excise taxes levied on (a) social and athletic clubs and (b) wagering such as lotteries are only a minute part of the total tax field, every citizen early in his career is faced, either as an individual or in a group, with the moral question of such taxes. Such clubs dot every city and town. The multiform variations of a lottery, drawing, or raffle are commonplace.

3 The many prominent cases which result in actual litigation and are easy to detect are indicative of the many other taxable enterprises—lesser, possibly, but which nonetheless pose the question of moral obligation to the participants.

4 The taxable amount actually involved is not the chief criterion of the importance of the matter, especially where the

young are concerned. More important is the attitude of mind developed in solving such questions according to the theory of the penal law and the effect that such solutions will have on the respect for all law, especially the important areas affecting the common good, serious rights of others, fundamental justice, the criminal code, marriage, and familial obligations.

5 Irrespective of all considerations of practicality, the theory itself should be studied thoroughly and accepted or rejected with finality.

6 Fundamental to the right order of the nation is the proposition that this right order, in tax collection or anything else, can never be achieved by the external force of the police power but must in the end be almost wholly dependent on the self policing of a citizenry conscious of moral values and the moral obligation of law. The Internal Revenue Service, for example, could not expect to police all the areas under its surveillance.

## The Thesis: The Civil Law Obliges in Conscience

It is the firm thesis of this study that the civil law, duly enacted and promulgated by a properly constituted state, induces in the citizenry a conscience obligation to obedience.

In the process of reaching this conclusion, it will be demonstrated in successive stages that the purely penal law is (1) an historical happenstance, (2) nonexistent in fact, (3) founded on premises intrinsically inconsistent with the proper notion of law, and (4) designed to meet problems which can be solved by traditional principles of law and moral theology. This fourth point is particularly important to the reader in forming his attitude, preconceived albeit, as he embarks on his way through this book. It should mollify the apparent hardness of the thesis to know that the application of tried-and-true ethics and morality will achieve the very result so earnestly sought by the purepenalists. Chapter IX will lay out eight avenues, notably that of equity, which lead to the same conclusion—no moral obligation—yet

follow different, but approved, routes. Chapter X should soften
any last harshness.

The problems posed by these propositions and the thesis set
for proof will find treatment in the chapters named for the following divisions:

# Lex Pure Poenalis

## The Concept

The intensive analysis of the penal law stands poised midway between the natural-philosophical and moral-theological concepts that precede it, and the practical application to action in the civil law and the day-to-day conduct of the lawyer and client, the priest and penitent, that follows it. There are, therefore, certain postulates[1] that must be assumed if the specific question is to be treated in detail: (1) There is a God. (2) His plan of the total governance of the universe was embodied from all eternity in the eternal law. (3) God created man. (4) In this man there is a human nature. (5) This human nature is the same in all men. (6) Through and in this human nature God's eternal law is efficaciously promulgated, and this is the natural law. Jacques Maritain expresses this thought appositely:

> I am taking it for granted that you also admit that man is a being gifted with intelligence, and who, as such, acts with an understanding of what he is doing, and therefore with the power to determine for himself the ends which he pursues. On the other hand, possessed of a nature, being constituted in a given, determinate fashion, man

15

obviously possesses ends which correspond to his natural constitution and which are the same for all—as all pianos, for instance,
whatever their particular type and in whatever spot they may be,
have as their end the production of certain attuned sounds. If they
don't produce these sounds, they must be tuned, or discarded as
worthless. But since man is endowed with intelligence and determines his own ends, it is up to him to put himself in tune with the
ends necessarily demanded by his nature. This means that there is,
by very virtue of human nature, *an order or a disposition which human reason can discover and according to which the human will
must act in order to attune itself to the necessary ends of the human
being. The unwritten law, or natural law, is nothing more than that.*[2]

(7) Among the precepts of the natural law is the mandate that
man obey the ordinations of the duly constituted authority.

## WHAT IS LAW?

Building on the foundation of these postulates and yet obviously fundamental to the concept of the purely penal law is the
notion of law itself. The definition of Aquinas is followed by
most moralists: "an ordinance of reason for the common good,
promulgated by him who has the care of the community."[3]
Suarez (1548-1617), the greatest Jesuit theologian to the present day, who has without exception the fullest treatment on the
subject of the philosophy of law and *lex pure poenalis*, adopts the
Thomistic definition.[4] The Jesuit Vermeersch, probably the foremost moralist of the twentieth century, has very little substantial
difference: "Law is every norm by which a legislator, using his
power of ruling society, that is, exercising his jurisdiction, intends efficaciously to prescribe a rule for his subjects."[5] He
further pertinently remarks: "There is found in every law some
kind of an ordination of the subjects to the common good. The
legislator determines a certain order according to which either
acts are to be done or matters disposed in accordance with the
goal of society. The legislator moreover intends that this be an
efficacious ordination."[6] Blackstone, in his *Commentaries*—

which inevitably reflected the Blackstone of the thirteenth century Henry of Bracton,[7] the lawyer-priest through whom all English law "passed as through a funnel"[8]—rephrases the traditional definition: "a rule of civil conduct prescribed by the supreme power in a state, commanding what is right and prohibiting what is wrong."[9]

The consensus of these definitions and of the traditional thinking resolves law into four essentials: (1) a code of conduct whether denominated an "ordinance" or "rule of civil conduct" or "rule for subjects," (2) promulgated with efficacious intent, whether expressed as a command, a prescription, an intention, or promulgation, (3) by a God-given authority—the "supreme power in a state," "a legislator with jurisdiction," "the duly constituted state," (4) just and reasonable, commanding what is right and prohibiting wrong.

### The Sanction of the Law

At the conclusion of the primary lawmaking process, the lawmaker generally issues a second command which prescribes a sanction for violation or observance of the law itself. The several nuances which distinguish sanction from obligation, from motive, and even from the purposes of the sanction itself, have serious relevance to the criticism and analysis of the penal-law doctrine.

Etymologically, *sanction* signifies according to Webster "to render sacred or inviolable." This signification reflects the purpose of the sanction rather than the sanction itself. In essence sanction is a reward given or penalty imposed by the lawmaker at some time subsequent either to obedience or to disobedience by the subject. Most commentators incorporate in the definition of sanction, which is limited strictly to the imposition of reward or penalty, one or more of its purposes, since a knowledge of the purpose of something is generally conducive to a more exact understanding of the essence defined. Thus does Vermeersch in his definition: "Thus, sanction is the infliction of punishment which is added over and above the law in order to bolster the law or to compensate for the harm to society which is the effect of the violation of the law."[10] Such inclusion is a praiseworthy practice but should not thereby lead to a confusion of the sanction with its purposes. These purposes could be expressed as fourfold: (1) restoration of the order disturbed by the violation of the law, (2) vindication of the honor of the state, (3) prevention of violation through the example to others, (4) punishment of the convicted malefactor.

*Only 4th!*

The sanction, as reward or punishment, may follow (1) necessarily or (2) accidentally. The loss or attainment of the very end and goal of the law itself is the necessary sanction. Thus, peace of mind is the automatic reward for obedience to the natural law, and the opposite follows disobedience. The accidental sanction is superadded as, for example, fine and imprisonment for fornication.

Above all, sanction must not be confused with motive. Many reasons may converge to induce the citizen either to obedience or to disobedience. No one of these motives, and this is an important distinction, is the sanction itself, either necessary or accidental. It is possible, even probable, that the contemplation or the reflection on the possible subsequent imposition of the sanction may be one of the motives, but the sanction proper remains consequent on obedience or disobedience and is the actual reward or penalty.

Of compelling importance is the realization that sanction is distinct from the law. The law is valid and complete, true law, when the legislature efficaciously promulgates a just, reasonable rule of conduct.

Whether the end and purpose of the law, the necessary sanction, is attained or not does not affect the validity of the law. The lawgiver has passed a binding law upon promulgation, and neither he nor his subjects are required to await the attainment or loss of its end (for example, the improvement of traffic conditions consequent on lowering the vehicular speed limit) before pronouncing on its validity.

The accidental sanction is even more remote from the essence of the law. In fact, the lawgiver need not append any accidental sanction—fine or punishment—if the circumstances so warrant. In the words of the Court of Appeals of Georgia: "under the Code definition of a crime, neither the imposition of a fine nor sentence of imprisonment is essential to make the act a crime. Penalty is no part of the crime but is simply a consequence flowing from its commission."[11] The proper essence of law is complete without reference to the accomplishment of any of the four purposes of the accidental sanction. If it is argued that some sanction is required as a supplement to the law, this requisite is achieved by the necessary sanction, which remains nonetheless outside the essence.

> While the term "law" is generally understood, and is quite generally defined, as "a rule of civil action prescribed by the supreme power in a state commanding what is right and prohibiting what is wrong," there has been a good deal of discussion as to whether such rule is of any force or effect unless there be a penalty, or sanction, affixed. But we regard much of this discussion as academic, and are persuaded that either the Congress or the Legislature may make a perfectly valid statute a rule of action, without providing any penalty or sanction.[12]

Webster's definition concurs with this commentary of the Supreme Court of Iowa and supports the traditional analysis of the distinction between law and sanction: "the detriment, loss of reward or other coercive intervention, annexed to a violation of a law as a means of enforcing the law."

In general, therefore, the citizen governed by law faces four theoretical stages in his approach to a given law: (1) the law itself as promulgated, (2) reflection on the motives, (3) observance or violation, and (4) the sanction.

## Does the Law Oblige?

The obligation intrinsic to the law is a moral necessity, laid upon the will of the citizen, constraining him to perform or to refrain from performing some specific act. This command he can, however, physically refuse to follow. Suarez, in treating the nature of obligation, is less detailed and simply refers to it as a moral necessity imposed on the subject by the law. "Concerning law, however, properly so called, and with respect to a rational creature, although it is settled that it does not induce simply that [instinctive natural] necessity [of brute animals], the question is whether it induces that moral necessity which is called obligation."[13] To this he adds: "Nevertheless it first must be said that there is no law properly so called which does not induce obligation, that is, a certain necessity of acting or not acting."[14]

Obligation, from the Latin *ligare* (as also is *lex*, "law"), "to bind," gains its efficacy, as will be seen, from the command (1) of the duly constituted authority (2) to adopt a determined means to a necessary end, the common good.

Confusion between obligation and sanction has engendered much of the difficulty in approaching the problem of the penal law. Meditation on the matter indicates indisputably that obligation is antecedent to violation or observance, because it concerns the precedent moral necessity of a choice; and sanction is subsequent, a consequence, reward or punishment for obedience or disobedience. Obligation, therefore, is markedly distinct from motive and sanction, a matter for later fuller discussion.

### *"Hobbes, Holmes and Hitler"*[15]

The long history of the school of legal realism has demonstrated with varying degrees of candor a willingness to place no obligation of a moral nature behind the law but to rest its efficacy solely in the force of the strong arm of the state—which is in fact a motive, not an obligation. The men who grouped themselves around Hobbes and Bentham, the predecessors of Holmes

and his followers, certainly placed the authority of the government in the power of the dominant group. There is no moral
"ought," only compulsion. Holland characterized the period:

> That which gives validity to a legal right is, in every case, the
> force which is lent to it by the State. Anything else may be the occa-
> sion, but is not the cause, of its obligatory character.[16]

With the advent of Oliver Wendell Holmes, Jr., came the
full flower of the school and the most unabashed and forthright
reference of the authority of the state to physical force.[17]
Holmes, whom Jerome Frank described as the completely adult
jurist,[18] spoke of law in these terms:

> I know that much has been written on this subject, but taking law
> as what I call it in *American Banana Co. v. United Fruit Co.*, 213
> U. S. 347, 356: "a statement of the circumstances in which the pub-
> lic force will be brought to bear upon men through the courts,"
> ...[19]

Of all Holmes's statements concerning the nature of man—hence
indicative of the essence of any law that Holmes would conceive
as governing a man—the most categorical and outspoken pronouncement places man on the level of the brute:

> I only mean that when one thinks coldly I see no reason for attrib-
> uting to man a significance different in kind from that which be-
> longs to a baboon or to a grain of sand.[20]

Highly consonant with Holmes's equation of man to the brute
was his attitude toward sin, which of course is nothing other
than the refusal to obey a command binding in conscience: "I
should be glad if we could get rid of the whole moral phraseology which I think has tended to distort the law. In fact even
in the domain of morals I think that it would be a gain, at least
for the educated, to get rid of the word and notion Sin."[21]

The sole purpose that Holmes saw in the study of the law
was "prediction, the prediction of the incidence of the public
force through the instrumentality of the courts."[22]

> Sovereignty is a form of power, and the will of the sovereign is law, because he has power to compel obedience or punish disobedience, and for no other reason. The limits within which his will is law, then, are those within which he has, or is believed to have, power to compel or punish.[23]

The deeper one penetrates into the writings of Holmes, the clearer it becomes how completely convinced he was that force was the sole base—one might even say "essence"—of the law. "I used to say, when I was young, that truth was the majority vote of that nation that could lick all others."[24] One could see the practical expression of this philosophy in Holmes's commentary on the conduct of the German nation in World War I.

> I don't believe that it is an absolute principle or even a human ultimate that man always is an end in himself—that his dignity must be respected, etc. We march up a conscript with bayonets behind to die for a cause he doesn't believe in. And I feel no scruples about it. Our morality seems to me only a check on the ultimate domination of force, just as our politeness is a check on the impulse of every pig to put his feet in the trough. When the Germans in the late war disregarded what we called the rules of the game, I don't see there was anything to be said except: we don't like it and shall kill you if we can. So when it comes to the development of a *corpus juris* the ultimate question is what do the dominant forces of the community want and do they want it hard enough to disregard whatever inhibitions may stand in the way.[25]

As years passed, Holmes's successors in the school of legal realism abandoned the blunt attribution of force to the law, but the concept remained, if only "suggested and hinted at."[26]

Were one to consider the late Jerome Frank as the prototype of the modern realists, and it would seem justified to do so, the conclusion would be that the present-day school has varied the fundamentals of its philosophy only in accidentals, since "Frank's principles, which he accepts from Holmes without qualification"[27] are reducible to the same notion that physical force, and not moral obligation, is at the base of the law.

## The Scholastic Position

Aquinas stands at the antipolar extreme to Holmes and the realists. In his treatise on the essence of law, Thomas unqualifiedly places some obligation at its base. "Law is a rule and measure of acts, whereby man is induced to act or is restrained from action: for *lex* (law) is derived from *ligare* (to bind), because it binds one to act."[28]

Aquinas, moreover, specifies the nature of this obligation:

> Laws framed by man are either just or unjust. If they be just, they have the power of binding in conscience, from the eternal law whence they are derived, according to Proverbs 8:15: "By Me kings reign, and lawgivers decree just things."[29]

It is almost universally held among scholastics that no law is properly a law which does not carry some obligation.[30] (As will be seen later, however, there seem to be exceptions to this general holding in some rare cases, particularly Vermeersch, Rodrigo, and Ford.) Suarez was dogmatic on the point, stating that it was "virtually a matter of faith" (*proxima fidei*).[31]

This reference to the scholastic position was not intended to be exclusionary. As would be expected, many who would not be termed scholastics placed moral obligation in the law. Thus, clearly and notably, did Blackstone.[32] Pollock is unqualified: "And thus among civilized people, after the distinction between law and morality is fully established, it comes to be understood that it is a specific moral duty to obey existing positive law, not only when we cannot see the reason for it, but when we think the reason a bad one."[33]

## THE KINDS OF LAW

Considered strictly from the aspect of the type of obligation under which it binds, the law is generally separated by the scholastics into three divisions:[34] (1) merely moral, (2) mixed, and (3) purely penal.

When the ordination of the lawgiver binds in conscience only, with sanction neither of fine nor imprisonment annexed, the law is denominated "merely moral."[35] Patently, examples of this type of law are found in the internal forum: Thou shalt not covet thy neighbor's wife. Thou shalt not covet thy neighbor's goods. Among the ecclesiastical laws, the obligations to attend Mass on Sunday, to abstain from meat on Friday, to fast before receiving Holy Communion—all these mandates—have no accidental temporal sanction attached to their violation. The punishment for the breach of such laws is reserved to God. Instances of the merely moral law will not be found in the legislation of the civil authority, because in every case the civil law adds a penalty for violation.

When a sanction of some kind, usually a fine or punishment, is superadded to the law but in no way affects or diminishes the moral obligation in conscience, the result is a "mixed" law. A violation of the Church's proscription against attempted marriage by a duly ordained priest of the Latin rite breaches the conscience obligation and results in subjection to the penalty, that is, excommunication from the body of the faithful. The law called "mixed" obliges under sin, obviously, but also has a supplemental sanction.[36]

Opponents of lex pure poenalis would class the laws of the state in this category, holding that the state adjoins a sanction to give added force to the moral duty inherent in the command. Thus, the many examples of federal excise taxes on wagering and social and athletic clubs would be cited as extremely appropriate examples of "mixed" laws. They receive no binding force from causes intrinsic to themselves, as would statutes, for example, prohibiting libel and slander (where the clear rights of others would demand obedience) or adultery and fornication (where the divine law has already imposed a conscience obligation). Rather, their binding force derives solely from the legislative command. The law of the state has in turn received its force from God through the natural-law principle: Obey competent authority.

The third class of law is the "purely penal." Perhaps the sole element to which all adherents to the general theory would subscribe is that there is no obligation in conscience to obey the command itself, although there may or may not be a conscience obligation to submit to the consequent sanction once imposed. Because an understanding of the many facets of the major variations of the theory is conducive to a proper understanding of the total problem, some descriptive treatment of the various approaches is in order.

### THE THEORY IN MUTATION

Since the doctrine of *lex pure poenalis* took root in the mid-1200s, it has developed three major branches (with many buds on each branch).

#### *Either Obey or Pay: The Disjunctive Approach*

By no means the oldest and certainly not the majority view is the variant of the theory proposed by authors of the 1800s in which the prospective delinquent was presented with a choice: Either obey the law or submit to the sanction. The choice itself was binding in conscience but neither the one nor the other determinately.[37] Thus, one is not bound in conscience to obey the law if he chooses the sanction, but he is bound in conscience to whichever of the two he chooses. Nor is one bound in conscience to the penalty if one chooses to obey the law, but he is bound in conscience to obey whichever one he determines. The subject, therefore, is bound in conscience to accept one or the other of the options. He is bound to either one indeterminately in conscience but to neither determinately. Hence, it could be said that the lawmaker's principal concern is neither obedience to the order itself nor fulfillment of the sanction once imposed but rather to one or the other equally at the election of the subject.

The disjunction is between the law and the sanction. Only in the sense that one need not obey at all can it be said that he is not bound in conscience under this theory.

Vermeersch distinguishes this from his own particular elaboration by remarking:

> This theory has been abandoned today, and with good reason. No lawmaker equates or favors equally the observance of the law with the undergoing of the penalty. He intends to impose the ordination most efficaciously, at least by means of the penalty.[38]

Dunn, whose recent commentary is a modern defense of the Suarezian position and the theory in general, agrees with Vermeersch that the "disjunctive" type is untenable,[39] but he also rejects Vermeersch's own position.[40] Few writers today would deny that the primary object of the law is obedience to the mandate itself and that the payment of the penalty is a consequent sanction and distinct from the command. A sanction is a means, not an end in itself. A lawgiver would not equate the principal with the subordinate, the end with the means. This disjunctive type is obsolete.

### Obligation, Sanction, and Suarez

The full flowering of the doctrine and of the second and clearly majority approach came with Suarez (in the mid-1500s). This theory of the conditional moral obligation has continued to the present to be the consensus. Very simply, the Suarezian system stipulates that the ordination itself does not bind in conscience but that the second command, the sanction, once the law has been violated and the penalty imposed, does carry a moral obligation.[41] Dunn remarks, considering the chief flaw in the disjunctive system, that

> the advocates of this [Suarezian] position concede that a legislator principally intends and consequently primarily obliges his subjects to the action prescribed by his law, but with a merely juridic non-moral obligation. Conditioned upon a lack of compliance with

this principal object he obliges his subjects to undergo a penalty. This secondary obligation of submitting to a penalty is a moral obligation derived from the penal law itself.[42]

For present purposes this capsule presentation of the Suarezian system will suffice. It should be remarked, however, that all major proponents of the doctrine, with few exceptions, build on the foundation of Suarez. Nor can the stature of Suarez be minimized. Not only was he preeminent in the elaboration of *lex pure poenalis* but, far more important, in the initiation of a modern jurisprudence. "The second of the books of *De Legibus* is for us Suárez' *magnum opus*, dealing as it does with the eternal law, the natural law and the *jus gentium*, in the consideration of which he assumes his rightful place as the founder of the philosophy of law in its various phases . . ."[43]

More by way of illustration than intrinsic content, the purely penal philosophy of Blackstone's *Commentaries* recommends itself as an instance of the probable influence of Suarez.

> So also in regard to *natural duties*, and such offenses as are *mala in se*: here we are bound in conscience, because we are bound by superior laws, before those human laws were in being, to perform the one and abstain from the other. But in relation to those laws which enjoin only *positive duties*, and forbid only such things as are not *mala in se* but *mala prohibita* merely, without any intermixture of moral guilt, annexing a penalty to non-compliance,[1] [reference to a footnote of Blackstone's "See Vol. II. page 420."] here I apprehend conscience is no farther concerned, than by directing a submission to the penalty, in case of our breach of those laws . . .[44]

### Obligation without Responsibility

The third variation of the system, Vermeersch's, seemingly eliminates all obligation in conscience whatsoever, either to the law itself or to the sanction once the law is violated. "Merely penal law . . . in its totality does not oblige in conscience."[45] Any obligation that Vermeersch might impose, and it certainly is not in conscience, is in the purely "juridical order, that is, in the external forum."[46] This is an apparent change of attitude in Vermeersch, as his first two editions of *Theologia Moralis* placed him with the adherents of the "disjunctive" type.

Quite logically, Vermeersch cannot understand how a legislator could intend the principal and chief part, the law itself, not to bind in conscience but still hold the citizen under pain of sin to the lesser and dependent part, the sanction.[47] Vermeersch, as a consequence, removes all obligation in conscience regarding either law or penalty. Furthermore, he is apparently standing alone. He cites no authorities and seemingly has no major adherents. His preeminence as a moralist and the strong impulse to adopt his reasoning in rejecting the other two theses are not, however, sufficient to avoid the conclusion that Vermeersch finds himself, in the end, with no law at all but merely sovereignly admonitions. His theory, nevertheless, is mentioned with respect in any thorough treatment of the subject. Lucius Rodrigo, S.J., is one example.[48] In fact, Rodrigo, who undoubtedly has the most complete modern treatment and who, moreover, is deserving of respectful attention, considers that his own analysis has taken the best of both Vermeersch and the Suarezian system.[49] The approach of Rodrigo is not sufficiently distinct from the others or of such intrinsic cogency to warrant special treatment, in spite of the excellent work.

The only conscience obligation connected with the Vermeersch theory is neither to the law nor to the sanction but to the command of the duly constituted authority in imposing the penalty. Presumably, this command is issued pursuant to the provisions for its imposition annexed to the law. Moreover, this obligation does not spring from the penal law itself but from the order of the superior exacting the punishment as specified. Furthermore, the obedience to this order is not referable "to the force of the human law itself but rather to the force of the divine law which imposes obedience to just laws."[50]

There is no doubt that this seems self-contradictory and is difficult to understand. Vermeersch, however, certainly says that the penal law causes no moral obligation. This would seem to controvert the fundamental premise that any proper law must induce some moral obligation. In the end, the law itself apparently only serves as the occasion and not the cause for the moral obligation. Once there is a violation, the superior intervenes, and by a completely independent act his command effects the imposition of the penalty. Thus, Vermeersch founded the obligation in the legitimate command of the superior. He is adamant, however, that his system involves only a juridic obligation. Ford, though, who certainly commands present-day respect, has reportedly said:

> The fundamental point at issue is whether the very concept of law, properly understood, necessarily implies moral obligation, i.e., an obligation binding in conscience under pain of sin. . . . The basic and essential issue, Father Ford continued, is a metaphysical and philosophical one. Every philosopher will admit, no doubt, that it is of the essence of law to bind, to impose a necessity on the human agent. But not all will admit that this necessity must from the nature of the case be that absolute and imperative *ought* which is derived from a consideration of man's essential relation to God as his last end. Some continue to believe that a merely juridical or penal necessity satisfies the formal concept of law. The question of the possibility of a merely penal law cannot be satisfactorily decided unless one comes to a conclusion or takes a stand on this ultimate issue.[51]

\* \* \*

The Suarezian system will serve as the representative of the penal-law theory in the major arguments, critiques, and analyses of this treatise. The "disjunctive" type has been abandoned on all sides and, hence, is at best an historical study. The third theory, that of Vermeersch, has found virtually no support except from Rodrigo[52] and the hesitancy on the part of Ford in condemning its philosophy. Vermeersch, unfortunately, leaves one with the clear impression that the system not only removes all obligation in conscience but also removes all law.

Finally, the Suarezian approach is so universally accepted by penal-law advocates as to warrant readily its selection as the prototypal system. Henceforward, therefore, the Suarezian system will be synonymous with the doctrine of the purely penal law in this study.

## CHAPTER III

# What Laws Are Purely Penal?

Since there is little dispute as to what laws in general are purely penal (albeit considerable difficulty in specifying exactly this or that law), the study of the norm for their discernment will be made through the eyes of the Suarezian system. All systems, however, generally agree on the approach to the task.

## WHAT LAWS ARE NOT!

It will become increasingly apparent that the compass of the penal law is in fact most limited. Exclusion after exclusion reduces the total body to a highly circumscribed class.

The first great exclusion from penal-law possibility is the natural law itself, which is divided into the natural moral law governing human acts and the law governing irrational creatures. As a matter of fact, the term *natural law* is used almost universally to mean the "natural moral law" (which governs all but irrational creatures). The exclusive concern here is rather with the positive law—laws not imprinted in the heart of man but promulgated after the creation of man and of his nature.

Cathol.

This positive law is divided, according to the norm of the type of legislator, into human and divine classifications. The mandates of the divine positive law may or may not, dependent on their nature, be reiterative of the natural law. For example, all of the Ten Commandments (except the third: Keep holy the Sabbath day) are not only divine positive-law mandates, enacted by God Himself and promulgated through Moses on the Mount, but they are also restatements of the natural law. In the case of the third, however, the law is divine and positive but certainly not also a command of the natural law. God might as well have said that Wednesday was to be the day of worship. (Do not, however, confuse the specification of the day with the natural-law command to worship God at least some time during one's life.) There is a consensus that no divine positive laws are penal.[1] It should be noted, moreover, that those divine positive laws which are simply declaratory of the natural law are doubly excluded from consideration.

Once the orbit has been narrowed to the human positive law, the next logical excision is the ecclesiastical law (such as attendance at Mass on Sunday, fast and abstinence, and the like), which rarely if ever permits penal interpretation. "Purely penal laws are rarely found in ecclesiastical law,"[2] and never, according to Arregui.[3] These laws certainly have no intrinsic moral content but gain their binding force solely through the act of the legislator. The *Codex Juris Canonici*, moreover, always binds in conscience unless specifically noted otherwise.[4]

As with the divine positive law, so too with the civil (non-ecclesiastical) human positive, there is a considerable body of legislation which is merely reiterative of the natural law. Patently, this is also excluded.[5] Thus, as it generally does, the state specifically prohibits by statute murder, adultery, fornication, abortion, and burglary, for example. All of these prescriptions are merely restatements of the natural law. The citizen was bound in conscience irrespective of the positive-law statutes of the legislature. Without benefit of a legislative enactment, these laws would be classed as merely moral. The source of the binding force is primarily the natural law, not merely the authority of the legislator.

Only certain laws among the civil human positive can be considered purely penal. They involve actions which are otherwise perfectly indifferent and gain their efficacy (if one maintains they have any) from the fact that they are prescribed by the law of the duly constituted state and not directly from the natural law.

By way of further limitation, those laws among the non-divine, nonecclesiastical positive-law enactments which directly affect the rights of others (for example, smoke-abatement ordinances, laws of descent and distribution, statutes affecting minimum living-wage requirements) always bind in conscience.[6] Even here, however, there are exceptions. Many such laws are held not binding in conscience *ante sententiam judicis* ("prior to the court's pronouncement"), even when they seem to declare an obligation before an adjudication.

It should be noted, moreover, that special circumstances, completely apart from the essential nature of the law, may render a command obligatory in conscience.[7] Thus, for example, there may be nothing intrinsically wrong in leaving firearms about the house (which is to say that it would be permissible except for the statute prohibiting it), but if it is clearly understood that a subnormal fifteen-year-old son with a known penchant for firearms is presently in the home, a moral obligation immediately arises without regard to any statutory provision.

Finally, the common good itself, again unrelated to the intrinsic morality of the law, may impose an obligation in conscience. This is true where the purpose of the statute is so intimately connected with the common good that it shares in the necessity of the final end of the common good itself[8] (for example, certain municipal health provisions, condemnation orders, narcotics legislation). But even in this class of legislation the merepenalists may regard certain specific approaches to the legislative goal or certain aspects or sections of the statute as purely penal. As long as the objective of the common good is respected, legislation which is not necessarily directed to that end, which may be simply one of several indifferent, possible means, may be penal. The minutely specified details of the manner of purchase and sale of narcotics will not go to the essence of the statute. Hence, they are not excluded by this criterion. This is not so, however, with the essence of the legislation—that is, the protection of the general public from the ravages of addiction.

From all this it can be seen that the scope of the purely penal law is limited indeed (which, however, neither derogates from its intrinsic importance nor means to say that there are few instances or applications of the law). Within this confined area (outside the natural-law prescriptions, the divine and ecclesiastical positive law, and exclusive of laws involving substantial rights of others and areas essentially affecting the common good) do the proponents of the penal laws locate that legislation which they maintain does not bind in conscience. Subject henceforward to these limitations, how does one discern a penal law?

### The Will of the Legislator

Although the distractions of discussion and the mazes of some of the arguments have led commentators to forget or ignore the fact, there is only one controlling norm generally established for discerning the purely penal law: the intention of the legislator.[9] Suarez himself stresses this point.[10]

(One overriding distinction should pervade every consideration of the penal-law doctrine in specific reference to the so-called will or intention of the lawgiver. The intention to legislate—to pass a valid law—is one thing. The intention to oblige—to bind in conscience—completely another. All competent moralists will concede that the binding force of a law ceases if there was no legislative intent to pass any law at all, or that the mind of the lawmaker is a valid norm in the interpretation of the content of a law [hence the value and necessity of the legislative history in statutory interpretation]. The penal-law proponents do not mean to signify this when they refer to the intent of the legislator. Their reference is to legislative intent to oblige in conscience. Their theory permits the lawgiver to intend to legislate but also to intend not to oblige. The Suarezians always posit the intent to legislate. Recall throughout, therefore, that the Suarezian system is concerned with the legislative will to oblige, not to legislate.)

To the merepenalist it is the will or intent of the lawmaker which is the immediate cause or reason for the obligation in conscience.[11] Did he intend that the subject obey, bound by duty? Or did he mean that there was no obligation to obey the law itself but that there would be a moral obligation to submit to the sanction attached to the law, the penalty? If the latter, the law is purely penal. If the former, it is not. Even in those areas where the system would permit of a purely penal law, the legislator may determine otherwise (a consideration worthy of reflection). In the beginning and the end, there is one, sole criterion of the purely penal law. As Vermeersch so succinctly states it, "Consult the will of the lawmaker."[12] The following *indicia* are almost universally employed to discern that will.

(A fuller explanation, betimes, of the psychology of will and intellect will account for this reliance on the will as the sole norm of discernment.)

### THE INDICIA OF THE LEGISLATIVE INTENT

It perhaps should be noted that some authorities would go so far as to maintain that the lawgiver must say expressly that his positive-law command does not oblige in conscience.[13] A competent Belgian moralist, however, counters and expresses what is probably the consensus.

> The direct criterion of the merely penal law is generally not nor
> could it be the expressed declaration of the will of the legislator
> . . . For he thus would really be acting at odds with himself by de-
> claring that his law did not oblige in conscience.[14]

At this point, therefore, nearly all the penal-law moralists have
resort to the so-called *indicia* to find the will—implied and not
expressed—of the legislator. Obviously, if it is express there is
no need for *indicia*.

(Vermeersch almost naïvely adds a further difficulty to the
problem by noting that today one rarely finds a one-man legislator and that, hence, there is the added burden of finding the will
of a parliament.[15] With the elaborate and meticulous compila-
tions of the legislative history of every enactment—minority and
majority reports in committee, introductory speeches on the floor
of the proponents, Congressional debate, and so forth—the correct and exact legislative intent is spelled out with precision.)

If any caution should be stressed, it is the following: These
criteria are designed not to discern the purely penal law itself,
but rather to determine the will of the lawmaker. Did he intend
not to hold the citizen "duty bound" to obey? Many authors soon
forget this and even list the "will of the legislator" as one of the
several *indicia* of a penal law, rather than *the indicium*. These
are *indicia* of the will, not of the law. Of the will, furthermore,
to oblige, not to legislate.

Because the line of demarcation is occasionally thin between
the norms for determining the will of the legislator and the arguments adduced in support of the doctrine (and since many proponents confuse them), these *indicia* should not only give some
considerable insight into the essence of the purely penal law but
also, to some extent, plead the case for its intrinsic possibility.

### 1   *The Object of the Law*

This is the most important criterion but is in fact merely a
restatement of the exclusions, narrowing the scope to nonnatural-

law and nondivine, nonecclesiastical positive-law legislation. Purely penal laws may have as their object[16] only a temporal purpose whose sanction is confined to this life rather than the next. The object, of course, cannot impinge substantially upon the rights of others or the common welfare.

## 2  The Manner of the Law's Public Reception

According to penal-law lawyers, probably the most secure and universal test of the will of the legislator is the manner in which the law is commonly received by the people.[17] In other words, the citizenry best knows the mind of the legislator. Does the average citizen consider that he is duty bound to obey the law or rather that he is not held to obey the law itself but is later held morally to submit to the sanction if apprehended? It would not seem that each person would be expected to express his estimation of the nature of the obligation in the same way. Some would call it "moral obligation"; others, "bound in conscience." Many would probably be expressing the same sentiment if they simply said that a conscientious citizen "ought" to obey or that surely he "should," or he would not feel "right" if he did not, or it would not seem "honest" or "decent." The conscience of an individual expresses itself in subtle and varied ways. The question could profitably be posed in connection with the excise taxes for athletic and social clubs and wagering. Do the people, by and large, have the conviction that they have a "bounden duty" to pay these excise taxes?

## 3  The Godless Legislator

As unlikely as it may seem, some purely penal schools hold that since the foundation of the law for most modern legislators is divorced from God and morality, such godless legislators could hardly intend to bind in conscience.[18] How could they, since they would not even admit of a conscience at the outset? It must be admitted that this would be true of Holmes and those

who have clearly followed him.[19] Certainly, this argument or
norm would be tenable if the legislature of a given state were
known to be completely Holmesian in its philosophy of law. This
would not mean, however, that such legislature could, thereby,
succeed in withholding the moral obligation from a law if it intended to legislate. That is the very point for proof and argument. This *indicium*, therefore, might point to a desire on the
part of a lawmaker to withhold the obligation. Whether he is
able to attain his desire is the question to be answered.

### 4 *The Enormity of the Penalty*

If the penalty is beyond all proportion to the offense, so the
reasoning goes, the legislature certainly did not intend to bind
the malefactor in conscience and annex a sanction. The penalty
would seem to be clearly sufficient. The penal-law lawyers admit
that this index applies sometimes but not always.[20]

### 5 *The Terminology of the Law*

Some systems maintain that the intent of the lawgiver can be
divined from the manner in which he couches the terms of the
law.[21] Some laws, it is alleged, offer a choice and make no outright command, as "Whosoever shall commit . . . shall be fined
$10.00." These laws the legislature intended to be penal. On the
other hand, other laws seem to command: "No one shall . . ."
or "It shall be unlawful . . ." These possibly would indicate a
lawmaker's intention to oblige, at least under this criterion.

These are the *indicia*. They are the criteria not of the penal
law itself but of the will and intent of the legislature to oblige or
not, which is itself the ultimate and sole determining norm of the
purely penal law.

---

# PART TWO

# Tradition against the Law

*Historical Arguments for a Penal Law*

## CHAPTER IV

# The Case for the Defendant Theory

$A$lthough the *indicia* do carry implicit argumentative force, the penal-law lawyers have over the years arrayed a series of special arguments designed expressly to rationalize the system. These approaches to the problem can be appropriately classified according to their intrinsic and extrinsic aspects. As will be evident, the intrinsic arguments are by far the more important. On them, in fact, and on Suarez rests the whole. So large does Suarez loom that it could safely be said that no succeeding author to the present day has substantially altered the Suarezian system or contributed appreciably to the doctrine.

## The Suarezian Intrinsic Argumentation

In elaborating his system, Suarez has developed the intrinsic argument in three distinct stages: (1) the psychological nature of the lawmaking process, (2) "civil" or "political" culpability, and (3) the preservation of moral obligation in the sanction. It is most intriguing to remark the development of this reasoning. Each step embodies fundamental concepts. Each is a separate unit yet coheres essentially and from necessity with the whole. And each has been severely impugned by his antagonists.

### The Psychological Nature of the Lawmaking Process[1]

Of all the considerations fundamental to the purely penal doctrine, one stands out as the most important. It is the conviction of Suarez that the moral obligation intrinsic to the law is induced by the will, not the intellect, of the lawgiver. Once grant Suarez this point, and he has established one, if not the most important, of the three bases of his system.

The Suarezian psychology envisages the interaction of intellect and will in the mechanics of legislation, culminating in the act of the will as the proximate cause of the law and, hence, of the obligation of the law.

The legislator begins his process by clearly establishing the final cause, end, objective, of good government. This is the common good and welfare. All law, if it is to be reasonable and just, must contemplate peace, happiness, and domestic tranquillity—the common good. This is the work of the intellect.

By legislative hearings, inquiry, and investigation, the legislature next surveys the many possible statutory means to this end. At this juncture, the intellect formulates a judgment—a reasoned conclusion from its study—that a particular bill will satisfactorily (but not necessarily most satisfactorily) meet the demands of the common good.[2]

This proposed legislation the intellect then submits to the will in the form of the judgment: This statute adequately conduces as a means to the end.

Following this judgment of suitability, the all-important act of the will adopts the judgment and commands that the subjects must observe the legislation judged practical by the intellect. Suarez is meticulous in warning that there is no command (*imperium*) in the intellect, so important is it to him to place this command in the will: "there is no command in the intellect

directed at the will, except by way of judgment. Nor can the intellect force or move the will other than by its cognition or judgment."³ As a matter of fact, Suarez has two distinct acts of the
will in the lawmaking process. The first, the election (*electio*), is
the choice of one possible legislative proposal over another. This
efficacious act selects one from many possible statutes. The second act of the will, the use (*usus*), commands the execution of
this choice.

> In its proper sense *consent* signifies the embrace by the will of some
> definite means. This follows the preceding deliberations of the intel-
> lect. This selection, if it is efficacious and chooses one means from
> the others by way of a preference, is called the election. Once this
> election, however, has been made it is necessary that those means be
> reduced to execution, which is accomplished by the acts of "use"
> [*usus*] . . .⁴

Since there is no intervening act of the intellect in the nature of
a command between the *electio* and *usus*⁵ and since the command (*imperium*) is in this election or choice⁶ and, finally,
since it is this *imperium* that is the law,⁷ there is no necessity for
present purposes to dilate on the various substages of the lawmaking process. This command, therefore, of the will, which
Suarez calls the *imperium*,⁸ is both requisite and sufficient to induce moral obligation in the citizens. The will to command and
to oblige are effected in the same will act.⁹

But most important, and this is the nub of the entire matter,
Suarez adamantly maintains that the will is completely free,
even after the judgment of the intellect, to command or not to
command. There is no necessity in the will to follow the judgment of the intellect. Should the intellect have decided that legislation should embody old-age-pension provisions, the will may
determine on the contradictory position and refuse to legislate
altogether. (In logic, a *contradictory* is "a term which is the exact negative of another"—to legislate or not to legislate, white
and nonwhite.) Should the intellect have determined that a stat-

ute should establish an income tax on all males between eighteen and thirty years of age, the will may take the contrary stand and pass a law taxing the income of all males between thirty and sixty years of age. (In logic, a *contrary* is "either of a pair of terms that cannot be affirmed of the same subject"—to legislate this or legislate that, black and white.)

> The will is able not only in a contradictory way not to will what has thus been judged but also may in a contrary way will the opposite. Therefore the will remains free both as to action and specification.[10]

It is essential to the Suarezian position that the will should in no way be determined by the judgment of the intellect to one particular form of legislation rather than another. The intellect merely submits for the will's choice a proposal suitable to the end to be achieved.

> If the intellect were to judge that a particular means is useful or worthy of choice, although it also were to judge some other means to be useful, the will might make a choice of one of them. Nor is it incumbent upon the intellect to judge determinately beforehand that one must be chosen, nor for that matter that one is more suitable than the other.[11]

Facing a consequent problem, Suarez next reasons that the judgment of the intellect should not be thought to be completely "undetermined." This would leave the will with nothing at all, as it were, upon which to operate. The judgment of the intellect has at least indicated the feasibility and acceptability of a proposed statute—which is something. The will is left, of course, with the choice of acting or not acting. In the cases where the intellect has submitted several possible legislative approaches, the will is completely free to determine for itself upon one of the many possibilities presented in the judgment of the intellect.[12]

Ultimately it is this undetermined nature of the intellect's judgment that is the foundation of freedom. The intellect submits a choice so undetermined that the will is not necessitated but retains full liberty.[13] In a word, Suarez firmly maintains that the freedom of choice rests in the will alone.[14]

Suarez makes it clear that he rejects the doctrine that maintains that the command or *imperium* is in the intellect and that the intellect, after weighing the possible means at hand, makes a definite judgment that a particular statute must be passed. (This is the intellectual *imperium* of Thomas, which will be delineated later. The Thomistic *imperium* is, of course, made efficacious by a previous and perduring will act.) This, according to Suarez, denies liberty to the will since the will could do nothing but accede, under these conditions, to the judgment of the intellect.[15]

Certain Thomistic opponents to the Suarezian psychology have endeavored to place a second act of the intellect following the election of the will. Suarez clearly denies this and maintains strongly that the actual command is in the election of the will.

> Indeed, once the doctrine concerning the command [*imperium*] of a person to himself has been presupposed, it necessarily follows in considering the command of one to another that, after the will-act of the lawmaker . . . it is only requisite and necessary that the legislator make known his decree and judgment—promulgate it to those subjects to whom the law applies. . . . However, that this suffices is patent, because the will of the ruler is of itself efficacious, since it flows from sufficient power and, according to the present supposition, is issued with an absolutely obliging decree. Therefore, if the law is adequately promulgated to the citizen, it accomplishes its purpose. It induces obligation. With that the law is effected. Therefore nothing further remains to be done.[16]

In support of his stand, Suarez lists an impressive group of theologians who place the essence of the lawmaking process in the will: Henry of Ghent, Gabriel Biel, William of Occam, St. Bonaventure, John Medina, William Durandus, Gregory of Rimini.[17] A strong strain of nominalism can be noted throughout.

With this, the Suarezian process of lawmaking has reached a conclusion. The will of the legislator is in receipt of the judgment of the intellect, accepts the judgment, makes its election and, in the very act of election, commands the obedience of the citizenry, and in commanding, induces the moral obligation in the subjects. With this efficacious will of the lawmaker, the process is complete. This act constitutes the law itself. Only promulgation remains.

The implications of this freedom of the will to accept or to reject completely, to choose one means or another, should already be clear. The most fundamental and far-reaching concept in the Suarezian psychology of the legislative process is the absolute liberty of the will of the legislator in legislating or not, in legislating this or that, or (most important of all) in obliging the subject or not.

In summary, this *imperium* of the Suarezian legislative act, since it is purely volitional, contains no intellectual content ordered to a final end. As a result, the law-act does not of itself contain ontological obligation and can, therefore, be specified as obligational or not at the whim of the positive-law legislator. This gives him complete freedom in dealing with the sanction.

The immediate result of this psychology is the first of the three postulates on which the doctrine is founded: The total freedom of the legislative will renders the legislature completely free to select this legislation or that, to oblige the citizens or not to oblige them—in a word, to pass a law without moral obligation: "the precepts of both the divine and human positive laws do not possess of themselves any intrinsic necessity but derive their necessity from an extrinsic will."[18] On the assumption that the will, therefore, is the proximate cause of obligation in the law, Suarez resolutely takes the next step toward the intrinsic possibility of a purely penal law.

*Liability without Culpability*

The second fundamental conclusion of Suarez is of almost equal importance in the total structure of the doctrine: The legislator may justly punish, for disobedience of this nonobligatory law, any citizen. He bases this on a nonmoral guilt which he calls "civil" or "political" and which he founds to a great extent on the omnipresent aphorism *Sine culpa, non tamen sine causa.* That is, punishment may be imposed "without fault—not, however, without cause." This maxim is of notable importance to the penal-law doctrine. The story of its origin in history will be told in appreciable detail.

The elaboration of this important premise finds Suarez progressing through several stages of intricate argument and adverting throughout to the dependence of moral obligation on the intention of the legislator.

Suarez begins by categorizing, from the specific standpoint of the gravity of obligation induced by the will of the legislator, three kinds of law. It is the will of the lawmaker to legislate (1) without reference to obligation, (2) with obligation but with an unspecified degree thereof, or (3) without any obligation in conscience. Suarez, in fact, lists a fourth category which is not sufficiently relevant to the present discussion to include it: a law to which the lawmaker wishes to attach an obligation under pain of venial, rather than mortal, sin.

In regard to the first class, this "law undoubtedly obliges in conscience, since a true law by its very nature has this effect if it is not specifically excluded."[19] It is pertinent to note that Suarez presumes that a moral obligation intrinsic to true law is present rather than that it is absent.

When the lawmaker expresses an intention to bind in conscience but does not specify the degree, the gravity of the legislative matter will be determinative—either mortal or venial.[20]

(In either of these first two ways, the legislator may append an accidental sanction or not, as he wishes. The result will be either a purely moral law or a mixed law, as the case may be.)

It is in elucidating the nature of the purely penal law that Suarez makes the important distinction between the law proper and the sanction.

That law, indeed, is denominated mixed which is at once moral and penal. It includes in effect two commands: one, to perform an act or to shun it, the other, to submit to a specified penalty upon disobedience . . . That law, however, is called purely penal which is enunciated in only one, as it were, hypothetical command: to undergo a certain *poena* or discomfort, if this or that is done, although a command is not imposed relative to the act itself to which the condition is attached.[21]

Special attention should be called to the fact that Suarez conceives of the mixed law as containing two separate commands: (1) Obey the law itself. (2) Accept the penalty, the sanction. On the other hand, when he discusses the purely penal law, he refers to only one command which he calls hypothetical.

The extent to which Suarez relies on that *indicium* of legislative intent, the terminology of the law, can be assayed from his discussion of the mixed law.

Therefore, it must be stated that a law which is expressed as a command, in explicit terms or in the manner of its adoption, although a penalty is attached, obliges in conscience, either under mortal or venial fault, according to the nature of the matter and other signs . . . unless it appears from other evidence that it is the express will of the legislator not to bind.[22]

Suarez manifestly places great importance on the presumption of the presence of moral obligation, rebuttable only by other evidences of the express intention of the legislator not to oblige.

Unlike Vermeersch, Suarez was extremely conscious of the necessity of some moral obligation in law. In his own excogitation of the penal law, he met this problem by placing the conscience obligation on the sanction rather than on the law. Thus, when the legislator expressly intends a penal law,

that intention changes the matter of the law and is in the power of the legislator. He may prescribe this or that content of a law, either determinately, or disjunctively, or absolutely, or under a certain condition, although he may not exclude all conscience obligation completely if he wishes to pass a true law. Therefore when it is stated that the legislator intends not to bind in conscience, but only to the penalty, this must be understood to refer to the act directly commanded or prohibited. By this very fact, however, this act is not the complete content of the law but rather this disjunction: Either perform such an act or undergo a certain penalty. Or (and it comes to the same thing) the law is conditional, with a penalty attached if a certain act is done. This then does not exclude the conscience obligation from the total disjunction.[23]

With this, Suarez has thrown down the gauntlet. He finds himself with a true law, a command to obedience, unaccompanied by moral culpability in disobedience.

> It can be proven, however, that strictly speaking those who violate the purely penal law are not guilty of sin. This is due to the fact that, acting prudently, they conform the dictates of their conscience to the intent of the lawgiver. He, however, has declared that there is no moral fault in such a violation by reason of the very law itself. Therefore the subjects form their conscience prudently, so that no sin follows in that context. In truth they do not sin, therefore, because that which flows from an honest conscience is no sin.[24]

To the problem implicit in this conclusion, Suarez replies, citing St. Thomas,[25] by drawing a parallel with the rules of religious orders. The rules for religious do not bind in conscience but may carry a penance for infraction.[26]

Suarez reaches the culmination in his proof when he adduces three arguments in support of the intrinsic possibility of the penal law. His first two reasons are not compelling.[27] On his third rests his entire case. It is as would be expected:

> In the third place, although some obligation is essential to law, the kind of obligation depends on the intention of the lawgiver. Wherefore, although the content of the law may be grave, the legislator may prefer not to bind under pain of mortal sin. Likewise he may prefer not to oblige in conscience, but only under some other kind of necessity or physical force.[28]

Through this logical elaboration of his psychology of the legislative process does he build his second on his first premise.

Suarez recurs to the seriousness of the necessity of some conscience obligation. Thus,

> penal law can be reduced to some conscience obligation, of paying
> or undergoing the penalty, and this meets the requirement of a true
> law, even though there is no conscience obligation to the condition
> under which the penalty is threatened and in respect of which it is
> called purely penal, although in regard to the penalty itself it has
> the force of obliging.[29]

Suarez here finds himself with an extremely clear-cut position:
The legislator has passed a true law—a command to obedience
—which carries, nonetheless, no moral guilt but induces a nonmoral obligation which he calls "civil" or "political." For disobedience the legislator can, in spite of the absence of moral
culpability, impose a sanction in the form of a punishment.

It is certainly logical, in the light of the Suarezian psychology of the lawmaking process (but only in the light of it), to
envisage a lawmaker by a free-will act withholding the conscience obligation. Nevertheless, it was painfully clear to Suarez
that he faced a mountainous obstacle in the age-old Augustinian
dictum of no liability without culpability, no punishment except
for sin. "Every penalty, however, if it is a just one, is a penalty
for sin and is called punishment."[30]

In response to this pressing difficulty, Suarez has resort to
(1) Thomas Aquinas, particularly in two of his treatises:
(a) on the state of religious life and (b) on the virtue of vindication, (2) the parallel between the regulations of the religious
life and the laws of the civil state, and (3) the oft-quoted *Sine
culpa, non tamen sine causa.*

One of many references to Thomas and the parallel with the
rules for religious comes early in the *De Legibus*[31] as support
for the thesis that the lawmaker can command the citizen to obedience and yet withhold any culpability before God in the disobedience.[32] Suarez seeks support here from the Thomistic
treatise on the state of religious life.

At a later point Suarez again recurs to this parallel. In Chapter IV of Book V of *De Legibus*, he asks "whether penal laws, which do not oblige in conscience but only under a penalty without subsequent fault, either exist in fact or are possible in theory."[33] To this he responds that the rules for religious often oblige to the penalty but not under pain of fault.[34] He continues with an example from church administration:

> An interdict and an irregularity [ecclesiastical disciplinary measures] are often incurred without fault . . . pain [*poena*] is sometimes incurred without fault, although not without cause [*sine culpa, quamvis non sine causa*] as also the inspired Thomas says in the *Secunda Secundae*, Question 108, Article 4, to the second objection, citing examples.[35]

Here Suarez has resort to the second of the famous Thomistic treatises constantly cited in support of the penal-law doctrine. This tractate, in Question 108, treats specifically of the virtue called vindication located in the general treatment of virtues and vices. Note that he also cites *Sine culpa, quamvis non sine causa*.

This reliance of Suarez on the parallel with the rules for religious, discussed in a nonlegal context by Thomas, cannot be overemphasized. Thus, in a religious community, Suarez attributes the immediate source of obligation to the will of the religious superior:

> Some laws are purely penal, and do not oblige in conscience, but rather to the penalty . . . first, since they are possible, because they are often more apt for governing the citizenry with less danger and harm in some matters in which a greater onus is unnecessary. It would seem to be reasonable that penal laws are often passed in this way. Second, because in certain religious orders clear examples are found of such laws. . . . in human laws, a law which imposes a penalty for escaping from prison, for cutting wood in the public wood and the like is considered purely penal.[36]

Suarez again adverts to this parallel in his justification of the imposition of unequal punishments by the lawgiver.[37]

Nor can the equally great dependence of Suarez on the reasoning inherent in *Sine culpa, non tamen sine causa* be minimized. It is by the use of this maxim that Suarez explains the imposition of punishment upon a citizen who acted without guilt. Treating the maxim as an exponible proposition, Suarez elaborates on the principle and arrives at nonmoral guilt, which he calls "civil" or "political," and which Vermeersch and others[38] after him refer to as "nonmoral and juridic."

> Although it imposes some pain [*poenam*] (that is, some inconvenience or evil) without fault, it is not, however, without cause [*sine culpa, non tamen sine causa*], or although it imposes it without moral guilt, it is not, however, without civil or political guilt, and this suffices.[39]

Suarez develops this concept of nonmoral civil guilt, explaining it in Thomistic terms derived from the tractate on the virtue of vindication, Question 108. From this treatise, Suarez distinguishes two totally different kinds of *poena* which, incidentally, later writers on occasion have termed "vindictive punishment" and "preventive punishment." Thus, Dunn remarks: "The twofold guilt and punishment of which Suarez speaks is a reecho of St. Thomas' distinction between vindictive punishment, 'quae non debetur nisi peccato' ['which is not due except for sin'], and preventive punishment, which is 'preservativa a peccato futuro vel promotiva in aliquod bonum' ['preservative against future sin and promotive of some good']." Dunn cites the same famous Question 108, Article 4.[40]

Calling on the support of Thomas, Suarez faces head-on this problem of liability without culpability.

> As is said in Deuteronomy 25: According to the measure of the crime will be the manner of the punishment and . . . Augustine . . . Every penalty, if it is just, is a penalty for sin and is called punishment; and, therefore, Gerson said that fault and penalty are correlative . . . therefore, when the penal law justly punishes, it supposes fault in the transgression of the law. However, this argument

cannot prevail, for although *poena* in a certain more rigorous signification implies an order to moral guilt, however, in a broader
sense, taken as any suffering or loss or inconvenience, it can justly
be imposed because of a just cause without moral guilt [*causam
sine culpa*]. . . . Moreover, it can be said that although every *poena*
is imposed because of fault, it does not always follow that the fault
is against God, but sometimes it suffices that the fault is as it were
civil and human.[41]

With the possible exception of the Suarezian psychology of the
lawmaking process (placing the source of moral obligation in
the will of the legislator), no other area of the penal-law reasoning is as important as this reliance of Suarez on the two Thomistic tractates and the maxim, to explain the imposition of
punishment on a citizen admittedly free of moral guilt.[42]

### Conscience, Obligation, and the Sanction

Suarez was highly preoccupied, as well he might be, with the
possible deficiency in his system which would violate the fundamental premise that all true law must essentially have some
moral binding force. "[The legislator] cannot completely exclude all obligation in conscience from the matter, if he wishes
to pass a true law."[43] How does he save true law? By making the
sanction, albeit not the law itself, bind in conscience.

This last of the three Suarezian stages of progress is perhaps
not so important as the previous two. It is in some way rather in
the nature of a rebuttal. Suarez admits the need for some conscience obligation and forthwith attempts to meet the problem.

Therefore, when it is stated that the legislator intends not to bind in
conscience but only to the penalty, this must be understood to refer
to the act directly commanded or prohibited. By this very fact, however, this act is not the complete content of the law but rather this
disjunction: Either perform such an act or undergo a certain penalty. Or (and it comes to the same thing) the law is conditional,
with a penalty attached if a certain act is done. This then does not
exclude the conscience obligation from the total disjunction.[44]

This is the manner in which Suarez preserves the moral obligation requisite for true law. He moves it to the sanction. There is no doubt of Suarez' firm adherence to this thought. He repeats it in other places.

> In the second place, the purely penal law is a true law, as is patent, and yet it need not bind in conscience. Therefore it is not an essential of a law that it bind in conscience. The minor is evident, first, because it is enough to meet the requisite of a law that it bind in some way or other and, second, because it is also in operative force, as shall be seen, in many regions in which true laws or statutes are in effect, and in these laws it is declared that they do not bind under sin but only to the penalty.[45]

Suarez faces the question squarely in his discussion of the third of the three arguments in support of the intrinsic possibility of purely penal law.

> In the third place, although some obligation is essential to law, the kind of obligation depends on the intention of the lawgiver. Wherefore, although the content of the law may be grave, the legislator may prefer not to bind under pain of mortal sin. Likewise he may prefer not to oblige in conscience, but only under some other kind of necessity or physical force.[46]

Later, in the fifth book of the *De Legibus*, Suarez again returns to an explanation of his specific approach to the problem.

> Penal law can be reduced to some conscience obligation, of paying or undergoing the penalty, and this meets the requirement of a true law, even though there is no conscience obligation to the condition under which the penalty is threatened and in respect of which it is called purely penal, although in regard to the penalty itself it has the force of obliging . . .[47]

Thus has Suarez constructed a unified system of the purely penal law: (1) He begins with the premise, founded on his psychology of intellect and will, that the will of the legislator can freely withhold the conscience obligation in the subject. (2) Next, with the support of two notable Thomistic citations, the parallel with the rules for religious and *Sine culpa, non tamen sine causa,* he develops a juridic, nonmoral obligation which he calls "civil," "political," or "human" and which condones punishment without corresponding culpability. (3) Finally, he saves the requisite of some conscience obligation in the law by attaching it to the sanction even though he removed it from the law proper. This last, the preservation of moral obligation in the sanction, caps the intrinsic argumentation.

*   *   *

Later generations of supporting commentators have adduced further reasons in support of the penal law, some in embellishment of old Suarezian arguments, others in new elaborations with minor variations.

### The Docility of the People

Fundamental to the reasoning that permits the legislature to remove the conscience obligation from the law yet place it on the sanction is the understanding that the lawmaker may so act licitly only as he is acting reasonably. In short, reasonableness is in fact the norm of legality in withholding the conscience obligation from the law proper.

This reasonableness, it is argued, would always be present whenever there is sufficient docility and general amenability to law on the part of the citizenry.[48] In effect, the execution and observance of the law would be forthcoming in general without the added necessity of an obligation in conscience. Such docility would clearly be referable to: (1) a wholesome innate sense of obedience and the overall orderliness of the law-abiding community, and (2) the adequacy of the means of external force and the conscientious vigilance of the law-enforcement agencies (this is stressed by penal-law lawyers as important), joined with a forceful sanction appropriate to the gravity of the situation and (3) buttressed with the moral obligation to undergo the sanction once imposed. There seems no need to add a moral obligation to obey the law itself when the ultimate goal of the law is achieved by the other three factors.

Besides, does such a ruling not place an unjust burden on the conscientious? Reasoning from somewhat extrinsic considerations, the adherents proceed to argue that if

> . . . the theory of penal law is denied in a civilization such as ours, the burden of civil obligation will fall disproportionately on those who recognize such a thing as an obligation in conscience, for violation of which one must answer to God. Those who deny all such obligation will be burdened by the law only to the extent of a legal sanction—an inequality in violation of the demands of distributive justice.[49]

This is the age-old argument of those who feel that a moral obligation as well as a sanction would put conscientious citizens at a disadvantage in their dealings with those unprincipled persons who have lost all religious scruple and are led to obey the law only out of the most lowly motives.[50]

Closely akin to this last argument is the allegation that the multitude of present-day statutes would place an intolerably

> . . . heavy burden on the shoulders of honest citizens. It would be imprudent. Civil laws are too multiplied and too complex. Every time a man turned around he would become guilty of a venial sin. A sane and happy life under such conditions would be next to impossible. Some people would become affected with a bad case of scrupulosity. Others would become as punctilious as the Scribes and Pharisees of old.[51]

Herron is quoting a fictitious adversary. Dunn joins this argument with the one immediately previous by quoting this statement of Blackstone:

> The good only would regard the laws, and the bad would set them at defiance. . . . the multitude of penal laws in a state would not only be looked upon as an impolitic, but also would be a very wicked thing; if every such law were a snare for the conscience of the subject.[52]

Dunn himself continues, "For if in a civilization such as ours the penal law theory be denied, civil obedience will impose a disproportionately greater burden on those who believe in such a thing as moral obligation, while those who repudiate such a notion will be burdened only to the extent of a legal sanction."[53] Vermeersch adds, "There are so many civil statutes today that it would be an intolerable burden to be held in conscience to obey all of them, or even many of them."[54]

*   *   *

This concludes the outline of the Suarezian position in its major aspects: (1) the theory proper, (2) the *indicia* of the legislative will to oblige, (3) the intrinsic arguments in support of the system.

# PART THREE

# The Civil Law Binds in Conscience

*Reasoned Arguments for the Moral Binding Power of the Law*

Two distinct avenues lie open in the attack on the penal law: proof that such a law (1) has never existed in fact and (2) could never exist in theory. Albeit by no means conclusive of the matter, the extrinsic argument—that the penal law is non-existent—will give considerable support and likelihood to the intrinsic —that such a penal-law concept is essentially impossible and inconsistent with the very nature of law.

These two broad avenues will be traveled in the succeeding four chapters. The extrinsic argument in Chapter V, "The Brief for the Civil Law I: A Question of Fact," asserts the *de facto* nonexistence of the penal law. The intrinsic argument is elaborated in the next three chapters. Chapter VI, "The Brief for the Civil Law II: From Gratian (1140) to Suarez (1581)," is historical. Chapter VII, "The Brief for the Civil Law III: The Intrinsic Argumentation," cuts to the core of the reasoning. And Chapter VIII, "The Civil Law Appears *Propria Persona*," is a direct rebuttal but is integral to the intrinsic argumentation.

## CHAPTER V

# The Brief for the Civil Law

## I

### *A Question of Fact*

Has there ever really been enacted a purely penal law? Has there ever in fact been a lawmaker who has intended to withhold the conscience obligation to obey?

Scrutiny of the question from the positive aspect would seem to indicate that the legislature, after reasoned legislative investigation, considered debate, and the inauguration of a mandatory statute, has ineluctably intended that the citizens have a firm duty to obey. It seems almost unreal to conceive of lawmakers enacting serious legislation with the concomitant will that the subjects be held only to the sanction if apprehended. It is difficult to imagine a lawgiver so speaking, "for thus he would act against his own purpose by declaring that his law did not oblige in conscience."[1]

It is true that perhaps no legislature has fully elaborated or even adverted to the intimate nature of the conscience obligation that it does intend. But it could be thought that, at least implicitly, the legislature would will an obligation superior to no obligation at all (and not be satisfied with the secondary sanction—

the penalty) and that conceivably it would express its understanding of the obligation in words such as "ought," "should,"
"have a patriotic duty to obey," "bound in honor," "bound to
obedience," "the duty of a citizen." If a lawmaking body principally wanted the sanction—the punishment—it reasonably
would have legislated in this manner from the outset.

## The Weakness of the *Indicia*

From the negative aspect, this position—that any thoughtful
lawmaker would inevitably expect obedience as a duty—is corroborated by a rebuttal of the alleged *indicia* of the contrary
intention not so to bind. An attack on the reliability and validity
of such criteria would, if successful, seem to indicate that such
a will was nonexistent and consequently that the penal law itself
was also nonexistent in fact. If each *indicium* failed to indicate,
the cumulative effect would be the destruction of the initial
thesis (to wit, the existence of such a legislative intent) and with
it the penal law.

### Common Acceptance by the People

There are several approaches in rebuttal to this norm.
(1) Should the people be in a moral decline, they might well be
violating all laws promiscuously. The moral estimate of the people in Tiberian or Claudian Rome, for example, could offer no
valid criterion of legislative intent. This norm, it is true, is confined to the reputable and sincere citizens, but even under this
consideration the scope for laxity is broad. (2) Should the majority of the conscientious citizens reasonably be violating the
law, the law probably would be unjust or contrary to the common good or invalid for other reasons.[2] (3) Responsible members of society do in truth see some kind of obligation behind the
law that corresponds, albeit loosely, to the description "moral."
The eminent Cooley, who could not be considered a scholastic
theologian, couched the concept in the term "mischief": "Where

an act is forbidden under penalty, it must in general be assumed that some degree of public mischief or private injury was meant to be prevented . . ."[3]

## The Godlessness of the Lawmakers

In any *ad hoc* consideration of a specific nation this is a question of fact and of history. A theoretical study, however, with examples of extreme, middle, and extreme, should expose the arguments against such a criterion.

In Ireland, with a constitution setting up a state religion, there would seem to be little doubt that the legislature, constituted in the main by men steeped in a background of scholastic philosophy and cognizant of the implications of the natural law as the source of the authority of the state, would presume that the Irish citizenry considered their enactments to have moral force. Some recollection, however, recalls four centuries of the purely penal law and suggests that the Irish would be merepenalists. The answer to this dilemma lies in the extent to which the rank and file would (1) learn of such a doctrine (some moralists caution not to explain the theory to the uninitiate) and (2) reason to it—both of which are unlikely.

As much as the moral reformer in viewing the United States might be inclined to berate the morals of the nation and cry for the return to ethics and religion, the fact remains that the country is at base a religious one, founded on God as Creator and on justice as the norm. Perhaps the finest statement of its tradition[4] can be found in the masterful dissent of Mr. Justice Reed in *McCollum* where he traces over many pages the deep religion of the people and the extent to which the founding fathers and the Government have fostered this religion.[5]

> By directing attention to the many instances of close association of church and state in American society and by recalling that many of these relations are so much a part of our tradition and culture that they are accepted without more, this dissent may help in an ap-

praisal of the meaning of the clause of the First Amendment concerning the establishment of religion.[6]

Continuing with detailed references to the religious principles of Madison and Jefferson, Justice Reed enumerates instance after instance of the reliance of the nation on the three great religions of the country. He emphasizes Congress,[7] the Armed Forces, the service academies.[8]

With some notable exceptions, the courts have maintained this tradition, and the legislators have been God-fearing. It would be gratuitous to say that the legislators of the United States intended to divorce the law from God in the manner of Holmes. Holmes is an unlikely representative of the culture.

In the light of this history, the only essential difference that could be posited between the United States and Ireland, for example, would be one of terminology (assuming that Holmes and the realists have had an effect on the United States comparable to that of the merepenalists on Ireland). The Irish legislature would, no doubt, if asked, couch its expression of the moral obligation of the law in scholastic terms. Members of Congress would suit their speech to their own backgrounds, expressing the concept variously but nonetheless describing some obligation beyond the sanction.

Even in the case of Russia, it could be argued that the lawmakers intend their laws to have a binding power consonant with the obligations of human nature. Soviet legislators, professing atheistic materialism, could admit an obligation to follow the dictates of the law of nature excogitated without advertence to a supreme being. A highly controverted question in natural philosophy is whether an obligation can be founded on the nature of man in complete precision from a supreme being. The tendency is to say that it can. Even in an atheistic nation (which most thinking people deem impossible), there is substantial argument that the legislators intend to bind their subjects to their commands under an obligation that could be called "moral."

Finally, as the intrinsic arguments will show, it is not within the power of even the godless legislator to withhold the conscience obligation from the law, if he has once determined to legislate. (Here again, it is pertinent to recall the distinction between the will to legislate and the will to oblige.) Merely his conviction that there is no God does not destroy Him, nor his wish that there be no moral obligation forestall it. Both are present regardless.

### The Gravity of the Sanction

It is difficult to agree with the reasoning of this argument. If the penalty were so great and so disproportionate as to be unjust, the law would not be binding in any event. It would be no law at all. But this would be founded on unreasonableness alone. If the law, however, is just and reasonable, the higher the penalty, the stronger and more sincere the intent of the legislature. There would be no adequate reason for a greater or a lesser penalty if it were not proportioned to a precedent fault. The gravity of the penalty would be an excellent gauge both of the seriousness of the offense (which would be all the more reason to assume a moral obligation) and of the legislative intent to bind in conscience as well. McGarrigle argued in the same vein:

> Disproportionately severe punishment may mean, as Suarez himself notes, that the temptation to break it is exceptionally great, so that only heavy penalty will obtain some semblance of obedience to the law. Far from making a law "merely penal," this is only a greater indication of the lawgiver's command to be obeyed, which always induces a moral obligation.[9]

### Statutory Phraseology

Legislators vary the formulae of introductory and prohibitory phrases: "All . . . are strictly forbidden," or "No one shall . . ." These would presumably be indicative of moral obligation. At the other pole is the disjunctive form so common in ancient codes: "If the citizen shall . . . he will be fined," or "Whosoever shall commit . . . shall be imprisoned." In actual practice these formulae help very little. The terminology has to-day become almost totally irrelevant.[10]

> The form of every important law in our time is penal in the sense that a penalty is imposed for its violation. In fact, a civil statute which carries no penalty is not now regarded as a law at all. It is merely a directive rule, a more or less persuasive ideal or a civil counsel of perfection. From the form of a law it is almost impossible to draw any reference concerning the extent or restriction of its morally binding character.[11]

The phraseology of the United States Code relative to espionage in time of war, for example, is at odds with the philosophy of this criterion.

> Whoever, in time of war, with intent that the same shall be communicated to the enemy, collects . . . any information with respect to . . . the Armed Forces . . . of the United States . . . shall be punished by death or by imprisonment for any term of years or for life.[12]

This terminology presumably should indicate that the lawmaker intended only the sanction. Yet it would be difficult to assume that Congress did not intend to hold every citizen to a duty in conscience not to undermine the cause of the nation in wartime. Furthermore, the citizen would be bound by the dictates of the natural law in a matter seriously involving the welfare of the country—which is further evidence that the legislature has not, at least in this particular context, been concerned with the formula in relation to the moral obligation. Text and terminology, therefore, may indicate nothing at all about the intent, except that the lawmaker intends to pass a law for the common welfare and conceivably wants it obeyed.

Two things in conclusion can be said about the *indicia*: (1) they do not in fact "point out," but (2) if it were conceded that they pointed to something, it would not be to an intent to remove all moral obligation but to the opposite. In short, how valid are these criteria as indicative of the legislative intent?

Considerable difficulty would be removed were the adherents of the theory to follow meticulously their own norm of determining a penal law. If the sole question asked were "What does the lawmaker intend?" the answer would invariably be "An obligation in conscience," unless, perchance, he intended not to legislate at all. Where the penal-law theorists use the so-called *indicia* as criteria of the purely penal law itself, difficulties indeed arise. Those moralists err who list the intent of the lawmaker as one of the criteria of the penal law instead of the sole norm.[13] According to the system, the criteria are necessary only because the legislature's intent to oblige or not is not clear. If it is clear, what need is there for criteria? Suarez was strong on this point.[14]

\* \* \*

This frontal assault on the very existence of a penal law— initiated by (1) the fact that no lawmaker would ever so will, and buttressed by (2) the collapse of the *indicia* as indicators— lays the ground for further corroboration in the extrinsic arguments against the doctrine.

### EXTRINSIC ARGUMENTS *Contra*

#### A Tractable Citizenry

The argument that a conscientious citizenry would render an obligation in conscience unnecessary would seem to beg the question. Obedience by the people springing from a sincere religious and patriotic sense of what is right, just, and owing to the state does not indicate either (1) the absence of a moral obligation (and, hence, the presence of a penal law), or (2) the legislature's intent not to bind in conscience. Rather, orderliness and law-abiding habits of the people indicate that the moral force of the law is having its calculated effect and that the citizenry is obedient out of respect for the law itself, not in fear of the sanction. One might turn the argument about and conclude that therefore no sanction at all is necessary.

### The Penal Sanction Alone Fulfills the Purpose

The overall health and well-being of a nation must ultimately depend on a responsible habit of self-policing by the people rather than on the vigilance, strength, and all-seeing eye of the enforcement agencies. This does not mean that the police arm of the state should not be firm, vigorous, and alert. This would be to deny the efficacy and purpose of all sanction and would be as untenable as the other extreme of placing all reliance on the penalty. It has been well contended, however, that the penalty is in fact a very weak deterrent to violation of the law. Rather, fear of disgrace, timidity, lethargy, and, principally, moral obligation are the controlling forces. Both the moral obligation to obey the law itself and the subsequent sanction for disobedience do, nonetheless, have their proper place—whatever may be the proportion—in the total scheme of the order of the law. Each complements the other. Set off the multitude of occasions where the citizen finds himself the only policeman at hand against the few instances (for example, the excise-tax examples) in which law-enforcement officers are able to detect and apprehend violations of the law. Obedience and right order, therefore, depend on the individual's conviction that he should obey—not out of fear of the sanction but out of respect for the common welfare.

A heavy penalty or a robust enforcement arm can never alone effect order in a state; nor would they render an obligation in conscience unnecessary. They certainly do not indicate a legislative intention to remove the duty of obedience for the majority of the citizenry who would never be apprehended and to impose the sanction alone on the few whom the vigilance and diligence of the police might detect and convict.

In examining the suggestion that obedience was meant to spring solely from the arm of the magistracy (thus rendering the further obligation in conscience unnecessary), first consider the positive arguments against the possibility of the penal law, and then ask: If such were the intent, why did not the legislature state openly that its only concern was the sanction? When has one heard a legislature first command obedience and then openly demand only the penalty upon conviction? Since the assumption would seem to be (it is for Suarez a presumption) that the law does oblige in conscience and not to the contrary, a valid norm for the absence of a penal law would be the absence of an express declaration by the lawgiver that it was such a law. (With the *Codex Juris Canonici* this is exactly the case, since it is assumed that no penal law exists.)

### Undue Burden on the Good

When one bears in mind that (1) only just and reasonable laws are binding, (2) restrictive statutes are strictly construed in favor of freedom, (3) a sizable body of principles of conduct has grown over the centuries designed specifically to cope with any harshness in the law (as Chapter IX will show), there is little reason to fear that the absence of the penal-law theory would place a disproportionate burden on the honest and conscientious and leave unscathed the unscrupulous and disobedient. Do not be misled, however. The honest and the good in this life often appear to have and often do have the more difficult lot. That, however, is not attributable to the absence of the penal law but rather to the presence of a strict moral code of conduct which does impose a burden at times painful and repugnant. Thus, Herron says:

> No one can deny that to observe the dictum of Christ, to render to Caesar the things that are Caesar's, is not always easy. But life in this world was not meant to be a bed of roses. The objection that it creates great burdens for honest people is useless. After all, when

St. Paul gave his famous admonition to the early Christians, even though the pagans then living knew of no such thing as conscience [sic], that did not deter him. He knew the burden he was placing upon the Christians but he also knew that justice demanded obedience to lawful authority, and he insisted upon it. Confessors and pastors must do likewise today. They must not minimize the obligations of civil law, but rather teach men that the commands of their civil magistrates are sanctioned by God and that submission to their salutary commands is necessary in order to please God and avoid sin. After all, civil obedience is part of the law of God. Pastors and confessors must teach the law of God in its totality.[15]

## The Multiplicity of Statutes

There seems to be a fallacy latent here which presupposes that the laws allegedly penal are in some way unjust or unnecessary or passed at the whim of the legislature. If this were true of a law, it would not be binding in any event. If, on the contrary, it is necessary and useful and just, questions immediately arise: Why should it not be obeyed? Why should the citizen not be bound in conscience? It could be added, moreover, that the intricacy and the multiplicity of regulations in matters affecting the natural law, the divine positive law, and the ecclesiastical law are equally burdensome and discouraging—more so—and yet there cannot be found in this an argument for removing the moral obligation. In short, this abundance of legislation is the high price that the citizen of today pays for the luxury of democracy and the complexity of modern living.

## Retrenchment

At the conclusion of their treatises, many moralists have given an intimation of a retreat by strongly deprecating and discountenancing the broad dissemination of the doctrine in writings and public preaching.[16] To the contrary, they maintain, all good citizens should be encouraged to observe the law and follow fully any just and reasonable legislation.[17] Implicit in such disapproval of widespread broadcasting of the theory, especially to the less educated, lies an attempt to rebut the allegations that the doctrine will undermine all law and right order. They are, in fact, embarrassed to hold the theory.

There is an unwarranted desire to make capital of this. But prudence is a virtue, and there are many instances, in moral theology especially, where dissemination is inadvisable (for example, the doctrine of occult compensation). It is nonetheless arresting to read Sabetti-Barrett: "However that may be, it is certain that nothing of this should ever be mentioned to the people, especially the less educated. They ought to be sweetly persuaded to follow all laws."[18]

### Internecine Opposition

Some validity can be given to the argument that the internal disagreement and confusion within the school itself is at least indicative of inherent weakness. With one variant of the theory condemning another and another, another, it would be possible to eliminate all of the varied approaches by the authority of the proponents themselves. Self-extinction is predictable. It should be somewhat unnerving to an adherent to cope with the fundamental disagreement within the fold and to realize that each proponent would exterminate the other. At best, such a state of affairs should warn that a thorough investigation is in order.

\* \* \*

From all this, the very existence of the penal law can be questioned. Grant, however, its nonexistence in fact, is it intrinsically possible? Although one would be inclined to argue from nonexistence in fact to impossibility in theory, it is fundamentally not a valid illation.

## CHAPTER VI

# The Brief for the Civil Law

## II

*From Gratian* (1140) *to Suarez* (1581)—*The History*

Undoubtedly the most intriguing area of an already engrossing subject is the highly improbable history of the purely penal concept. One suspects some sort of metempsychosis. It is as if the theorists over the centuries—from Gratian, through John the German, Penafort, Aquinas, Henry of Ghent, de Castro, and to Suarez himself—concluded to a conspiracy; as if they reasoned that the concepts of conscience, obligation, and the law, and of fault, punishment, and pain would eventually metamorphose themselves into other concepts, concepts with the same names but with altogether different meanings.

This, of course, is pure fantasy, but it serves to highlight a genuinely fascinating birth and evolution, and transformation, of an idea. It also serves notice that there has been in cold fact, apart from metaphor and simile, a very real, and in the eyes of some an incredible, transmutation. One can scarcely recognize in the mature concept of 1600 the one first formed centuries earlier. But most of all, it serves to emphasize the importance of this history. Only by means of a step-by-step study of the origin in history and earliest beginnings of the penal-law theory[1] can one gain any insight into the intrinsic illogicality of its nature. When one knows the origin of the theory and follows its growth over the centuries, the later attack by Bellarmine and his adherents will carry more cogency. This is the role of the history in the progress of the intrinsic argumentation.

There are in this history of the concept four marked stages, each with distinctly different fact situations, governing principles, and philosophies: (1) the work of Raymond of Penafort (1222-1237), the gloss (1234) on the canon of the *Decretum Gratiani* (1140), and the text of the *Decretales Gregorii IX* (1234), (2) the concept applied to the rule of religious (1272), (3) the Thomistic application in the personal life of man (1272), and (4) the final evolution in the civil law (1581).

Only through the knowledge of the essential facts and an intimate understanding of the radically different meanings attached at each stage respectively to law, violation, *culpa*, and *poena* can there be a full realization that each transition from one historical period to the next is a major leap to a level of legal analysis, interpretation, and rationalization essentially different in kind—not merely in degree—from the precedent one.

At this point, moreover, it should be understood that the phrase "purely penal-law theory" cannot be applied to all four stages. That there is a nonlegal, purely penal concept in all four is possible, but what is nonlegal in the first stage[2] cannot become legal in the fourth by the mere employment of some jurisprudential legerdemain. Note also from the beginning the meanings attached to the various key words, notably *poena*—"penalty" and "punishment" or "pain" and "hardship."

### RAYMOND OF PENAFORT

The focal figure in the earliest genesis of the theory was the celebrated lawyer-priest, Raymond of Penafort (1175-1275). Saint, general of the Dominicans, professor of canon law at twenty, Penafort brought his influence to bear at three extremely important points of impact, centering in (1) his revision of the Dominican constitutions (1228-1236), but perhaps more seriously influencing the incipient theory through (2) his masterful *Summa de Poenitentia* (1222-1237) and (3) his compilation of the historic *Decretales Gregorii IX* (1230-1234).

## The Dominican Constitutions

It is conceded that the concept had its very first appearance in the constitutions (specifically in the prologue) of the Order of Preachers[3] revised and reedited by Penafort. In the prologue it was specifically stipulated that the friars were not to be bound in conscience. The relevant wording: "In order therefore that we might provide for the unity and peace of the whole Order, we wish and we declare that our Rule and our Constitutions should not bind us under sin but only to a penance, unless out of contempt or on account of an order of the superior."[4] There is little doubt that this is the earliest mention in history of such an approach.[5] This work was concluded at the latest in 1236. The original Dominican constitutions of 1228 had no mention of the concept. Thus, the clause ("*[Constitutiones]* *non obligent nos ad culpam, sed ad poenam*—[The Constitutions] do not bind us under sin but only to a penance") expressing the purely penal theory was formulated between 1228 and its first appearance in Penafort's revision in 1236, the year of the General Chapter at which this new insertion was promulgated.[6]

Of far greater interest, however, than the specific words of the prologue is their background and the factors that contributed to their appearance.

## The Summa of Penafort

As the practice in the Church of external penances gradually gave way to auricular confession and the treatment of sin in the internal forum, the ancient *libri poenitentiales* (formbooks of sins and prescribed penances) passed into desuetude and were supplanted by a new genre of ecclesiastical literature—moral casebooks and treatises to guide the confessor in solving questions of conscience in the confessional. The most successful of these *summae* was that of Raymond of Penafort.

In his *Summa*, written over the years 1222 to 1237,[7] two outstanding points explain the thinking he carried to the constitutions and, of course, thus also explain the first faltering steps of *lex pure poenalis*.

In the section of the *Summa* where he treated the moral obligation of impost taxes—important clearly because of the central role of taxation in the mature doctrine—Penafort took a firm and conservative position: Pay the tax if just.[8] Hence, no application of the penal concept to the civil law could be attributed to Penafort in his *Summa*. This traditional view on imposts was followed by later *summistae*, not an insignificant consideration.

Most important of all historically, however, and a point of the greatest interest to those studying the growth of the doctrine is the appearance in Penafort's writings of what was to become the celebrated maxim of *lex pure poenalis* and the keystone of its philosophy: *Sine culpa, sed non sine causa*—"Without fault, but not without cause."

In his *Summa*, Penafort treated of certain hardships (*poenae*) of day-to-day living, major or minor visitations from God which can come to all and which are incurred without fault (*sine culpa*) on the part of the recipient but (*sed*) do have some underlying rationale or cause (*non sine causa*) for their being. The sole reference to these afflictions of human life was cursory, but it had relevance to the birth of *lex pure poenalis*:

> By way of continuing this subject, moreover, it should be noted that there are six cases [*sex casus*] in which a person suffers [*punitur*—the verb companion to *poena*] daily—justly and licitly—without fault, but not without cause [*(sine) culpa, sed non sine causa*]. Whence . . . [the verse, an hexameter in the Latin]: Poverty [*Pau-*

*pertas*], dislike [*odium*], prejudice [*favor*] and human failing, crime, and rank—these deprive persons and places of their rights.⁹

This reference in the *Summa*—produced during the years 1222-1237—to the maxim (*sine culpa, sed non sine causa*) and the notion of hardships suffered without fault are directly referable to another work of Penafort, his monumental compilation of canon law, the *Decretales Gregorii IX*.

### *The* Decretum Gratiani (*1140*) *and the* Decretales Gregorii IX (*1234*)

Historical research encourages the thesis that Penafort's maxim can be traced directly to a well-known marginal commentary on a canon in the *Decretum Gratiani*. The Italian Gratian, a learned Camaldolese monk of the twelfth century (he died *circa* 1158), collected and attempted to order the entire mass of ecclesiastical legislation extant. The result was his *Concordantia Discordantium Canonum*, popularly called the *Decretum Gratiani*. This concordance of the "discordant" canons (disciplinary laws, pronouncements of the popes, decisions of the councils) was completed about 1140 and was the outstanding work on canon law of the time. In a certain sense, Gratian could be said to be the founder of the science of canon law.

The canon in question in the *Decretum* had effected the promotion of the church of Constantinople to the rank of the second patriarchal see over that of the church of Alexandria, which theretofore had held that rank. This canon was a reformulation by Gratian of the original Canon XXI of the Fourth Council of Constantinople (869-870).¹⁰ The canon in Gratian read:

> C. VI. The church of Constantinople ranks second to Rome. . . . Restating the decrees of the holy council of Constantinople, we petition that the see of Constantinople should receive privileges similar to those that Rome, its superior, possesses (not however that it should have the primacy in ecclesiastical affairs that Rome has) and that since this see is second after Rome, it should be ranked before

[*prius quam*—opposite these words the commentary was appended]
the see of Alexandria; then Antioch, and after that, Jerusalem.[11]

The relevant commentary to the canon is attributed to Joannes
Teutonicus (1170-1245[6]),[12] who had inserted at the page
edge the following remark:

> Before. Thus, therefore, a certain church may be deprived of one of
> its rights without any fault on its part, and this may happen some-
> times through prejudice [*favorem*], sometimes through dislike
> [*odium*] . . . Otherwise the rule is that no one should be deprived
> of a right without fault. . . . And note that although someone may
> lose a privilege without fault [*sine culpa*], never is it without cause
> [*numquam sine causa*]. Whence the verse: Poverty [*Paupertas*],
> and the rest.[13]

The obvious connection between this gloss by Joannes Teutonicus, estimated for the year 1234 (on the words *prius quam*
[before] in the canon in the *Decretum Gratiani*), and the
*Summa* completed in 1237 does not, however, establish who
might be the original author or whether each had resort to a
third. The use of the maxim in both gloss and *Summa*, the parallel in thought and examples, the resort to the aphoristic hexameter, may not reveal original authorship; but the fact that
Penafort adds *loca* (places) in his *Summa* to the *personas* (persons) who might suffer some loss of their rights leads one to
attribute this to a reference to the church at Alexandria and the
gloss of Teutonicus. Penafort, furthermore, accepted the six
cases (poverty, dislike, prejudice, and the rest) and the reasoning as well-known and established, and entered into no additional explanation of the hexameter, assuming perhaps the
knowledge by the reader of the details in Teutonicus. This explanation is buttressed by reference to the estimated dates of
publication—1234 for the gloss, 1237 for the *Summa*. Any res-
ervations about Teutonicus' gloss on *prius quam* in *Distinctio*
XXII of the *Decretum Gratiani* caused by the absence of a critical edition of his *Glossa Ordinaria* and the frailty of medieval

scribes (and more to the point, by the unbridled enthusiasm of armchair glossators) are somewhat offset by another gloss by Teutonicus on *Distinctio* LVI of the *Decretum Gratiani.* Here is the same basic thought.

> . . . in a case in which a person suffers a deprivation without fault. However, one should realize that many times a person suffers a deprivation without fault but not without cause.[14]

At worst, paleographers have a rebuttable presumption that John the German employed the maxim and the thought in the year 1234.

### *The* Decretales

The most coherent synthesis is also the most intriguing— that Joannes Teutonicus received the maxim itself and the germ of the idea which he employed in his glosses on Gratian from the broadly circulated *Decretales* of Gregory IX compiled by Penafort himself and finished in 1234, the year of the gloss and three years before the completion of the *Summa.*

Pope Gregory IX (1145?-1241), farsighted and vigorous, entrusted to Raymond of Penafort the four-year (1230-1234) task of collecting all the multiform legislation of the Church. These *Decretales Gregorii IX,* completed in 1234, were the first authentic collection of church law and were outstanding as the first major compilation (there were five intermediary collections) since the *Decretum Gratiani.* Both the *Decretum* and the *Decretales* were used as textbooks in the schools of canon law and were subjected to the glosses of the leading authorities of the day (for example, Joannes Teutonicus).

In the small intellectual world of the day, Teutonicus the canonist could hardly have failed to study the latest collection of canon law concurrently with his annotation of the earlier work of Gratian.

The *Decretales* contained in the body of the text the possible source of the maxim and the penal-law keystone. Here was an

instance of "hardship suffered without fault" so perfectly parallel to the demotion of Alexandria that Teutonicus would be unable to pass it by. The maxim, furthermore, was also present in
the very text itself, adduced in explanation of the subject under
treatment in the specific decretal. The pertinent wording concerned a privation occasionally incumbent on parties to the marriage contract.

> . . . wherefore in marriage many cases occur where the spouses are
> forced to continence—without fault, but not without cause.[15]

Here was another example of a *poena* undergone *sine culpa, sed
non sine causa*.

With this the circle is complete, since it was Penafort who
collected the *Decretales*, which, of course, was the first major
companion to the *Decretum Gratiani*. Thus, Penafort first studied
the canon in the *Decretum* (1140) when he compiled the *Decretales* and then later read Teutonicus' gloss of that canon when it
appeared in 1234. There is, moreover, no reason to suppose that
he did not then employ the reasoning of the gloss (which was
much more elaborate and detailed, patently more fully thought
out) and the maxim in his *Summa*. The date of the completion
of the *Summa*, 1237, however, favors the explanation that the
references in the *Summa* were made subsequent to the completion of the constitutions. Since the *Summa* was fifteen years in
the writing, this is by no means necessarily the case.

Although the thesis may be ill-founded that Teutonicus
(1234) received the maxim and the principle from the text of
the *Decretales* (1230-1234) and that Penafort in turn incorporated both in his *Summa* (1222-1237), the important and incontrovertible fact is that the maxim *Sine culpa, sed non sine causa*
and the examples and reasoning it supports (whether culled
from the spouses in the *Decretales*, the demotion of Alexandria
in the Teutonicus gloss on the *Decretum*, or from the *sex casus*
in the *Summa*) were at the base of Penafort's formulation of the

Dominican constitutions (1228-1236), where the penal concept appeared for the first time in history.

The better reasoning would seem to credit Teutonicus with the original and elaborated thinking, joined to the maxim, that Penafort took to his work on the constitutions.

The parallel between the *poena* suffered by the guiltless Alexandria and the "penal affliction undertaken for the good of the spirit [a penance]" (as Bellarmine described the *poena* imposed on religious[16]) was sufficiently pat to suggest to Penafort the appropriation of the reasoning of Joannes Teutonicus as expressive of the Dominican conviction that the Rule should not bind in conscience. Thus, what was said of a see become regulative of religious and seemingly matured into the maxim that was to be so prominent in the penal-law concept and to go down over the centuries to support the most fundamental notion of that system: a penalty—*poena*—inflicted *sine culpa, non sine causa.*

There are four major reflections relevant to this first transition from the gloss of John the German to the Dominican rule for religious: (1) Neither in the demotion of the see nor in the *sex casus* nor in the continence of the spouses nor in the prescriptions of the monastery was a true law to be found. Certainly the papal announcement classifying the various sees only remotely resembled a law. The other cases were more remote. Although it is a highly controverted matter, the majority and better opinion classifies the rules for religious as nonlaws—about which in detail later. (2) A violation in the proper sense was certainly in no way present in the facts involving Alexandria, the *Summa*, or the spouses. Only if the rules for religious are denominated laws can it be said that the failure of a religious to follow the rule is a violation. Rather, the neglect of the rule is simply the failure of the religious to select the better and more perfect course of action. (3) In no case was there a true fault (*culpa*). In all, however, there was a cause (*causa*) for the hardship— the lesser importance of Alexandria, mortification, probation, health, self-discipline, and the refusal to choose the better course. (4) Most important of all, none involved a genuine penalty (*poena*) in the strict sense.

This fourth reflection leads logically—perhaps belatedly—to a fuller discussion of one of the most disturbing areas in the Suarezian elaboration of the doctrine of *lex pure poenalis*. There is a seeming distortion of the Latin word *poena* and its offspring the verb *punio* (*poenio*). If there is any sleight of hand involved in the development of the system, it seemingly occurs in the juggling of the two meanings of *poena*. At a certain point in the reasoning, *poena* in the primary sense becomes *poena* in the transferred sense. Later, Thomas for his part held true to the double meaning. His followers made the transposition.

Harper's sets off the two meanings vividly. The primary meaning of *poena, ae,* f. is "indemnification, compensation, satisfaction, expiation, punishment, penalty."[17] The correlation of *poena* in this strict sense to fault is highlighted by the Harper's illustration of the meaning in Horace: "*Poenas aequas irroget peccatis*, Hor. S. 1. 3, 118 [He inflicts penalties proportioned to the sins]."[18]

On the other hand *poena* in the transferred sense has no intimation of a penalty or of fault: "II. Transfer., hardship, torment, suffering, pain, etc. (post-Aug.)."[19] The usage in Pliny confirms the distinction: "Plin. *In tantis vitae poenis* [In the great hardships of life]."[20]

These distinctions have relevance at every stage of this study. Since *punio*, "I punish," is of the same stem, its usage must be consonant with *poena* (for example, "I undergo the punishment or penalty," "I suffer the pain or inconvenience").

Although the parity between the hardships suffered in the several examples and the imposition of pain in the form of a penance upon monks is by no means intimate, there would be nothing reprehensible in the use by Penafort of the parallel and the maxim, unless it was maintained that the rules for religious involved (1) true laws, (2) true violations, (3) true fault, and (4) *poena* in the strict sense.

### Thomas Aquinas

The next major transition in the gradual growth of the theory came with the various commentaries of St. Thomas. As expected, both proponent and antagonist enlisted his support.

It is submitted that the proponents neglected to expose adequately the mind of Thomas and that he was opposed in principle to the theory.

Although the major, if not the exclusive, teaching of Thomas on law is found in Article 90 and following articles in the *Prima Secundae* of the *Summa Theologica*, the adherents of the theory place great, perhaps complete, reliance on two treatises elsewhere in the *Summa* relating to (1) the religious state and (2) the virtues.[21] Both treatises are in the *Secunda Secundae*. The two most reliable sources place the date of their composition between 1268 and 1272, some forty years after the *Summa* and *Decretales* of Penafort.

Thomas (1225-1274), as a Dominican living during the earliest years of the order and intimately acquainted with Raymond of Penafort (1175-1275) and his writings—his *Summa*, the *Decretales*, *Sine culpa, sed non sine causa,* the revision of the Dominican constitutions—used the rule of his own order as the focal point for his treatise on the nature of religious life, an understandably engrossing subject of the day.

The general context from which the purely penal concept is extracted concerns broadly—as the title of the discussion states —"Whether a religious always sins mortally by transgressing the regulations contained in the rule." This is the short Article 9 of the *Secunda Secundae* of the *Summa*.[22] It is clear from the total treatment that there is here no reference to the civil law. The treatise is only evidence that Thomas employed the purely penal notion, although not in application to the civil law, at least to the rule for religious. This rule, Thomas says (indicating that he appreciated fully the difference), "is imposed on the religious as something in the nature of a law."[23]

Thomas approaches his analysis in his usual fashion, beginning with three hypothetical objections followed by a substantive treatment of the question. He then undertakes to answer each objection in turn. In his answer to the first objection, Thomas begins by listing certain areas of religious life governed "by precept" which do bind under pain of mortal sin. He then instances other regulations binding under pain of venial sin. To these, finally, he compares the policy of his own order, which employs the purely penal approach.

> In one certain religious institute, however, to wit, the Order of Friars Preachers, such a transgression or omission by its very nature does not oblige under pain of sin [*non obligat ad culpam*] neither mortal nor venial, but only to submission to the penance [*solum ad poenam*] imposed, because the religious are bound in this way to observe the rules. They may, however, sin venially or mortally through neglect or concupiscence or contempt.[24]

Once Thomas has laid out these three gradations of culpability within the religious rule, he makes it unmistakably clear in his response to his second hypothetical objection that he has no reference to the civil law. (He, in fact, sets off the rule for religious against the civil law.) To understand Thomas' reply, it is best first to read his objection:

> 2. Besides, the Rule is imposed on a religious as something in the nature of a law. But he who transgresses the precept of a law sins mortally. Therefore it seems that a monk in transgressing those regulations of the Rule sins mortally.[25]

To this Thomas answers (in the reply to the second objection, immediately following his reference to his own order in his response to the first hypothetical):

> To the second objection it must be said that not every regulation contained in the law [*lege*] is set down by way of precept, but

some things are expressed in the form of a certain kind of ordination or statute obliging a definite penance [*poenam*]; thus in the
civil law transgression of a legal statute does not always render the
subject deserving of death. So also neither in ecclesiastical law do
all ordinations or public statutes bind under mortal sin. And likewise is it not so with the statutes of the Rule.[26]

It is clear that *lege* in the first sentence is not civil law, inasmuch
as Thomas specifically qualifies the word "law" by the adjective
"civil" later in the same paragraph. Rather, he is using it in the
wide sense as referring to the religious rule. This is what he
meant when he referred to the rule as "something in the nature
of a law [*lex quaedam*]" in Objection 2, to which this is a response. From this it can be seen that Thomas is setting off the
civil law from the religious rule. He makes the parallel between
the two insofar as each has distinct grades of importance and,
hence, culpability, but at no point does he include in the civil
law a body of purely penal regulations, as in the religious rule.

## THE SPECIAL PROBLEM OF THE RULES OF RELIGIOUS

Because of the important role in the history of the growth of
the penal concept, the question of the nature of the religious
rule[27]—law or otherwise—has obtruded itself into every analysis of the penal law. The question has historical implications as
well as an intimate relation to the penal-law nature of the civil
law. If these rules are adjudged true laws, there is some force
to the argument that St. Thomas would be prepared to apply to
the civil law his specific reasoning in their regard. There would
then be, moreover, some suasive force in comparing the civil law
to the rule for religious institutes where, over the centuries, the
purely penal concept has received almost universal application,
acceptance, and success.

If one grant *ex arguendo* that the rules for religious are true
laws, it must be said, however, that all of the same responses,
arguments, and rebuttals adduced against the theory in general

will nonetheless apply with equal force to the rules for religious and, hence, not enhance the position of the opposition from the aspect of intrinsic logic. The religious is simply bound in conscience to the rule, if it be a law: an important point which might easily be overlooked in the great attention paid by the merepenalists to the argument from the rules for religious.

It is here contended, however, that these rules are not in fact laws. It might be possible merely to say that they are nonlaws and leave it at that. The Dominican Gonzalez took that approach: "Nor should it be said that the statutes of many religious institutes are purely penal laws. . . . such statutes should be called simply nonlaws, rather than purely penal laws."[28]

Bellarmine analyzed the relationship between monk and order as one of contract and hence would not call the rules laws in a proper sense.[29] According to this line of thinking, the agreement that would result upon the entry of a monk into a monastery would permit stipulations exculpating the subject for violations of the rule and yet countenance the infliction of penances in the nature of disciplinary mortification or as a penitential practice (but unrelated to true moral guilt) or, as Bellarmine termed this penance, "a penal affliction undertaken for the good of the spirit."[30] He prefaced this definition by remarking, "It is not properly a penalty [*poena*] . . ."[31] This reasoning would be consonant with the interpretation and analysis of the historical development of the concept thus far elaborated —especially in relation to the distinctions between *culpa* and *causa* and between *poena* (punishment) and *poena* (pain).

Others would call these rules merely domestic precepts with none of the true binding force of law. According to this approach, the subject would do better if he followed the precept but still would commit no sin if he did not. His conduct would be deemed an imperfection (using the term as completely nonsinful in contradistinction to its use as the least category of true venial sin). Any disciplinary penances that the monk would receive would be theoretically unconnected with the failure to follow the precept and would be considered within the terms of the original contract willingly embraced by the entry into the order. Repeated and continued failure to follow the precepts would result in the "contempt" referred to by all commentators and ultimately the subject's dismissal from the order, inasmuch as this protracted conduct would be tantamount to a breach of the original agreement and an effective declaration that the monk had determined to sever relations with the organization.

In this regard, the antimerepenalist McGarrigle makes a seemingly incomprehensible conclusion in regard to the violation of the rule by a religious. "It is not a sin, yet morally wrong; and for it, the Religious is rightly punished, as for a fault, and rightly confesses it."[32] This is particularly puzzling in the light of McGarrigle's generally unassailable position.

Suarez is highly conscious of the problem but supports strongly the position that the rules for religious are true laws, although he acknowledges that there is a genuine controversy "whether such an ordination if existent should be called a law or not."[33] On this he takes a firm stand: "Some reply that these are not laws but only counsels or some kind of conventions and as it were pacts. But this is asserted gratuitously."[34]

Perhaps the most widely accepted analysis emphasizes the basic difference between the two societies and denies the essential parity between the nature and origin of a religious order and that of the civil state. It is upon this distinction that the approaches in this treatise are based.

A society in general, encompassing societies of every kind (the state, the family, the church, a social club, a business enterprise), is a stable, moral union of many persons. Its purpose is the common good of all, to be attained by mutual cooperation.

Probably the most fundamental distinction categorizing societies and the one relevant to present purposes regards their origin and goes to their most inner essence. Ask: Whence the society? From God? From man? The answer will determine much of the purely penal problem and specifically the nature of the religious rule.

A society which has its origin from God (there are only two —the state and the family) has had its nature and essence already formed and determined by God. It is a natural society and gains its efficacy, nature, and rules from the natural law. It is rooted in, and is an exigency of, the nature of man—man's natural need to live in society. It is about this natural society, specifically the civil state, and the nature of the law emanating therefrom, that this volume has concerned itself and will so concern itself in detail over the coming pages.

The positive society (there can be and are a multitude), however, can now be considered only out of the necessity of its comparison with the natural, the civil state, and must be relegated to the background. Far from having its essence, as it were, ready-made by God and the law of man's nature, the positive or arbitrary society finds its origin and its nature in the free agreement of men. A literary club? Then the nature may conform to whatever is the delectation of the literati. The members? All men, irrespective of differences? No, only those *selecti quidam* who meet the test. The rules? Whatever the membership wishes.

When one realizes that the religious order is not a natural, necessary society, which the state certainly is, it is possible to conceive of the applicability of the purely penal concept. The members of the order may establish any norms they wish by the contract of formation and entry. They may elect to membership or determine to withdraw at their own choice. This, of course, is what Bellarmine meant when he founded the rules for religious on contract. This can hardly be said of membership in the human race, in a civil state.

This explains, moreover, why Thomas could permit an exception to the moral binding force of religious rules and did not so do in the case of the civil law.

All of the nonlaw solutions to this problem are reducible to the same thing. The religious order is an arbitrary, free, positive society. Hence, its members can govern their actions by arbitrary agreements and, therefore, by rules and obligation as well. If they wish to exclude conscience obligation by agreement, no matter. Since the order is not a natural society, the members may determine its nature and essence. (It is interesting to note that some are ready to admit that the religious institute is only a positive society but counter that religious orders are empowered to enact laws properly so-called because they share in the jurisdiction of the Roman pontiff, who gains his power from divine, albeit positive, law.[35])

Whatever may be the true essence of the rules of religious orders,[36] the impact on the intrinsic nature of the penal concept cannot be great. If they are true laws,[37] then they bind in conscience but are subjected to all of the mitigations and qualifications (to be treated at length in Chapter IX) applicable to those civil laws which also bind in conscience. If they are not true laws, as it appears they are not, the probative value both historically and intrinsically of the arguments for the penal law is considerably weakened.

\*    \*    \*

The Thomistic treatise on the religious state illustrates the nexus with Penafort and in turn with the gloss of Teutonicus. The transition has yet to be made, however, beyond the limited application to the monastic rule.

### THE THOMISTIC APPLICATION TO MAN'S PERSONAL LIFE

The next stage in the growth of the concept is a major advance—from application to the monastic code to a special category in the personal life of man. At this point, moreover, *Sine culpa, sed non sine causa* and the principle which it embodies have been fully canonized by Thomas and will henceforward be found in every commentary on the doctrine. Thomas, in the second of the purely penal treatises, employs the maxim, the reasoning of the gloss, and the Rule in his discussion of so-called "vindication" (*De Vindicatione*) or "vengeance"—one virtue in his broader study of the virtues and vices. The English Dominicans translate this "On Vengeance." This is infelicitous. The word "vindication" is possibly more apt, as will be seen from the references to the virtue of *vindicatio*.

In the first 170 questions of the 189 of the *Secunda Secundae* of the *Summa*, Thomas has devoted himself to the theological (faith, hope, and charity) and cardinal virtues. In the heart of this section is Question 108, *De Vindicatione*. This tractate is concerned with that virtue which governs the acts of those in authority (chief of state, judge, bishop, governor, mayor, teacher, parent) in their treatment of those under their governance who have transgressed the rules of their respective authority. "Vindication [or 'vengeance'] consists in the imposition of a penal evil on one who has sinned."[38] "Therefore, it should be said that he who imposes a vindicative penalty on the sinful, in keeping with his rank and position, does not arrogate to himself what belongs to God, but rather exercises the power bestowed on him by God . . ."[39] The norms of this virtue are directed to the guidance of the personal conduct of the person in charge and secondarily to the subject. Scarcely could they be said to involve the civil law. A study of the Thomistic reference to man's personal life is essential to an evaluation of the legitimacy of the penal-law resort to Thomas and of the concept's validity as applied to the civil law.

The now-crystallized principle is the one pronouncement in the dissertation on vindication of paramount interest to the purely penal concept: "And according to this, a person sometimes suffers [*punitur*] without fault [*sine culpa*], not however without cause [*non tamen sine causa*]."[40] On this slightly more elaborate form of the maxim is placed almost exclusive reliance for the Thomistic position and for support of the doctrine. To whatever extent this advertence by Thomas to the concept could be said to be "in a moral setting,"[41] to that extent only can he be said to approach the use of the concept in the field of the civil law. It rather is spiritual advice (1) to the one in authority—counseling him as to the degree of hardship, discomfort, pain, which can be inflicted on or be permitted to a subject and (2) to the subject—apprising him of the occasions on which he can justifiably expect such distasteful visitations from God at the hands of His ministers, those in authority.

But the unqualified quotation of the maxim, without a study of the context and an analysis of its correct intrinsic meaning as intended by Thomas, is deceiving. It must be concluded, in fact, that Thomas intended to apply the principle to the moral life of man only in the most remote way—more properly to his spiritual life—and indubitably in no way to the civil law.

Two distinct considerations make clear the extent to which Thomas meant to employ the so-called "purely penal" concept in man's spiritual life: (1) the marked advertence Thomas made to the two meanings of *poena* and (2) the applications of the maxim and the concept, as seen by his examples, which are as distant from true law as is the demotion of the see of Alexandria.

### Two Kinds of Poena

The English language has inherited two completely different concepts from the one Latin word *poena*, and they admirably illustrate the two meanings of *poena* distinguished by Thomas. The first translation is "punishment" or, perhaps better, "penalty"— in the sense that both denote a sanction and connote the presence of culpability. The second, and the more obvious etymologically, is "pain"—the same sound as *poena*. There is no intimation or necessity of "penalty" or "punishment" in "pain," although it would be an unusual punishment or penalty that carried no pain. It should be clear that *poena* in the strict sense of a sanction, "penalty," led to the post-Augustan usage of *poena* in the wide sense ("pain," or some kind of inconvenience, hurt, affliction, visitation, or suffering—all legitimate renditions of *poena*).

Thomas makes these distinctions between *poena* and *poena*, and in so doing defines their inner nature by including the notion of fault in the one as of the essence—and excluding it in the other as equally outside the essence. Culpability is as much a necessary prerequisite to sanction as it is abhorrent to the unqualified notion of pain.

> *Poena* can be considered in a double sense. In one way, according to the very essence of a penalty. And under this aspect a penalty is not due except for sin, because through a penalty the equality of justice is restored, insofar as he, who by sinning follows his own will to excess, suffers something that is contrary to his own will. Wherefore, since every sin is voluntary . . . it follows that no one is punished in this way unless for something which was voluntarily done.[42]

Corroborative evidence of the Thomistic definition of *poena* in the strict sense can be found in an altogether different part of the *Summa*, in the *Prima Secundae*, in his specific treatment of the question "Whether every penalty [*poena*] is imposed on account of some fault [*culpam*]."[43] To this question comes the unequivocal response:

> If one is speaking of *poena* in the strict sense, according to which it partakes of the essence of penalty, thus always does it have a relation to antecedent fault.[44]

Thus, penalty connotes fault. It can properly be referred to law. It is the sanction for the law's violation. Set off against this strictly legal notion of penalty is the second meaning, about which the treatise on the virtue of vindication concerns itself.

> Secondly, *poena* may be considered as a medicine, not only healing the past sin but also preserving from future sin, or conducing to some good. And according to this a person sometimes suffers [*punitur*] without fault, not however without cause.[45]

And this *poena* is pain, something unpleasant or distasteful, as Thomas continues, citing the first of several examples:

> And thus sometimes a person suffers in regard to his temporal affairs without fault, such as the many hardships inflicted by God in this present life for our humiliation or probation.[46]

It is only by reflection on Thomas' applications to specific fact situations that one can appreciate fully the nature of *poena* in the wide sense. The next three examples give further conviction to the double definition.

> Reply to Objection 2 . . . Wherefore a person ought never, at the judgment of a human court, be subjected, without fault, to the punishment of flogging, so that he be killed or mutilated or wounded.
>
> The hardship, however, of some deprivation may be imposed on a person, even at the hands of another human being, although without fault, but not without cause [*sine culpa, sed non sine causa*]. And this in three ways: First, a person may be disqualified, without any fault of his own, from the acquisition or retention of some advantage. Thus, a person afflicted with leprosy must be removed from the administration of a church. Another person, for bigamy or because he has pronounced the death sentence on someone [as a judge], incurs an impediment to the reception of sacred orders.[47]

This impediment of "bigamy" goes back to St. Paul, who stipulated that the ordinand be *"unius uxoris vir* [a man of one wife]"—that is, as the *Codex Juris Canonici* puts it, he may not have contracted *"duo vel plura matrimonia valida successive* [two or more valid marriages successively]."[48] The reprobation expressed implicitly in the impediment, therefore, is not simultaneous bigamy, which is sinful and would warrant punishment, but consecutive, which is not only not sinful but may be commendable under other circumstances.

> Second, because the particular advantage that a person forfeits is not a personal possession but is common to all. Thus, whether a certain church has the status of an episcopal see is a matter affect-

ing the entire city and is not a question only of the aggrandisement of the clergy.[49]

Thomas was here rebutting an objection to the effect that "a church ceases to be an episcopal see because of the depravity of the people. Therefore [concludes Thomas *ex arguendo*], *vindicatio* is imposed only for voluntary sin."[50]

> Third, because a benefit inuring to one person may depend on the integrity of another. Thus, in the case of high treason, a son loses his inheritance through the sin of his parent.[51]

The best—or the worst—that could be said of these various *poenae* is that they were afflictions or inflictions bearing pain, hardship, suffering, or unpleasantness, but were totally unrelated to fault. The visitation from God, the loss of his pastorate by the leprous priest, the denial of sacred orders to the bigamous ordinand or the judge-would-be-cleric, the demotion of the episcopal see, the loss of the treasonous inheritance—all are of a piece with the see of Alexandria, the *sex casus*, the spouses, with the religious who chose not the better course.

The parallel throughout these cases is the same. No true law has issued in any one of them. The act of God, demotion of a see, removal from a pastorate, denial of orders, loss of inheritance, penance imposed on a monk, have no essential relation to a law. They could range from the order of parent to that of pope.

In none of them was there a violation—let alone a true law —except in the analogous sense of calling the religious rule a law.

More important, in none was there a *culpa*. A cause, true, else the act would be unreasonable and absurd.

As an inexorable consequence, there can be no sanction. Nor was there any. The *poena* that may logically and justly be imposed for such nonculpatory cause can only be nonsanctive, can be no more than some visitation from God—directly from God, perhaps (as the leprosy), or indirectly through man (as the treason of a parent). This *poena*—pain, suffering, unpleasant-ness—may have some healthy, curative spiritual effects known to God or the superior. It may be designed as a disciplinary help or, as Thomas says, a humiliation or probation, but it must not be confused with a sanction in the strict sense imposed as a consequence on the violation of a law.

This, and no more, is what Thomas meant when he employed the celebrated principle *Sine culpa, non tamen sine causa.*

One might justifiably refer to the reasoning of Thomas in this treatise as the application of some kind of a purely penal concept to the personal life of man, if one understood the correct meaning of "penal," but he scarcely would connect it with anything legal or involving civil-law sanction. Thomas would be in wonderment at the thought of applying the *poena sine culpa* of the leprous cleric to a "tax dodger."

This is the whole of Thomas on the matter. It can now be judged to what extent, if at all, he used even the purely penal concept—let alone the penal-law doctrine.

## THE CONCEPT APPLIED TO THE LAW

The purely penal concept contented itself, in the main, for over two centuries with applications to the rules for religious and analogies similar to those begun by Joannes Teutonicus and elaborated on by Thomas. In 1355 the assembled fathers applied the concept to the provisions of the Provincial Council of Toledo which, of course, contained ecclesiastical legislation: "That transgressions of the provincial constitutions shall bind transgressors, not under pain of sin, but only to a penalty."[52] The tradition against the theory in application to ecclesiastical law has been so clear-cut, however, that this one isolated instance cannot carry weight. Thus Arregui says unqualifiedly: "In ecclesiastical law they are not, in fact, found."[53]

Henry of Ghent (1217?-1293), writing shortly after Thomas, has been considered an exception. He used the maxim not only in application to the religious state but also, allegedly, in a limited way to the civil law.[54]

Later and more intensive research,[55] however, has reached the clearly tenable conclusion that "Although sometimes regarded as the father of the purely-penal-law theory, Henry of Ghent is more eligible for the title of earliest known opponent of the theory."[56] He paralleled Thomas closely in applying the penal concept to the religious rule and concluded his treatise on the subject: "Although he [the religious] undergoes the *poena* in this instance without fault, it is not without cause [*sine culpa, non tamen sine causa*]."[57]

It was Alfonso de Castro, O.F.M. (1495-1558), who took St. Thomas' work and the commentaries of Henry of Ghent[58] and formulated the first formal application of the concept to the civil law.[59] Although his work was a major breakthrough, it was too thoroughly overshadowed by Suarez to warrant special study. He placed prime reliance in his reference to the civil law, as would Suarez after him, on the omnipresent maxim: "But *poena* . . . does not necessarily depend on fault. Because although *poena* is never imposed on someone without cause [*sine causa*], frequently, however, it is imposed on someone without his own fault [*sine culpa sua*]."[60]

Thus, from the gloss of John the German that Penafort first read along the page of the *Decretum Gratiani*, the purely penal law burst into full bloom in the complex system of Suarez.

## CHAPTER VII

# The Brief for the Civil Law

## III

### *The Intrinsic Argumentation*

Toward the end of the sixteenth century, the doctrine had reached its maturity, and the lines of protagonist and antagonist were clearly drawn. From the simple gloss of Teutonicus, it developed to forthright application to the civil law, at least in the limited area indicated. It is interesting that the leaders of the two camps were towering theologians, exact contemporaries, and Jesuits: Francis Suarez (1548-1617) and Robert Cardinal Bellarmine (1542-1621).

With Suarez, the chief expositor and major proponent,[1] the vast majority of theologians over the centuries have aligned themselves. Notable supporters among the moderns are D'Annibale,[2] Lehmkuhl,[3] Billuart,[4] Janssens,[5] and, certainly, Vermeersch.[6] The most recent is Dunn,[7] but it ought to be noted that Rodrigo,[8] among the very modern proponents, has the most thorough contemporary treatment. And, of course, Calvin held firmly that the civil law was not binding in conscience.[9] The modern German Schilling could speak for the present-day consensus of merepenalists.

> The human lawgiver has the authority, within his own proper competence, to impose an obligation on the will, either under sin, or under sin and punishment, or even to impose no obligation. Therefore it is incomprehensible why he should not possess at the same time the lesser competence to oblige merely in an imperfect and indirect way—namely, to oblige only under pain of punishment—with the view of satisfying the public welfare.[10]

The great Bellarmine, on the other hand, had very few supporters. As Litt put it: "The adversaries [of the theory], known and avowed, could almost be numbered on the fingers of the hand."[11] Litt, however, was speaking more than twenty years ago, and one would like to think that these adversaries have increased in the very recent days. Slightly antedating Bellarmine, both Sylvester[12] and Soto opposed the theory. The Dominican Dominic Soto (1494-1556) attacked the purely penal laws on the basis of intrinsic impossibility.[13] The principal support to Bellarmine and the early opponents has come in the twentieth century with such as Koch,[14] Renard,[15] Lopez,[16] Litt,[17] Woroniecki,[18] Davitt,[19] McGarrigle,[20] and Häring. Although not so thorough as Rodrigo or Litt, Häring presents the thinking of a modern German opponent to the theory: "According to the theory which defends the existence of purely penal laws, the subject of the law has a species of free choice. He may either fulfill the precept itself or accept the penalty for violating the law. He may choose either alternative without sin. This theory I look upon as entirely false."[21] The work of the Frenchman Litt, in two parts, is one of the finest treatments on the subject and would seem to represent the best modern thought antagonistic to the theory.

The editors of *America* had this to say regarding the penal-law theory: "We very much doubt its validity, because all true law, being designed to promote the common good, simply specifies the general obligation we all have to cooperate to that end. So if purely penal law is ever embalmed, we'll applaud."[22] *America* was prompted in its comment by the incisive polemic (brashly but well written) against the doctrine by McGarrigle,[23] to which in mild rebuttal appeared a nontechnical response by John R. Connery, S.J.[24]

Though somewhat less a theologian than a controversialist (his works number twelve volumes in folio), orator, and leader, Robert Francis Cardinal Bellarmine, S.J., was one of two Jesuit saints (Canisius was the other) whom the Church made doctors. He was raised to this status in the early days of the order, troublous times for the Church.

Just as it is indisputable that the Suarezian system is the prototype of the doctrine, so will the synthesis of the nature of law of Bellarmine, with its positive attack on the grounds of intrinsic impossibility, serve as the outline of the arguments against the theory. Throughout, resort will be had to Aquinas who is in spirit and fundamentals deeply opposed to the concept.

It is further submitted that had the theory reached any recognizable form in Thomas' time, he would have rejected it.

## The Eternal Law

The ultimate foundation of all law begins with the very beginning of things. God as the Creator of the entire universe projected from all eternity, as a part of the Divine Essence,[25] the divine plan for the governance of all things. Thomas shows the relationship between the Divine Wisdom and the law expressing that Wisdom governing the universe.

> Just as in every artificer there preexists an exemplar of the things that are made by his art, so too in every governor there must preexist the exemplar of the order of those things that are to be done by those who are subject to his government. . . . Now God, by His wisdom, is the Creator of all things, in relation to which He stands as the artificer to the products of His art. . . . Moreover, He governs all the acts and movements that are to be found in each single creature . . . so the exemplar of Divine Wisdom, as moving all things to their due end, bears the character of law. Accordingly, the eternal law is nothing else than *the exemplar of Divine Wisdom, as directing all actions and movements.*[26]

It is from this all-embracing government of the Eternal Legislator that all law derives its force and efficacy. As St. Augustine says, referring to the eternal law:

> . . . that law, which is called the highest reason, which must always be obeyed, and through which all the bad merit misery, the good a blessed life; through which, finally, that which we said ought to be called temporal is properly managed and changed. . . . I see this law as eternal and incommutable. . . . At the same time I also believe that you see that nothing is just and legitimate in that which we call temporal which man does not derive from the eternal.[27]

So, too, did Bellarmine begin his reasoning: "All law is a participation in the eternal law of God. . . . and a certain participation of the eternal law of God, which is the first and highest rule . . ."[28] Again: "For whether one violates the natural law or the positive or the divine or the human, he always sins against the eternal law, since all law is a participation in the eternal law."[29] Aquinas corroborates Bellarmine: "Since, then, the eternal law is the plan of government in the Chief Governor, all plans of government which are in the inferior governors must be derived from the eternal law. But these plans of inferior governors are all the other laws which are in addition to the eternal law. Therefore, all laws, insofar as they partake of right reason, are derived from the eternal law."[30]

## THE NATURAL LAW

In the same act of creation, God the eternal legislator promulgated the precepts of His eternal law in the natures of His subjects, whether animate or inanimate. Obviously, Bellarmine is concerned only with that division of the eternal law which governs man. Thus, the promulgation of the eternal law in the case of rational creatures is achieved through their rational natures. The eternal law of God is expressed by the natural law in man's heart.[31] "And this participation of the eternal law in the rational creature is called the *natural law*."[32]

Aquinas summarized these concepts admirably:

> There are present in all beings certain principles by which these beings are able not only to effect their own proper operations but also by which they direct these operations to their end . . . Thus in things acting from the necessity of nature there are principles of action proper to the essence of each by which their operations are directed conformably to their end; so in those beings which participate in cognition there are principles of cognition and appetite. Whence it follows that there is natural conception in the cognoscitive sense and a natural appetite or inclination in the appetitive power by which operation . . . is directed to its end. But man among all animals knows the true significance of finality and the relation of a work to its end, since a natural tendency is imprinted in his nature by which he is directed to act properly, and this is called the natural law or the natural right. In other beings, however, it is called a natural estimative power, for brutes are forced by nature . . . rather than regulated as it were by their own free will.[33]

All would agree, therefore, with Suarez that ultimately the norm of conduct, the expression of the natural law, is the rational nature as such.[34]

## Man a Social Animal

Bellarmine, hearkening back to Thomas and, in turn, to Aristotle, characterizes man as a social animal by nature,[35] and, accordingly, by the law of this nature are men joined together in society.

> However, it is natural for man to be a social and political animal, to live in a group, even more so than all other animals, as the very needs of his nature indicate. For all other animals nature has prepared food, hair as a covering, teeth, horns, claws as a means of defense, or at least speed in flight. Man, on the other hand, was created without any natural provision for these things. But, instead of them all he was endowed with reason, by the use of which he could procure all these things for himself by the work of his hands. But one man alone is not able to procure them all for himself; for one man could not sufficiently provide for one life unassisted. It is therefore natural that man should live in company with his fellows.[36]

### Legitimate Authority Must Be Obeyed

This society, Bellarmine continues, once established, is ruled by one receiving his authority from God through the consent of the governed.[37] "If, therefore, it is natural for man to live in the society of many, it is necessary that there exist among men some means by which the group may be governed. For where there are many men together and each one is looking after his own interest, the group would be broken up and scattered unless there were also someone to take care of what appertains to the common weal."[38] The natural law that brought men together in society also orders them to obey the duly constituted authority placed over that society.[39]

> Moreover, the highest duty is to respect authority and obediently to submit to just law. By this the members of a community are effectually protected from the wrong-doing of evil men. Lawful power is from God, "and whosoever resisteth authority resisteth the ordinance of God." Wherefore, obedience is greatly ennobled, when subjected to an authority which is the most just and supreme of all. But where the power to command is wanting, or where a law is enacted contrary to reason, or to the eternal law, or to some ordinance of God, obedience is unlawful, lest while obeying man we become disobedient to God.[40]

Thus, all authority comes from God through the natural law. In the natural-law principle "Legitimate authority must be obeyed" lies the foundation for the whole positive-law structure.[41] This authority is necessary for the proper ordering of the state, for the preservation of the peace of the community.[42] It augments the natural moral law, prescribes rules for those areas of human activity which are not directly provided for in the natural-law precepts already imprinted in man's heart.[43] The law then that the state inaugurates in furtherance of the divine plan must always be directed to this end—the common good. Man's reason looking at man's nature tells him what is just and right and consonant with this nature and this end.[44]

At this point, Bellarmine has narrowed the discussion. There has never been any question of the binding force of that area of the positive law which merely restates the natural—mere declarations[45] of the natural law. Leo XIII describes these reasoned conclusions of the natural law expressed by the positive:

> Of the laws enacted by men, some are concerned with what is good or bad by its very nature. They command men to follow after what is right and to shun what is wrong, adding at the time what is a suitable sanction. But such laws by no means derive their origin from civil society; because, just as civil society did not create human nature, so neither can it be said to be the author of the good which befits human nature, or of the evil which is contrary to it. Laws come before men live together in society, and have their origin in the natural and consequently in the eternal law. The precepts, therefore, of the natural law contained bodily in the laws of men have not merely the force of human law, but they possess that higher and more august sanction which belongs to the law of nature and the eternal law.[46]

About these restatements of the natural moral law found in the positive law, Bellarmine no longer concerns himself. Instead, he turns to that area of the positive civil law which determines how these natural-law precepts are to be effected, to the *ad hoc* specifications of the natural law. Thus, says Thomas:

> But it must be noted that something may be derived from the natural law in two ways . . . secondly, by way of a determination of certain common notions. . . . the second is likened to that whereby, in the arts, common forms are determined to some particular. Thus, the craftsman needs to determine the common form of a house to the shape of this or that particular house . . . (for example, the law of nature has it that the evildoer should be punished, but that he be punished in this or that way is a determination of the law of nature). Accordingly, both modes of derivation are found in the human law. . . . But those things which are derived in the second way have no other force than that of human law.[47]

It is in this vast body of enactments, the determinations of the natural law, that is found, so it is said, the body of penal law.

Leo XIII comments further about these particular determinations of the natural law found in the positive civil law:

> Now, there are other enactments of the civil authority, which do not follow directly, but somewhat remotely, from the natural law, and decide many points which the law of nature treats only in a general and indefinite way. For instance, though nature commands all to contribute to the public peace and prosperity, still whatever belongs to the manner and circumstances, and conditions under which such service is to be rendered must be determined by the wisdom of men, and not by nature herself. It is in the constitution of these particular rules of life, suggested by reason and prudence, and put forth by competent authority, that human law, properly so-called, consists. This law binds all citizens to work together for the attainment of the common end proposed to the community and forbids them to depart from this end; and the same law, in so far as it is in conformity with the dictates of nature, leads to what is good, and deters from evil.[48]

Such is the total dependence of the positive law on the natural. Its origin and being from the exigencies of nature are expressed in the precept "Live in society." Its vigor and obligatoriness come from that natural-law precept "Obey legitimate authority."

From these fundamentals can be deduced the intimate nature of the civil law.

## The Essential Nature of Positive Law

Immediately deducible from this foundation are the three intrinsic notes of the positive law which constitute the very heart of this treatise on conscience, obligation, and the law and, hence, of the philosophy of the civil law. On the validity of these premises, consequently, does the penal-law system stand or fall. Each goes to the heart of the law. Without each there is no law. With all three there must be law. (1) True law binds in conscience. (2) Violation results in fault. (3) Fault warrants punishment.

This positive statement, in three parts, of the moral binding power of the civil law serves, moreover, as the response to the

Suarezian intrinsic argumentation, in parallel three parts, in Chapter IV: "The Case for the Defendant Theory."

## True Law Binds in Conscience

The explicit explanation of the source of the moral obligation of the positive law can be found in the junction of (1) the necessary demands of the common welfare (the finality of the common good)—"Live in society," and (2) the divinely endowed authority of the legislator—"Obey legitimate authority."

The ultimate rationale of the conscience obligation in the law lies in the absolute moral necessity incumbent upon any government to reach, or at least strive to reach, the one goal of any state—the peace, happiness, and domestic tranquillity of the citizens—the common good.

In the case of the means which are absolutely necessary to attain this goal, there is no difficulty in understanding that a moral obligation to embrace those means when commanded by law devolves upon the citizen and gains its efficacy directly from the necessary end. When one and only one means can possibly attain a necessary end (here the common good), the necessity of the means is directly referable to the necessity of the end. Thus, since justice must be administered, there must be legislation establishing a judicial system.

When, however, the necessary goal may be attained by one of several indifferent means, the obligation demanding obedience to the one means actually chosen by the legislator springs not only from the necessity of the final goal but relies in addition upon the principle that competent authority must be obeyed. This is founded on the necessity of choosing at least one of the several indifferent means. The means become necessary not because they are the only means but because some means must be chosen. Since someone must choose the means, the choice devolves upon the person in authority chosen by the consent of the governed.

Furthermore, the means which the legislator chooses need not be the best. They need be merely adequate. Thereby, they satisfy the one necessity: that at least one means, some means, be chosen to achieve the necessary final goal.

Since the moral obligation has its source in the finality of the common good, the lawmaker has in no way control over its presence or absence. The legislator may well conclude that the common good does not demand any legislation whatsoever. He will then refrain from legislating. But if he determines that legislation is necessary, the given statute that he determines upon obliges in conscience whether he wishes it or not. His determination that some means must be chosen, and the further selection of that means, *eo ipso* induces the moral obligation.

> Although it may depend upon the legislator whether he will truly command and establish a true law or rather only point out what should be done, without any order, nevertheless, if he seriously wishes to command and set up a true law, it is not in his power to impede the obligation, either mortal or venial depending on the magnitude of the thing.[49]

Aquinas supports Bellarmine in this important fundamental:

> Laws framed by man are either just or unjust. If they be just, they have the power of binding in conscience, from the eternal law whence they are derived, according to Prov. 8:15, "By Me kings reign, and lawgivers decree just things."[50]

This is what Leo XIII meant when he said: "This law binds all citizens to work together for the attainment of the common end proposed to the community."[51] Pope Leo, as Aquinas and Bellarmine, referred the obligatory nature of the positive law to the eternal law: "The binding force of human laws lies in the fact that they are to be regarded as applications of the eternal law and are incapable of sanctioning anything which is not contained in the eternal law, as in the principle of all law."[52]

1 Just as the Suarezian psychology of the will was fundamental to the Suarezian system, so is Thomas' and Bellarmine's

psychology of the lawmaking process, in placing the source of
the law in the intellect, the base of the Bellarmine system.

Of all the explanations of the ultimate reason for this conscience obligation, Bellarmine's is probably the most cogent:

> First, the matter is proved by this that the force of obligation is of
> the essence of law . . . and to oblige is its necessary effect. There-
> fore, all law by whomsoever it is passed, either by God, or an angel,
> or man—and if a man, a bishop, king, or father—obliges in the same
> way. . . . because it is of the essence of man to be rational and a
> quality proper to him is risibility, every man is rational and risible,
> whether created by God alone, as Adam, or by God through another
> man, as Eve, or born of men, as Cain. . . . It must be noted that as
> other things depend on an agent for their existence, not, however,
> for their essence, since essences are eternal . . . so also law, as far as
> existence is concerned, depends on the legislator, for it will not be
> law unless passed by him, since he has the authority. But as far as
> essence is concerned it does not depend on him since the fact that
> law obliges is eternal and immutable and a participation, as it
> were, in the eternal law of God. . . . And although it is not possible
> that a true law should not come from God . . . however if (by an
> impossible supposition) a law were not from God, it would none-
> theless oblige in conscience, just as it would be true if (by an im-
> possible supposition) a man were to exist who was not created by
> God, that he nonetheless would be rational.[53]

In a word, whatever one may wish to call this unrational "man,"
he is not in fact a man. And whatever one may desire to call a
"law" that does not oblige in conscience, it is in truth no law.
Although one may have "something," without an obligation in
conscience it is not a law.

The lawmaker, whether he be absolute monarch, constitutional president, or legislator, has before him two alternatives in
conveying his intentions for the reasoned governance of the state.
He may in clear and open terms issue a firm mandate (that is,
pass a law) or he may confine himself solely to his preferences
or wishes in a certain matter. Thus, the Roman pontiff can
through one of his congregations legislate categorically in

regard to the nature of the Eucharistic fast. Or he may in a pastoral letter express his fatherly wish that the faithful take a more active role in the liturgy and append thereto numerous concrete suggestions as to the nature of this participation.

In the former instance, there is no doubt that the pope has issued a command and expects obedience. An analysis of the nature of his order would indicate that the subject matter itself contains no intrinsic moral content. It is neither a reiteration of a natural-law precept nor a restatement of a divine-law commandment, but is merely one of several possible regulations, any one of which would have achieved the ultimate purpose of the law (that is, seemly preparation for the reception of the Blessed Sacrament). It represents, therefore, the reasoned conclusion of the Holy See after mature consideration of all possible, indifferent means to the necessary end. It gains its efficacy not by intrinsic goodness or morality—although obviously it may not be bad or unreasonable and yet command obedience—but through the final end of the law, as the reasonable choice of the duly constituted authority.

If, to the contrary, the legislator determines only to express a preference, the subjects are faced with a choice not between good and evil, but between the good and the better. There is clearly no sin if one of the faithful contents himself with obedience to the letter of the liturgical law and prefers to forgo a fuller participation. Were he to heed the pontiff's wishes, he would be more virtuous; but the act would be nonetheless supererogatory, in any case.

(Although the family is not a perfect society, as are church and state, a homely parallel might illustrate the reasoning. If a father clearly and firmly orders his son to remain home for the evening, disobedience is a sin. If the parent, however, grudgingly permits the son to leave but exhorts him to remain, there is no sin if he departs, although there would be greater virtue if he did not.)

As Bellarmine said, once the intellect has determined on a proper course and has presented the materials of its judgment to the will, it is not for the will to determine whether or not the subject is to be bound in conscience.[54] This has been done by the intellect's perceiving the intrinsic reasonableness of the course. In summary, the procedure comes to this:

> The work of the will in this matter cannot be overlooked. "To direct to the end" [Aquinas, *S.T.*, I-II, q. 90, a. 1] has been designated as the work of the reason, and this is true. It is true, however, only in this sense that the reason recognizes the order that must be observed or followed, knows the means that will accomplish this end, and presents, as it were, the *rule* to the will. The reason *directs*, but it is for the will to *effect*. Once the proper order has been decided upon by the reason, the will must apply this order. Thus law is *formally* in the reason as the rule and measure, and *efficaciously* in the will.[55]

This is the Thomistic approach to the mechanics of the legislative process.

> From this it can be declared that the lawgiver must first make a judgment in which he concludes to the reasonableness of the law. Next he wills that the law become binding. Finally he actually ordains through an act of the reason that the law is law. This last act of the reason is the ordination itself.[56]

Thus, a legislature may determine that the traffic regulation for an intersection could equally be served by a blinker, a four-way stop sign, a traffic signal, a two-way stop sign, a viaduct, or by no specification at all. Since someone must regulate in regard to this matter, once the legislator has determined for a good reason that one particular means is to be used, the order that emanates from that legislator is binding in conscience. The Dominican Gonzalez has reference to the same concept:

> For Suarezians, who hold that law is the work of the will, at least logic is preserved. But for Thomists, who say that law is the work of reason and who hold that the end (or the common good) founds

and orders all morality,—the very existence of society, the union of men, authority, law, and all other things—the holding of purely penal law is something incomprehensible.[57]

Nor is Gonzalez alone in his conviction. The Dominican Gillet stoutly maintains that Thomas never envisaged the theory of *lex pure poenalis* in his treatise on *lex humana*.[58] Said Jesuit Davitt: "So, it is certain that St. Thomas did not hold the notion of purely penal civil law. Such a notion is contrary to his principles of law and his philosophy of intellect and will."[59] Among other reasons militating against the possibility of the purely penal law, Davitt, in summarizing Aquinas, Sylvester, Soto, and Bellarmine, maintains that it is of the essence of law to oblige in conscience.[60] The competent French Jesuit Brisbois, in his review of Georges Renard's *La théorie des "Leges mere poenales,"*[61] expresses this same concept aptly:

> Law, in effect, for St. Thomas, is formally an act of the reason judging what is required for an end to be attained, and expressing what an action must be in order to achieve that end. Thus we can see that for him the obligation of the law is derived from the necessity of the end and not from the will of the legislator. The legislative power is analogous, in the social order, to conscience in the sphere of the individual: it interprets for the members of society the requirements for the common good, in the same way as conscience expresses for an individual the requirements for his last end. And we cannot say that conscience creates these requirements; neither then does the legislative power create the requirements for the common good. Consequently it is not up to a legislator either to attach or withdraw obligation from his laws.[62]

There can be little doubt that the ultimate focus of the entire question of the moral binding power of the civil law lies in the true nature of the interaction of intellect and will in the lawmaking process. When all of the lesser arguments are heard and filed away, there remains the sword's-point clash of Thomas and Suarez over the decisive question: Where, at last, rests the responsibility for the actual act of legislation? In the will of the lawmaker? Or in his intellect? Answer the will, and the penal law is possible. Answer the intellect, and the resultant law binds in conscience.

2 Since Thomas is outstandingly the chief expositor of the civil-law position, his psychology should be traced in greater detail through the stages of the moral act of legislation.

Two preliminary adversions should prepare the way.

In the first place, considerable benefit can be derived by personal introspection and self-analysis, founded on the realization that the various conceptual stages in the process by which a lawmaker legislates are the same as those distinguishable in the constituent elements of a personal moral act. The only difference lies in the person commanded. In the former the legislator commands the citizen. In the latter the person commands himself. These constituent elements of the personal moral act, therefore, as segregated in the Thomistic analysis, will be adapted and applied to the legislative process.

In the second place, this breakdown obviously is conceptual. *Homo rationalis* has only one soul, the faculties of which are intellect and will. Hence in the legislative process it is the one soul acting. The particular activities of intellect and will are, therefore, performed concomitantly and with the most intimate interrelation. In this regard it is most important to understand that these various stages are not necessarily complete and distinct acts, although it is very useful in this way to bring out as clearly and distinctly as possible all the relations that are often obscured in man's ordinary activity.

The majority of Thomistic commentators conceive twelve specific and relatively distinguishable steps in the total legislative process. It will conduce to a more intimate understanding of the essentials, however, to consider these twelve in three general orders or categories, treating: (1) the end or objective of the law, (2) the statutory means to the end, and (3) the execution and promulgation of the law.

Thomas himself sets the broad outline for the first two of these three categories:

> Now, in the orderly sequence of actions, first comes the apprehension of the end, then the appetitive inclination to the end, next the deliberation concerning the means to the end, and finally the appetitive action in regard to these means to the end.[63]

Aquinas omits reference, here, to the order of execution and promulgation of the law which consists of the last four steps.

The lawmaker occupies himself first with the end of the law.

In the first four stages in the course of legislation, the lawmaker, in acts of intellect and will, concerns himself with the objective or purpose of a proposed law—both the ultimate end which is the common good, and the immediate, proximate goal which would depend upon the nature of the legislation (for example, the regulation of traffic, the financing of government through taxation, the control of alcoholic beverages).

First, the intellect perceives the end. The initiation of the lawmaking procedure consists in an intellectual recognition or apprehension of a certain goal as desirable. Since the will is incapable of understanding, it is the burden of the intellect to present or propose to the will an object discerned as worthy of attainment in and of itself—for example, the regulation of traffic. This first stage is strictly an intellectual perception and no more.

Throughout the entire series of the acts of legislation, the intellect directs its activity to the end (*finis*) of the proposed legislation. This is the finality of the intellect. "The intellect moves the will in the way in which an end is said to move; that is, it preconceives the knowable essence of the end, and proposes it to the will."[64] The intellect works not as an efficient cause, which is the role of the will, but as a final cause.[65]

At the first level, by proposing a generic good as a goal (traffic regulation in general) of some kind, the intellect attracts the will toward a legislative objective of the broadest compass.

As St. Thomas says, the intellect moves not by way of executing motion but by way of directing to motion, and this is in the order of apprehension.[66]

Second, the will inclines toward the end. It is of the essence of the will to tend toward the good. At this earliest stage the will of the legislator is not free, since it is impelled of necessity and by its very nature to embrace a general, known, and unqualified good. As yet the will has not been presented with any specific action toward achievement of this broad goal. Even the possibility of attainment has not yet been entertained by the intellect. The will simply wishes at this stage (carrying out the example) a system of traffic control. The will has not as yet intended anything. It rests, instead, in the general desire—which is called volition (*volitio*)—of an objective perceived as beneficial (that is, regulated traffic).

> For the movement of the will toward the end is not in its absolute sense called the intention, but simply wishing . . . One who wishes health is said to wish it without qualification; but he is only said to intend it, when he desires something on account of health.[67]

It would be appropriate to note, at this point of the *simplex volitio* of Thomas, that Naus in commenting on the simple volition points out that not all moral psychologists would so arbitrarily categorize the elements of the personal moral act.

> Among the best of recent analyses of the human act . . . is that of Servais Pinckaers, O.P., in which he rejects Charles Billuart, O.P.'s, array of twelve acts of intellect and will which proceed in psychological succession and proposes instead a simplified structure or causal order. He shows that for St. Thomas the initial willing of the end (*simplex volitio*) carries on dynamically through subsequent will acts to the choosing [*electio*] of a means [the statute itself] and its use [*usus*—the execution and promulgation of the law].[68]

Third, the intellect judges that the end can be achieved. Whereas the first act of the intellect was the simple apprehension—the goal as good only, no more—the second is a judgment (*judicium*) that the goal of the proposed legislation is feasible. This objective, perceived as attainable by the intellect, serves as an inducement to the will to perform on its part the next will act.

> When the reason proposes something to itself under the formal nature of a good to which other things may be ordered as to an end, then it tends to that end with an orderly relation . . .[69]

In this judgment the intellect has not yet determined the exact approach. It has merely reached the reasoned conclusion that the legislative objective—that traffic across the state can be regulated—may be achieved by *some* statutory means.[70] How remains to be seen.

Fourth, the will intends the end. When the intellect presents to the will the opinion that the broad objectives envisaged can be attained by some possible legislation—without specifying any particular statute—the will is drawn toward this end necessarily. The will is not free to refuse a general good submitted to it. If the regulation of vehicular traffic were undesirable or even an evil in itself or a specific statute had already been proposed which could be scrutinized and questioned, the matter would be otherwise. There is as yet no formal act of legislation, since the will has merely passed from the general wishing stage to the actual intention. "Intention is an act of the will in relation to the end."[71] The lawmaker intends definitely by a positive will act to legislate but has not yet chosen the statutory implementation.[72]

The second stage, therefore, concerns the means.

Once determined that some legislation is advisable, his intellect engages in an orderly deliberation—study, investigation, and evaluation of the various possible enactments which would be suitable to the determined objective. "And so a rational investigation is needed before a judgment can be made on the many possible choices, and this investigation is called *counsel*."[73] "Since, therefore, counsel is an inquiry, it is not of the end, but only of the means to the end."[74] It is as if the intellect takes counsel of the many possible statutory means to the legislative end and in turn gives counsel and advice to the will. Thus, if the legislature has determined upon general statewide traffic regulation, it must weigh the many possible approaches to this problem and conclude to one pattern rather than another (for example, one-way streets rather than two-way, definite speed limits rather than "the reasonable-man rule," and the like). At the conclusion of this discursive process, the legislature must arrive at a definite decision as to exactly which legislation should be instituted. This judgment only concludes that a certain traffic-control program should be inaugurated. The intellect has not yet determined that it shall be.

Sixth, the will accedes to the intellect's decision. The lawmaker next presents the results of this intellectual deliberation to the will. The legislator must will to utilize and follow this counsel of his intellect. St. Thomas calls this the consent (*consensus*) of the will—"the application of the appetitive movement to the determination of counsel."[75] This consent of the will is not the final choice but merely the approval of the intellect's decision that certain laws should be passed.

These six stages are preliminary to the essential act of lawmaking—the last practical judgment, when the legislator concludes that a definite law shall be passed. A brief pause summarizes the progress up to this transition point: (1) The intellect initiates the six-step process, which prepares the faculties of will and intellect for the last practical judgment (*liberum arbitrium*) and the act of choice (*electio*) and for the actual command of the law (*imperium*) and its execution (*usus*), with the apprehension of the legislative goal and objective. (2) The will responds with a desire, *simplex volitio*, for that end. (3) Next, the intellect reaches the conclusion that the objective is attainable. (4) This is followed by a desire for the end as the good toward which something is ordained. This desire is the intention. (5) The intellect then meditates upon the means in general. This deliberation is the act of advice and counsel. (6) These elicit immediately in the will a desire for the means. This approval by the will is in fact a general consent to the legislative means.[76]

Seventh, the lawmaker uses the practical judgment in the selection of legislation. The intellect of the lawmaker completes its deliberation and moves from the judgment that a certain means should be followed to the final judgment determining upon a certain course of legislation—a specific statutory means to the legislative end. This practical judgment (*liberum arbitrium*) is the denouement in the series comprising the acts of legislation. The election of the will "follows this decision or judgment, which is like the conclusion of a practical syllogism."[77]

This work of the lawmaker's intellect is the all-important instant of freedom in the lawmaking act. According to Thomas, free choice is not the sole prerogative of either intellect or will, but belongs to both in a close interaction in which the particular burden of the intellect is to arrive at the final decision, the practical judgment. It thus formally provides the content or object to the will by supplying it with the material of the choice and proposing a suitable means to the end.[78] When the intellect of the legislator concludes that this statute shall be law, the law has received its content. This act of the intellect is in the order of formal causality. The intellect has given the form, the substance, the content, to the law. This is the moment of intention.

At any point during this intellectual deliberation, the will may interrupt and stop at any practical judgment which the lawmaker favors. When, however, the will does actually make its act of selection (which is to follow), it must be guided by the practical judgment immediately preceding.

Perhaps the point most in need of emphasis in elucidating the nature of this *liberum arbitrium* (the free judgment) of the intellect in its final selection of the specific statutory means to the legislative end is the distinction between the essence, or content, of the law and its existence, or execution. In the *liberum arbitrium* the lawgiver's intellect has completed the draft of the law, has approved the legislative draftsman's final formulation. All the details are determined upon. Every provision is properly enunciated. It has its content. It has its completed form. (This is what is meant by the formal cause of the intellect in giving the content to the law.)

In addition to the formulation of the contents of the statute, the intellect of the lawgiver, from the aspect of final causality, has concluded that the provisions in the law conduce satisfactorily to the legislative goal. The intellect has approved the means as suitable to the end. This reasoning process—the *liberum arbitrium*—is exclusively an intellectual function, in the order of final causality.

Furthermore, the lawgiver has expressed his determination that no more changes in the substance are to be made. He has pronounced: This statute shall be law. But he has not yet executed the law. He has not yet said: This is law. That remains for another act of the intellect—the *imperium*. In other words, the *liberum arbitrium* has determined fully the substance and content—the essence—but there remains the execution and promulgation—the existence. The *liberum arbitrium* is in the order of intention. The promulgation (the *imperium*) is in the order of execution.

From this it is patent that there is no change in the provisions of the statute from this point on. The lawgiver merely translates the law from his desk, where it is in the order of intention, to the lawbooks through promulgation, where it is in the order of execution. One could speak of this as the end of the legislative road, but it would be inaccurate, because the draftsman's final draft is not a law in truth until enacted as such by the legislator. The prospective statute remains yet in the order of intention, not execution.

The term *intention* here has reference to the specific statutory means (for example, one-way streets) but not to the end (that is, traffic control) which was the intention in steps three and four. This intention in step seven is the intention in the concept expressed by the phrase "The intention of the lawgiver must always be followed."[79] The implications of this are great in the determination of legislative intent through the study of the legislative history. Obviously, from what has been said about the difference between the final draft in the order of intention and the promulgated statute in the order of execution, a study of the one is the study of the other. What makes this *liberum arbitrium* so important is the fact that this is the first stage at which the intellect of the lawgiver has completed the substance and content of the law, and approved it, albeit not yet actually enacted it into law.

Eighth, the will makes its choice of legislation. Simultaneously with the practical judgment of the intellect (*liberum arbitrium*), the volitional act of acceptance of or adherence to this decision is performed by the lawmaker's will. This act St. Thomas called the election (*electio*) or the choice. It is at this juncture, therefore, that the will, supplied with the work of the intellect, makes its consent to the judgment. This act of the will by which the legislator actively elects to abide by the last practical judgment of the intellect is in the order of efficient causality. The end product of this mutual causality, with intimate interaction—final and formal causality of the intellect, efficient of the will—is the free act of choice.

Through the combination of these two acts, the practical judgment of the intellect and the election of the will, the legislator is committed to a given statutory means (one-way streets and posted speed limits) to the final end (statewide traffic control). The union of these two acts is definitely the climax of the legislative process. All of the earlier stages were merely preparatory for the practical judgment and the choice. All that follows is implementation of the intention.

It is particularly important to note, relevant to the doctrine of the purely penal law, that the final judgment of the intellect,

the *liberum arbitrium*, is a very important element in the essence
of the legislative process. The *liberum arbitrium* of the intellect,
expressed in statutory form and herewith embraced by the will
in the election, will become, unchanged in form and substance,
the law. Since the intellect has already in the practical judgment
determined upon the specific legislation, it remains only to issue
the formal command of promulgation, the *imperium*. This implementation and execution of the law is in a way anticlimactic,
from the specific aspect of penal law. Manifestly, however, until
the draft of the law is executed, there is no law. In this sense
the all-important act is the execution and promulgation.

Ninth, the intellect issues the command. There remain now
only the procedures involved in carrying out the expressed intention of the lawgiver. In his last practical judgment he expressed his intention, and the will in the election embraced it.
The intellect now formulates the terms of the promulgation (the
execution of the law) in the form of the command, the Thomistic
*imperium*: Obey the law. "By the command [*imperium*] which
follows the election, the intellect supervises and directs the use
of the lower faculties in the realization of the choice."[80]

> To command, however, is indeed essentially an act of the rea-
> son. For the commander orders the one to whom the command is
> given to do something and this order is conveyed by way of a dec-
> laration or announcement. Now to order in this way, by means of
> some sort of declaration, is the work of reason. . . . such a declara-
> tion is expressed by a verb in the imperative mood, as when one
> would say to another: "Do this." . . . Hence it follows that to com-
> mand is an act of reason founded on a previous act of will [the
> election, the efficient cause], in virtue of which the reason moves by
> command [*imperium*] to the exercise of the act.[81]

Tenth, the will operates in execution. Inasmuch as the will,
throughout the mechanics of legislation, operates as the efficient
cause, it must now receive the order of formal promulgation of
the lawgiver and translate it into action—action that consists in
all of the details of execution of the law, culminating in formal

promulgation and operation. This is the work of the will operating concomitantly with the *imperium*. This concomitant action of intellect and will produces, at last, the law. Thomas calls it *usus*, the "use" or implementation of the command.

> The intellect directs the will in the election, by which it completely wishes the means, just as in the use (*usus*) which follows the election and tends to attaining the thing desired.[82]

For the final insight into the comparative roles of the two intellectual acts of the *liberum arbitrium* before the election and the *imperium* after it, some necessary comments remain.

In both instances the intellect is the responsible faculty. It reaffirms, in the order of formal causality, the reasoned conclusions of the *liberum arbitrium* by the ultimate, controlling step, the command to obey the law—the *imperium*. In this explicit command is the implicit reapprobation of the reasonableness of the content and form of the law. How more forcefully could the lawmaker attest to his approval of the provisions of the draftsman's final draft than by formally enacting the bill into law?

Furthermore, the intellect of the legislator in the *imperium* again relates the wisdom and necessity of the statutory provisions to the overall legislative objectives of the common good. Operating again in the order of final causality, the intellect restates the intimate relation of the instant means to the declared end. The *imperium* "Obey this law," therefore, is all that the *liberum arbitrium* was, and more. It confirms the intellect's satisfaction with the essence of the law by pronouncing that the law should now have existence as well. It passes on to the will its reasoned conviction that the law should be executed and promulgated. And it partakes of the dynamism set in motion by the intellectual acts formed at the outset of the legislative process.

One might possibly prefer to place the major emphasis in this analysis of the lawmaking process on the order of intention —the moment of the ultimate practical judgment of the intellect when the legislator declares his completed intention: There shall

be such-and-such a law, rather than on the order of execution—
the moment of the promulgation and execution of the law in the
command, the *imperium*, of the lawgiver: Obey this law. Such
shift of attention from the accepted point of emphasis does not
affect, however, the Thomistic approach to the penal law, since
the interaction of intellect and will is equally intimate and
simultaneous in both, with each performing the same role in
both. The intellect gives form and finality; the will effects execution and existence. "The underlying principles of interaction between intellect and will are the same in both . . ."[83] of the first
two categories, in the order of the end or objective of the law
and in the order of statutory means to that end. So, too, are they
the same in the third, the order of execution.

Naus indicates the parallel between the work of intellect and
will in the order of intention and execution: "But for this *praeceptum* to be fully practical presupposes that it is distinct from
the *imperium* which follows the election and introduces the dynamism of the intention into the order of execution."[84]

Although the intellectual ultimate practical judgment is generally referred to as the *arbitrium* and the intellectual command
or order of execution as the *imperium*, it is not the universal
rule. The last practical judgment is sometimes termed the *imperium*, as in Suarez[85] and in Lottin: "This practical judgment,
which can be called *praeceptum* or *imperium*, determines my
choice, the election. The choice is thus a truly human act, proceeding from the will directed, this time again, by reason."[86]

This undoubtedly concludes the legislative process for the
purposes of this study. St. Thomas and his commentators, however, include in the procedure two last acts: eleventh, an intellectual appraisal of the law once promulgated and in force, a
knowledge or realization of the suitability of the legislation,[87]
and twelfth, the parallel will act which rests in the enjoyment of
the fulfillment of the legislation.[88]

\*    \*    \*

The Thomistic psychology of the mechanics of legislation yields several extremely pertinent conclusions to this analysis of the penal law. Manifestly these conclusions group themselves around the two central, essential acts of legislation: the simultaneous interaction of the lawmaker's intellect in forming the last practical judgment (*arbitrium*) and of his will in adopting it (*electio*), and the repetition of this interaction in the intellectual *imperium* (obey the law) and the will's implementation of this command in the execution and promulgation.

Do not confuse the use, hitherto and hereafter, of the word *essence* as applicable variously (1) to the law in general, (2) to the specific statute enacted, and (3) to the legislative process. The word has a different sense in each.

The essence of law in general (one element of which is obligation in conscience) is determined by God and the exigencies of man's nature. It cannot be changed by the legislator's whim.

The "essence" of a given statute, enacted by the legislature, refers to the content, the substance (the statutory provisions of proscription or prohibition) of the specific law, and is used in contradistinction to its "existence," realized in the execution and promulgation. These provisions—the essence of a given statute —must conform to the nature—the essence of law in general.

The essence of the lawmaking process has reference to its central part, inner core, more important division, the point of major emphasis. It could be argued that it is in the order of intention when the lawmaker has formulated the essence of the law (the specific statutory provisions of the final draft) in the *liberum arbitrium*. Or perhaps more properly, it could be said that it is in the order of execution when the legislator has actually enacted the bill into law by the *imperium*, giving it existence in the execution and promulgation. Or, finally, it could be called a combination of both *liberum arbitrium* and *imperium*.

In the process of producing a law, both the intellect and will of the legislator have markedly defined burdens to bear.

The intellect is the formal cause. It gives the form to the law, supplies the content and substance. It forms the essence—the various elements necessary to a statute: (1) an ordination of reason (2) for the common good (3) promulgated. As formal cause the intellect operates in the order of essence. It specifies the will by presenting the content of its judgment. Precisely, the essence of the law is effected by the intellect.

The will, to the contrary, is the efficient cause. It gives existence to the law by embracing the content and form presented to it when it makes its choice or election. In this area of efficient causality, although the will is at complete liberty to act or not to act, to reject one statutory proposal after the other, it nonetheless must, finally, follow the last preceding practical judgment of the intellect. "The will is free to choose this or that, to act or not to act, to do moral good or moral evil. But it chooses this definite act precisely because the determination that comes from the ultimate practical judgment has been caused by its own influence upon the intellect in the formation of that judgment."[89] In other words, the will had, acting in the order of efficient causality, previously impressed the intellect to form the practical judgment.

"A man can, at the last moment, not choose what his deliberation shows him to be the best means. However, if the process continues unobstructed in its natural dynamism, the judgment which terminates deliberation becomes the practical judgment, the *praeceptum* [*liberum arbitrium*] of the election."[90] Although the will is free to interrupt the deliberative process of the intellect at any stage and to choose that legislation which the intellect in its last judgment has determined upon, the will is not free to alter the essence of the particular law that it does choose in its election.

For this reason, they [objectors] insist that the will does not need a practical judgment showing that this object, this act, is better or more suitable here and now. They would have the will—which is an appetite and therefore a noncognoscitive faculty—operate as if it were a complete intellectual supposit, capable of holding out against the conclusions of reason in the last practical judgment. This is contrary to the nature of the reasoning animal that is man.[91]

The lawmaker's will cannot think; it can only effect. As efficient cause it operates in the order of existence. It can bring the essence of the law into existence, but it cannot vary that essence. This is precisely what Bellarmine had reference to in his most penetrating analysis of the essence and existence of the law.

> It must be noted that as other things depend on an agent for their existence—not, however, for their essence, since essences are eternal . . . so also law, as far as existence is concerned, depends on the legislator, for it will not be law unless passed by him, since he has the authority. But as far as essence is concerned it does not depend on him since the fact that law obliges is eternal and immutable and a participation, as it were, in the eternal law of God.[92]

Confined as it is to the order of existence, the will of the lawmaker, precluded from altering the essence of the law, cannot either (1) vary the terms and content of the law (rethink the provisions), or (2) withhold the obligatoriness from the law.

Equally important is the role of the intellect in the area of final causality. In protracted deliberation (only the mind can think) the lawmaker's intellect determined on the end and the means to the end. It concluded that the demands of the common good required (1) a specific statute with specific provisions and (2) an obligation in conscience to obedience.

(Even were one to grant *ex arguendo* that a law could be a law without a conscience obligation, it would be the onus of the intellect so to withhold that obligation. Such exclusion of obligation is an intellectual act, a judgment of the reason. Conceding again that the intellect could make such an alteration in the essence, patently it would not, since it would be acting against its own reasoned conclusion that the statute determined upon was conducive to the common good.)

The will, *e contra*, is a noncognoscitive faculty and is incapable of rethinking the purposes and objectives of the law previously excogitated by the intellect. By such rethinking the will would do violence to the intellect, depart from its role as efficient cause and invade the domain of the intellect (the determination of the end and the means)—the area of final causality. Concisely, nothing whatsoever is added to the law by the will in giving it existence. Yet, in honest fact, Suarez and the Suarezians would have the will not only give existence to the essence of the law but add to it, rethink it, alter it.

The will as incapable of thought and reason may not, therefore, countermand the firm conclusion of the intellect that the end of the law, regulated traffic, demands (1) a particular statutory pattern and (2) obedience in conscience to that plan.

Note well: The very definition of an arbitrary act is that which has no reason except that it is wanted.

Thus in point of moral necessity, the intellect is not hindered from imposing upon the will the necessity of acting according to the demand of the objective relation of means to an end. This does not destroy freedom, because the will at any moment may be deflected from the choice presented by the intellect if it persists in concentrating on some good, albeit only apparent, other than the one proposed in the judgment of the intellect. Thus the legislator remains free to choose legislation recommended for passage by considerations of political expediency, in preference to other legislation founded on the manifest best interests of the common good. There is freedom in the will to legislate this way or that or not at all, but not to legislate without obligation or to vary the content of the law adopted.

\* \* \*

It is interesting for several reasons to know that Suarez in his earlier years followed Thomas and delineated the legislative process in these same Thomistic terms.

With this background I would conclude that the following is the more probable analysis of the matter: First, before the election there precedes a practical judgment, and there is no other act distinct from it which can be called a command [*imperium*]. This I said above and proved. Second, after the election, which abstracts from execution, before the act of use [*usus*] at least by nature there precedes and there is necessary another more practical judgment distinct from the judgment which precedes the election, because it reaches more immediately to the action and all determinate circumstances necessary for the execution of the action. Thus it is that it moves the will more vehemently not so much by any virtue of its own but by virtue of the election already placed. The reason is that before every action of the will must come a judgment of the intellect adapted to it, by which it is directed and enlightened. But the act of use is an act of the will which adds something to the election already made. . . . And this judgment is rightly called practically practical or altogether practical.[93]

Since some twenty years intervened between this young Suarez and his more mature elucidation in the *De Legibus*, scarcely could the sin of the youth be visited on the man. Suarez, at career's end, could hardly be conceived to be placing the essence of the lawmaking process in the intellect.

Some historical facts can enlighten the matter, although perhaps not explain it. In the year 1581-1582 Suarez presented to the students of the Roman College his current ideas on the interaction of intellect and will in the legislative process. The notes of the students, unrevised by Suarez for printing, were published eleven years after his death in a tractate called *De Voluntario et Involuntario*. The *De Legibus*, on the other hand, was, it is true, first taught (1601-1602) but later meticulously edited by Suarez (1611-1612) and published as *De Legibus* in 1612.[94]

### Violation Results in Fault

So inextricably intertwined with the first essential—true law binds in conscience—is the second, that the latter is really only a corollary of the former. Once the moral binding force of the civil law has been established through the twin premises of (1) the God-given authority commanding (2) a necessary means to the necessary end of the common good, the superstructure of the edifice virtually builds itself. Conceived as an exponible proposition, the moral obligation of the law ineluctably leads to a second essential proposition of the civil law: The violation of a true law engenders true culpability.

### The Positive Argument

The proof of a self-evident principle can be achieved only through meditation. So it is with the conclusion that culpability is a consequent on violation of a law. Culpability is intrinsic to violation. Disobedience is inherently sinful. In fact, the definition of sin is the refusal to obey. In the case of the fallen angels, of Adam, of any instance of sin, it is nothing other than the disobedience of a lawful command. Granted the obligatory nature of the law, there are only two requisites to culpability: (1) true law and (2) disobedience. The result is inevitably fault, culpability, sin. In what does the sin consist? (1) The disobedience of lawful authority and (2) the refusal to adopt a necessary means to a necessary end, the common good.

Sin is disorder and is unreasonable. When the subject refuses to follow the reasonable means established as law, he upsets the right order of the community, acts unreasonably, creates disorder. Augustine defines peace as the tranquillity of order. When the citizen disturbs this order by disobeying a law, the resultant disorder destroys the tranquillity that is peace. Such an act is sinful, a fault, and engenders culpability.

### The Negative Arguments

Proof of such fundamental principles (for example, as the principles of causality and that of contradiction) can often be realized by an analysis of the contrary position. Suarez at this specific point in the argument stated that although the citizen disobeyed the command of the lawmaker, nonetheless the transgressor was not guilty of sin. "It can be proven, however, that strictly speaking those who violate the purely penal law are not guilty of sin . . ."[95]

There certainly seems to be an intrinsic inconsistency in the conduct of a legislator who in one and the same act orders his subjects to a specified course of action and yet informs them that they will do no wrong, neither offend God nor himself, if they fail to obey. "The self-contradiction of 'merely penal' laws is apparent from the strange conclusion which must be drawn from them. Since no action in the concrete is indifferent, and since there is no moral wrong in violating a 'merely penal' law, such violation must be an act of virtue!"[96]

Suarez adduced, in support of this strange phenomenon of the nonmoral guilt, *Sine culpa, non tamen sine causa*. He reasoned from the maxim to what he termed a "civil" or "political" or "human" guilt[97] and what his successors called a "nonmoral" or "juridic" guilt.[98] Whatever it was called, however, it was also guilt. So presumably it contained some culpability, some sin.

Although it might occur to one to question at the outset the exact nature of this civil or human guilt, to query if it had any essence at all, it is more satisfactory to endeavor to compose its essence, as it were, by a synthesis of all the elements that have contributed to it. These elements can be discerned by a study of the applications and examples employed by Suarez and his progenitors in elucidation of this nonmoral guilt.

The virtual unanimity of analysis, from the gloss on Gratian to Suarez himself and beyond, presented no instance where the question involved either of the two essentials, a law or a violation of a law. It is understandable, therefore, that Suarez would conclude to an absence of culpability.

Consider first the question of the presence of a law. (1) The canon in Gratian merely announced the demotion of a see. (2) Not one of the six cases in the *Summa* of Penafort involved

a law—poverty, hate, political prejudice or preference, rob-
bery, rank. (3) Nothing approaching a law appeared in the
continence of the spouses. (4) The regulations of the religious
orders approached the nature of laws and yet upon analysis
lacked the true essentials. (5) Certainly, neither the visitation
from God nor removal of the leprous cleric nor the impediments
of the "bigamous" ordinand and the judge-would-be-cleric nor
the disinheritance of the treasonous son involved any law.
(6) Nowhere, in fact, in Suarez were there any examples different in kind.

Likewise is it true that there was no true violation. There
can be no violation where there is no law. But were it granted
*ex arguendo* that there was a law, what violation can be found
on the part of (1) Alexandria, (2) a person afflicted by poverty,
prejudice, and the rest, (3) the leprous priest, (4) the impeded
ordinands, or (5) the child who was born to a treasonous father?
Only in the case of the religious would a true violation be present—if there were a true law. Without a law, the religious
merely failed to choose the better. In all others, the principals
not only did not violate any law but for the most part remained
passive, were the unwitting denizens of this vale of tears.

It is equally clear that in none of the examples was any genuine culpability incurred, and rightly so. In the light of this
reasoning, an analysis of the maxim *Sine culpa, non tamen sine
causa* correctly leads in each instance to correlative conclusions.
First, there is no *culpa*. Second, there was, on the other hand,
some cause for the action inflicted upon each, whether that cause
was the changed circumstances of two patriarchal sees, disciplinary mortification, or orderly administration of a pastorate, a
diocese, or the universal Church.

To posit a parallel, however, between the several elements
in these examples, on the one hand, and true law and true violation on the other, is not justifiable. The option lies between a
true law and many another thing, from a papal edict to a pious

preference. If no law, no violation and, hence, no culpability. If a true law, however, the opposite persists.

From this, the true nature of the nonmoral, juridic fault can be discerned. It is, in fact, not fault at all. The emphasis should be placed on the words "nonmoral," "juridic," "civil," "human," or "political," which in effect negative any fault. There is no justification in joining the words "human" and "fault," if moral culpability is not intended. The only permissible phrase would be "juridic cause" or "civil," "human," or "political cause." This eliminates the element of fault completely.

Ultimately, the maxim should translate: A person sometimes suffers pain and hardship without fault but nonetheless for some good reason.

Both positively and negatively, therefore, moral culpability is intrinsic to the violation of the law.

Thus far in the reasoning the Suarezians would seem to have excogitated two conclusions: (1) A nonlegal edict, pronouncement, hardship, or affliction is not "binding in conscience." (2) The imposition on, or receipt by, a person of such edict, pronouncement, hardship, or affliction does not engender or carry culpability (although the imposition does not lack reasonableness, inasmuch as a sufficient cause was involved).

### FAULT WARRANTS PUNISHMENT

The third essential concept in the nature of civil law is also virtually a corollary of the other two and inextricably connected with them.

In a precise analysis of the correlation between guilt and punishment, between virtue and reward, there are two distinct approaches possible: (1) From the affirmative aspect, one could argue that culpability demands punishment, virtue reward. (2) On the other hand, the question could be considered from the contrary view that culpability never warrants reward or virtue punishment.

Since Suarez was solely concerned with (1) virtue (he firmly stated that there was no sin in transgression) and with (2) punishment (he maintained that the penalty must be endured under pain of sin), the only issue present is whether punishment may be imposed for virtue. In the interests of a deeper understanding, however, the affirmative approach should be rewarding and will leave an *a fortiori* conclusion for the contrary, if once proven. Therefore, the affirmative—that culpability demands punishment—will precede. A reflection on the opposite —that nonculpability never permits punishment—will follow.

### The Positive Argument

Reasoning as heretofore from the intrinsic nature of the concepts, it can be said that true culpability virtually demands punishment, as Thomas says: "The law of nature has it that the evildoer shall be punished."[99] Fault and punishment are correlative terms. Guilt seems to require satisfaction. More than that, all of the purposes of punishment must be achieved: (1) The lesion in the body politic must be healed. The order destroyed by disobedience must be restored. (2) The honor and position of the state must be vindicated. (3) The culpable subject must suffer and thus atone for his sin. (4) Punishment as preventative must be established as an example to the citizenry.

The ultimate intrinsic rationale of the necessity for punishment for sin lies in the eternal principle of right order in all things. This is another way, of course, of referring to the eternal law. This inherent necessity for right order, impregnated in all natures, is equally present in the right order of the state, the right order of the many means to the end of the common good. When the subject acts contrary to this right order in refusing to follow a means to the end, the resultant disorder demands righting. It is as fundamental as the law of gravity. The disorder created by the disobedience must be ordered. The threat, explicit in disobedience, to the total plan of right order, whether it be God's plan, the plan of the civil government, or that of a parent, must be removed in order to maintain the integrity of the order of the universe, the civil government, or the home. This integrity is restored by punishment in one or more of its aspects. Each of the purposes of punishment is directed to the broad principle of right order.

As with the other first principles, so with this. Only by reflective consideration can it be appreciated that the principle which demands the rectification of the disorder in the total plan of order is intrinsic to the nature of things. Just as two and two must inevitably equal four, man's nature and the nature of all things are driven naturally *ex intrinseca necessitate* to adhere to an order. Failure to follow this order is a sin, disorder, and automatically *ex sua natura* cries out for rectification.

This rectification is achieved in the imposition of the sanction—either necessary or accidental—which is not, however, part of the law itself. The intrinsic exigencies of right order can be achieved by the necessary sanction. The disobedient subject receives automatic and immediate punishment in the loss of the end of the law itself. There is no need for a superadded accidental sanction. Where the lawmaker, however, deems further rectification advisable he superadds the accidental sanction.

So much for the affirmative approach. The necessity of the imposition of punishment for violation of the law is not, however, the necessary concern in the refutation of the Suarezian argument. It may be conceded *ex arguendo* that the imposition of an accidental sanction is not an absolute necessity. There is valid argument, moreover, to this effect. The obverse, however, is essential and patent: Punishment can never be imposed without culpability. Virtue never permits punishment. From this aspect, if (1) restoration of order, (2) vindication of the honor of the state, (3) expiation, and (4) prevention are not needed, neither can there be a need for punishment. How, then, ought it to be required?

If the order of the state has been maintained, if the subject has accepted the means to the end, the common good, the necessity for punishment ceases. Punishment might be unnecessary for disobedience, but it is inconceivable as a necessity for obedience. Although punishment might not be an essential correlative to sin, it is intrinsically repugnant to virtue. It is a truism for Bellarmine to say that "it seems to involve a contradiction for a ruler to be able to hold a citizen to a penalty and not to moral fault, if indeed fault and punishment are correlative."[100] Without a moral fault no one can be punished. Cooley, commentator on Blackstone and one of the foremost American common-law jurists, expressed the principle in terms of the civil law: "Where an act is forbidden under penalty, it must in general be assumed that some degree of public mischief or private injury was meant to be prevented by the prohibition. The prohibition can have no other legitimate purpose. . . . it cannot be intended that a statute would inflict a penalty for a lawful act!"[101] As bumptious as McGarrigle may have been in his "It's All Right, If You Can Get Away with It," he turns this very thought delightfully: "The realm of 'merely penal' law is an ethical Wonderland, in which Alice does no moral wrong; yet the Queen of Hearts shouts: 'Off with her head!' "[102]

Dominic Soto, O.P., writing in the mid-1500s, couched his principal argument against the penal law in somewhat the same way. He argued that where there is no fault there can be no true penalty, since the essence and burden of a *poena* is to vindicate or rectify a *culpa*. "To vindicate, to avenge, to exact punishment, and thus to inflict a penalty, is by no means justifiable unless for fault."[103] Bellarmine quotes Augustine in this context[104] "Every penalty [*poena*], however, if it is a just one, is a penalty for sin, and is called punishment."[105] This Augustinian principle elicited understandable concern in Suarez.

As is said in Deuteronomy 25: *According to the measure of the crime will be the manner of the punishment*, and . . . Augustine . . .

*Every penalty if it is just is a penalty for sin and is called punish-
ment*; and therefore Gerson said that fault and penalty are correlative . . . therefore, when the penal law justly punishes it supposes
fault in the transgression of the law. However, this argument cannot prevail, for although *poena* in a certain more rigorous signification implies an order to moral guilt, however, in a broader sense
taken as any suffering or loss or inconvenience, it can justly be imposed because of a just cause without moral guilt. . . . Moreover
it can be said that although every *poena* is imposed because of fault
it does not always follow that the fault is against God, but sometimes it suffices that the fault is as it were civil and human.[106]

From its very nature, therefore, true punishment has only
one purpose: to right the disorder effected by the violation of
the law. It can accomplish its purpose in any of several ways.
When the goal set for punishment is absent, the *raison d'être* of
punishment ceases and with it punishment itself.

### The Negative Argument

Again approach the proof negatively. Suarez, his progenitors, and his successors concluded: Punishment may be imposed
without fault. It only remains to analyze the inner nature of the
"punishment" which the Suarezians are ready to impose on a
sinless citizen, since the essence of nonmoral, juridic guilt has
already been synthesized as lacking in fault or sin.

In every example, from the decree of Gratian, through Penafort, Thomas, and Suarez himself, the *poena* imposed was not
punishment, but rather the hardship, suffering, inconvenience,
or pain described by Thomas as *poena* "in the wide sense"[107]
and by Suarez as "in a broader sense."[108]

The point has been made that *poena* in the strict sense is
always a correlative to moral guilt, is translated "punishment,"
and "is not due except for sin."[109] This is the punishment that is
also called "vindictive,"[110] whereas "preventive" punishment,
the term of later writers,[111] is not really punishment at all but
more correctly a visitation from God that could come to anyone.

If the concept of *poena* is taken as pain, hardship, or suffering, the maxim *Sine culpa, non tamen sine causa* is indisputably sound, since the pain, hardship, or suffering inflicted on the many persons involved in the Suarezian examples were all imposed (without fault but) for good cause and sound reasons, whether the reason be the proper rank for a patriarchal see, the discipline or mortification of a religious, or the proper administration of a parish. To this extent Suarez and the Suarezians are perfectly correct.

It is even more interesting to note that if the analyses of the Suarezian examples have been justified, since in no instance was there true law, true violation, true fault, or true punishment, the pain, hardship, inconvenience, or suffering, if for good cause, was properly imposed throughout. And this is true, since there was a just *causa* in each.

The major difficulty comes, however, when the Suarezians endeavor to take this line of reasoning and apply it to the civil law, where there is true law, obligation, violation, culpability, and punishment. The nub of the error in the Suarezian approach rests (1) in the conviction that a true law is in fact involved in the many instances of application. The next major error follows (2) in the shift from the infliction of *poena* in the wide sense found in the examples to the *poena* in the rigorous sense imposed for breach of the civil law.

This twin sin of the Suarezians can be visualized by the juxtaposition of the two major conclusions of the theory:

Disobedience of a true law, yet no sin.

No sin, yet true punishment.

The phrase "no sin" in these two premises is the focus of the error. Removal of the word "no" would cure the difficulty in both instances. It would also destroy the purely penal law. The two premises then would read:

Disobedience engenders sin.

Sin warrants punishment.

From this it can be seen that there are two major analogies in the Suarezian system that are illegitimate: (1) that of comparing the edicts, pronouncements, or statements in the various examples to true laws, (2) that of equating suffering, hardship, and inconvenience with true punishment, which is the correlative to fault.

\* \* \*

These major arguments would seem to establish the three essentials of the positive law: (1) True law binds in conscience. (2) Violation results in fault. (3) Fault warrants punishment.

### THE ESSENTIAL NATURE OF SANCTION

The last remaining considerations fundamental to the Suarezian system revolve around the notion of sanction. Pursuant to the same pattern of positive and negative argumentation, an analysis of the essential nature of sanction and of the concepts immediately contiguous to it will lay the foundation for an enlightened inspection of the important role of sanction in the Suarezian system.

#### The Positive Argument

The cause of much of the confusion enveloping penal law and the apparent reasonableness of the doctrine surround the three distinct concepts of (1) obligation, (2) motive, and (3) sanction. Careful differentiation of the essential notes of each should reveal some further inconcinnities in the Suarezian system. This differentiation can perhaps be best approached by considering these three notions in what is certainly a conceptual, even a temporal, sequence. (This sequence itself emphasizes the distinct difference of each notion from the other.) Prescinding from the other elements in the process, the activity of the intellect proceeds through two separate stages prior to the will act of obedience or disobedience, after which, and only after which, is

the sanction imposed. These two stages are the successive appre-
hensions of obligation and motive.

Throughout the following study of the distinct natures of
these three concepts, bear in mind that purpose flows from
nature, and that the purposes of obligation, of motive, and of
sanction are likewise different. These differences in purpose emphasize the differences of their natures. The purpose of the law
is to achieve the final end, the common good, through the obedience of the subject to the means chosen. The purpose of motive
is to induce the subject to obedience. The purpose of sanction,
on the other hand, is fourfold: (1) to vindicate the honor of the
state, (2) to restore the order of the body politic, (3) to serve
as an example to others (and hence become a motive), and
(4) to punish the malefactor.

The following section will trace the three concepts of obligation, motive, and sanction as they arise conceptually in the
mind of the citizen subject to the law.

Immediately subsequent to the realization that he is faced
with a command of the legislator (for example, that traffic at
the sole intersection of the next small town on this highway is
regulated by a four-way stop), the citizen reasons to an obligation in conscience in a well-defined series of syllogisms.

Obligation (to be bound morally to obey the law) is the
knowledge that one must so act from moral necessity, that to act
otherwise would be against right order, the nature of things,
against one's own nature, that it would be a sin, wrong, to do
otherwise. This consciousness on the part of the subject is independent of all other considerations. He understands that the objective to be attained by the four-way stop is the common good
(in this case the safety of himself, his children, other people).
He further reasons that, although this end could have been attained by several other regulatory devices (that is, a green-and-
red signal, a two-way stop sign, a viaduct, and the like), there
is the necessity of some choice of a means to the necessary end

and that this was the purpose that God had in placing the authority in the legislator. He concludes, therefore, that his moral obligation to obey operates without reference to any extrinsic considerations or results but flows solely from the intrinsic demands of the right order of things and of his nature.

Convinced in his heart that he should obey the command because it is the right thing to do, the subject then enters upon a systematic investigation of the various motives which will impel his will to the act of obedience or disobedience, to help him decide whether he will obey. After a cursory consideration he lists six motives for obedience: (1) the possible loss of the end itself (that is, his own safety and that of his children and others) if he does not stop, (2) the probable disedification or scandal attendant upon disobedience, (3) the salutary effects of the reduced speed and the stop on the automobile, (4) the opportunity for closer inspection of the town which a slower rate of speed offers, (5) the payment of a fine and possible imprisonment which disobeying might necessitate, (6) the delay generally consequent upon arrest and judicial proceedings. It is an illuminating thought to consider further that the intrinsic right order of things, the essential finality of means to the end, which is the cause and source of obligation, can also, by a second and completely distinct act of the intellect, be considered from the standpoint of a motive. Thus, a citizen, once he has concluded that he is obliged to obey because of the essential right order of things, may conclude by a second act of the intellect that this same inherent right order is also an impelling reason or motive for obedience.

Over and against these motives for obedience, the subject lays out a set of antithetical reasons of a similar nature for disobedience. No one of the motives, nor the concept of motive itself, partakes in any way of the essence of obligation and, of course, a fortiori of the essence of law. The motive is a reason for heeding or not heeding the obligation to obey.

Once the subject has determined either to obey or disobey, driven by the respective motives, the will orders the subject to act. The result is either obedience or disobedience to the law. It is only after this act that the sanction comes into operation. For sanction is not only consequent upon obligation and upon consideration of the motives, but it is also clearly subsequent to obedience or disobedience. Sanction, either necessary or accidental, as an effect following upon obedience, is distinct from the law and, hence, not of its essence. An accidental sanction may or may not be superadded by the lawmaker, and even without such a sanction a law may be a true law and so possess formal obligation. The law may be a true law, moreover, whether or not the purposes of sanction are attained.

There is likelihood of confusion between motive and sanction, since the anticipation by the citizen of the possible imposition of a sanction upon disobedience is often a motive to obedience. But the anticipation itself, the realization by the subject that a sanction might very well be imposed after disobedience, is not to be confused with the sanction proper which is imposed *post factum.*

Thus, of the six motives of the subject-driver, one (the first) was the knowledge and reflection of the possibility of the resultant imposition of the necessary sanction, to wit, the loss of the end of the law, the safety of self and children. Another (the fifth) was the consideration and realization of the possible future imposition of the accidental sanction, superadded by the legislator, to wit, the fine and possible punishment. The antecedent anticipation or reflection, which is the motive, is completely distinct from the subsequent, actual (a) loss of safety and (b) fine and punishment.

A word of caution ought to be given here: Because of a long tradition of vagueness in distinguishing these concepts, constant advertence is necessary in applying them to the Suarezian arguments.

*The Negative Arguments*

Suarez and the Suarezians place two major allegations in dependence on their peculiar conception of sanction: (1) The moral obligation is not attached to the command of the law itself, but rather to the command of the sanction. "There is no conscience obligation to the condition [the command of the law itself] under which the penalty is threatened and in respect of which it is called purely penal, although in regard to the penalty itself it has the force of obliging."[112] (2) This conscience obligation to the sanction fulfills the rigid requisite of true law to bind in conscience. This is the last stage in the Suarezian system.

Suarez, however, does not conceive of the penal law as (1) a command to the law itself and (2) a command to the sanction, as he does in a mixed law, but rather as a single, hypothetical command with an option or a disjunction.

> That law, indeed, is denominated mixed which is at once moral and penal, and it includes virtually two commands: one, to perform an act or to shun it; the other, to submit to a specified penalty upon disobedience . . . That law, however, is called purely penal which is enunciated in only one as it were hypothetical command: to undergo a certain *poena* or discomfort, if this or that is done, although a command is not imposed relative to the act itself to which the condition is attached.[113]

Implicit in such reasoning is a denial of the fundamental distinction between law and sanction and a misconception of the respective purposes of the two. More detailed study will indicate that there are, in both fact and legal effect, two distinct pieces of legislation in every penal-law enactment.

In the illustration of the motorist, there were present both law and sanction. To the primary command, the law proper (stop at the sign), there was attached a supplemental, secondary command, the sanction (pay a twenty-five-dollar fine)—in truth a second law. Each enactment, the law proper and the sanction, is separate and distinct, a true law.

(Although by no means of highly probative force, it is not irrelevant to note as an instance that the legislature of the State of Missouri as a regular practice separates the law and the sanction into two separate acts of legislation. Thus, it passes two distinct laws stating, for example, "that it shall be unlawful for any person . . . to manufacture, sell . . . any article of non-alcoholic drink which is adulterated or misbranded."[114] and "Any person who shall violate any of the provisions of sections 196.125 to 196.145 shall be guilty of a misdemeanor, and, upon conviction thereof, shall be sentenced to pay a fine of not less than twenty-five dollars, nor more than one hundred dollars, or not more than six months in jail, or both."[115])

This sanction, the second legislative act, appended to the primary law, has in turn its own sanction attached to it, which is imposed upon violation of the secondary command, the principal sanction. In the instant example, refusal to pay the twenty-five-dollar fine would probably result in the imposition of the sanction's sanction: imprisonment for thirty days.

One might counter that this line of reasoning leads to an infinite series. This is true. The only obstacle to such a series is the finite nature of the malefactor. He has only one life to give in expiation of continued disobedience. A study of any given legal system will reveal that provision for an increasingly severe sanction has been made by the legislature for each repeated refusal to obey the law imposing the preceding sanction, either in the original statute setting the twenty-five-dollar fine, in a general criminal statute covering all failures to fulfill any sanction in the corpus of the law, or finally in the rules of the court permitting the judge himself to impose the second, third, or fourth sanction. Thus, if the motorist, first failing to pay the twenty-five dollars, by the second sanction is sentenced to thirty days and then eludes the custody of the enforcement officer, a third law of sanction will no doubt provide for more lengthy incarceration. *Sic ad infinitum.*

This should make it clear that there are in fact two laws involved in any penal law: the command of the law itself and the second command of the sanction.

In the case of a purely moral law, which is a law without a superadded extrinsic sanction, there is, to the contrary, only one law. Since the civil law rarely if ever indulges in such a purely moral law, an example in that area is impossible. In ecclesiastical law, however, there are many instances. Thus the Roman Catholic Church prescribes attendance at Mass on certain so-called holy days. These vary from country to country and are subject to change at the determination of the Church. To this law no second law of sanction has been attached. It is a true law which binds in conscience regardless of the absence of an accidental sanction or the failure to attain the sanction's objectives.

An additional cause for confusion is the failure to realize in the case of a mixed law (and, it is here argued, of the putative penal law) that there is a moral obligation attached not only to the law but also to the sanction, so that the citizen is bound in conscience not only to obey the law but also to submit to the sanction if apprehended.

The role that God plays in the matter of the sanction of a merely moral and a mixed law has been purposely excluded from discussion. It is true, however, that God does attach a sanction to every law which binds in conscience. This sanction is a second law, just as the sanction of the civil-law lawmaker is. (There is, of course, no question of a conscience obligation to this sanction since enforceability is not a problem with the Divinity.) This divine sanction, attached to the merely moral and mixed laws, is either an eternal one (if the violation of the subject was a total renunciation of God Himself—a mortal sin) or a temporal one (if the disobedience was of a venial nature, offending God but not renouncing Him). The latter sanction is undergone in purgatory, but only if, since the sanction is of a temporal nature only, the sanction of the civil-law lawmaker was insufficient to satisfy God (on the assumption, as with other sufferings here below, that it is undergone in the proper spirit and for the proper purpose) for the breach of the moral obligation attached to the civil law. Thus it can be seen that the presence or absence of this divine sanction does not impinge upon the considerations of the sanctions of the human lawmaker.

Further evidence of the distinction between law and sanction lies in their different purposes. The objective of the law is the common welfare (for example, safety through traffic regulation). The purpose of the sanction is to support the law, to promote obedience, or to right the wrong after disobedience.

The Suarezian thesis that a moral obligation attaches to the sanction but not to the law can be impugned in two distinct ways.

The first is the inversion of purposes. The only conclusion that might be drawn from such a premise could be that the leg-. islature established as its primary objective a fine or imprisonment and as its secondary one the common good, that the legislature was more concerned with the means, the fine, than with the end, safety. It would seem to be a damaging consideration that laws which attached a sanction of punishment only, without a fine, would thereby place primary importance on the punishment of the citizen and only secondary importance upon his obedience. According to Thomistic principles the final end, the common good, is determinative of moral obligation. It would be inconsistent for the lawmaker to place a conscience obligation on a command of secondary importance if he had removed it from the command of primary importance, to which the secondary is subordinated.

View the matter from the aspect of the common good. On Suarezian premises, presumably the rights of the commonweal have been so appreciably invaded that the malefactor is bound under sin to right the wrong. Yet the very act which so seriously invaded these rights is itself morally without blemish and free of culpability.[116]

Were the legislator to act in strict conformity to the dignity and gravity of the respective purposes (on the assumption that he wished to reduce the conscience obligation to a minimum), seemingly he would place the conscience obligation on the command of the law itself and remove it from the command of secondary importance, the sanction.

Vermeersch understood this and refused so to act. "As we have already said, it would be a thing of wonderment and scarcely appropriate for the will of the legislator to deny the force of conscience obligation to the principal part of the law, that is, to the command itself, only to attach it to the secondary part, the sanction, which is outside the law proper."[117] The system of Vermeersch placed no moral obligation either to the law or the penalty. Vermeersch was at least logical, although he left himself in an unenviable position, altogether bereft of any moral obligation.

The law can also be impugned for inconsistency. The question next arises: Why is the command of the sanction not also purely penal? Were one to apply all of the Suarezian *indicia* to the mandate imposing the sanction, the result should be, according to accepted Suarezian methods, a purely penal sanction. If the lawmaker saw fit to regard the law itself as penal, presumably his primary objective, should he not *a fortiori* remove the moral obligation from the second command?

(It is an understandable reflection that the godless lawgiver who would not bind the subject in conscience to the law could not be expected to bind him in conscience to the sanction.)

*E contra*, none of the Suarezian *indicia* point to a legislative intent to bind in conscience to the sanction. This approach should be pursued. Merely to enunciate it and pass on seems inconclusive. Each *indicia* of the will of the lawmaker should be applied to the sanction in the same spirit in which the Suarezians apply them to the law proper (for example, to the penalties attached to the evasion of the excise taxes). Could one then discern any *indicia* of intent to bind in conscience to the sanction that he did not find in the application of the same *indicia* to the law itself? It is altogether possible that this *reductio ad ultimum* might be the most cogent stratagem yet adduced for laying bare the true inner workings of the penal-law system.

Logically, if the law itself is penal, the sanction should be penal. So also should the second sanction, or the third, *ad infinitum*. As long as the doctrine attaches the obligation to the sanction and not to the law, the question will arise: Why to the sanction? The system is faced with a dilemma.

To satisfy the essential requirement of some moral obligation in all true law, the Suarezians place it in the sanction.

This thesis is tenable only if the sanction is an essential part of the law. Grant that the sanction is a second, distinct law superadded to the primary law, and it follows that the conscience obligation has no direct connection with the principal command of the law itself—were it admitted *ex arguendo* that the Suarezians could logically attach such a conscience obligation to the sanction without attaching it to the law itself. The command of the sanction, moreover, would constitute a true law since a conscience obligation was attached to it. But the command of the law would be no law since it carried no binding force. Yet there is, and always has been, unanimity in the doctrine that the sanction is not of the essence of law but is something superadded. This point has already been fully elaborated.

This further dilemma, then, faces the Suarezians: Either sanction is of the essence of law, or the moral obligation of the sanction makes a broad backward leap to the essentially distinct law, impelled by some hidden force hitherto unexplained.

\*  \*  \*

This concludes the arguments both extrinsic—that the purely penal law does not exist in fact—and intrinsic—that it is impossible in theory.

## CHAPTER VIII

# The Civil Law Appears
## *Propria Persona*

The merepenalists have consistently sought solace in the civil law itself for their inexplicable imposition of punishment without guilt, of a penalty leveled for a blameless act. They have responded affirmatively to the rhetorical question: Does not the civil law impose liability without culpability?

What are the Suarezian allegations?

The most recent penal-law protagonist to have resort to the civil law, Dunn, refers to Blackstone as an "unimpeachable witness"[1] and in another place quotes Holmes "as a contemporary testimony to the existence in the civil law of the notion of purely juridic guilt, a notion which was by no means original with him."[2] The quotation:

> While the terminology of morals is still retained, and while the law does still and always, in a certain sense, measure legal liability by moral standards, it nevertheless, by the very necessity of its nature, is continually transmuting those moral standards into external or objective ones, from which the actual guilt of the party concerned is wholly eliminated.[3]

As expressive of the youngest generation of moralists comes a concerned query about

> ... these contemporary examples of *poena* imposed *sine culpa, non tamen sine causa*:
> —Penalties imposed without regard to inadvertence or impossibility to fulfill the law—e.g., parking and some other traffic penalties in some jurisdictions (are they *poenae* or service charges?).
> —Tax penalties and even imprisonment imposed by a judge who regards as certain what the defendant regarded as dubious and therefore not binding.
> —Other criminal penalties imposed by a court which fails to recognize as excusing the causes which led the defendant to nonobservance.[4]

In a similar vein is the merepenalist statement of another present-day moralist: "There are many cases in which the civil law *de facto* inflicts penalties on citizens who are guilty of no moral fault, that is, no sin. Certain criminal statutes carry with them penalties even when violated unwittingly, for instance."[5] To this statement was appended the question that best sets the stage for this present inquiry: "Are there not many crimes where our law punishes for the mere doing of the act, without reference to the agent's knowledge or lack of knowledge, intent or lack of intent, to violate the law?"[6]

The answer to this question of liability without culpability in the civil law is not, like the suit for costs in *Jarndyce v. Jarndyce*, merely a bud on the parent tree. It is the philosophy of the civil law, as expounded in these pages, in practical application and expression in the Anglo-Saxon common law. It has, moreover, received such attention from the merepenalists as to warrant discussion in some detail.

First, the question must be placed in its proper context.

In truth, the only reason that the question ever entered anyone's head—to impose a punishment for virtue is fundamentally incomprehensible—lies in a series of *nonsequiturs* that terminates with the conclusion: A true punishment can be imposed without fault. The merepenalists feel that if this unlikely proposition can be proved and supported by some, any, evidence, it will somehow make the earlier, fundamental premises valid, will confirm the syllogism that resulted in the conclusion.

What is this series?

1 *The law proper does not bind in conscience.*

2 *Therefore, violation of the law is without fault.*

3 *But true law must bind in conscience.*

4 *Therefore, the sanction must bind in conscience.*

5 *But the sanction is punishment.*

6 *Therefore, punishment must be imposed without fault.*

Just as there is a fundamental difference in nature—a deep, essential chasm—between the law and its subsequent sanction, so too is there a bridgeless gap between the conclusion and the first premise:

6 *Punishment must be imposed without fault.*

1 *The law does not bind in conscience.*

(These and the following numbers refer, appropriately, to the six steps in the Suarezian series above.)

The Suarezians faced a razor-sharp dilemma:

1 *The law does not bind in conscience.*

3 *But true law must have some conscience obligation.*

Had they never determined to meet this dilemma with the theretofore unheard-of proposition that (4) the sanction binds in conscience, there would never have been the need to justify (6) the imposition of this sanction on a person who violated, blamelessly, (1) the law proper, which allegedly did not bind in conscience.

Ultimately, the explanation of the impossibility of reasoning backward from the last conclusion, (6) punishment must be imposed without fault, to the first premise, (1) the civil law does not bind in conscience, rests in the fact that there was no connection between the steps in the Suarezian reasoning forward at the outset. There is no logical progression or, more important, nexus between

1 *The civil law does not bind in conscience*

and

6 *Punishment may be imposed without fault.*

If there were such a connection, one could perhaps reason back from the last conclusion to the first premise. If there were, it might be advantageous to prove that the civil law did impose liability without culpability.

Stated in another manner, how does it follow that the imposition of punishment without fault leads to the conclusion that a person can disobey the law without fault? One false proposition does not prove another. Merely to punish innocent men does not prove that disobedient men are innocent. It is one thing to impose punishment without previous moral guilt and another to say that the law can knowingly be violated without guilt. These are two totally different questions—different because ultimately the sanction is not of the essence of the law and because there is no true, logical junction between the placing of the moral obligation in the sanction and the allegedly nonobligatory nature of the law itself.

Since it would aid immeasurably in this attempt to justify the imposition of a sanction on a sinless citizen (so it was thought) to show further that the civil law itself imposed punishment without culpability, there arose the basic question: Does the civil law so operate?

However, let it be argued elsewhere that the Suarezian principle of (4) a conscience obligation in the sanction, and its co-principle, (6) sanction without fault, have no connection with the foundation, (1) civil law does not bind in conscience. Let it be argued elsewhere that the act of placing the conscience obligation in the sanction is a *deus ex machina* to save the system. Let it further be argued elsewhere that one of several other solutions, equally unrelated to conscience, obligation, and the law, could have been excogitated. The fact nevertheless remains that the Suarezians did choose this particular solution. They adamantly maintain that the moral obligation in the sanction saves the essence of true law. They firmly conclude that true punishment can be imposed without fault, that there can be liability without culpability.

The matter therefore demands consideration, even as an isolated proposition, unrelated logically to the major premise: The law does not bind in conscience. It is incumbent to meet the Suarezians on their own ground, to rebut the outermost proposition, in the area in which they aver it can be found: the civil law itself. The primary purpose of this volume, to elaborate the philosophy of the civil law, is thereby achieved.

If it can be shown that there is no foundation to the allegation that the civil law imposes punishment without fault, doubt will correspondingly be (1) cast on the Suarezian imposition of a sanction on a sinless citizen. If doubt is cast there, it will also (2) fall on the essential premises that the sanction can bind in conscience and thereby save that requisite of the true law, some conscience obligation. In short, impugn the thesis of liability without culpability, and you impugn a substantial segment of the Suarezian system and, hence, damage the whole appreciably.

Within this total context it is not only justifiable but imperative to explore intensively the question of liability without culpability in the civil law. Were, however, the full context unknown beforehand, it could be misleading to embark on such an analysis. One could be deflected from the consideration of the morality of violating the law to a consideration of the justice in imposing a penalty without fault, as if the latter were the principal question and its answer would solve all.

With this understanding of the precise implications and the purpose and limits of the present investigation, what is the exact status of liability without culpability in the civil law? Let the civil law itself present a brief in its own defense.

Since the law indeed is a seamless web, it is readily possible to select two fields as representative of the whole in such a civil-law brief for the civil law. In particular reference to the question of the imposition of liability without culpability, the law of torts and the criminal law are in truth prototypal. The criminal wrong (the crime) and the civil wrong (the tort) are the civil-law, external-forum homologues of the moral-law, internal-forum fault or sin. It is understandable, therefore, that if the civil law is going to impose a penalty without fault, it will concededly do so in these two fields or not at all.

This could be misleading, since there is in fact a moral content in every field of the law.[7] Moral accountability is the base of the central structure of one of the more complex fields of the law, corporations. Some other fields, however, are less involved with moral considerations in proportion as they concern themselves, for example, with indifferent procedural matters, which, as in the case of pulling a tooth or removing an appendix, do not directly involve a moral issue. Nevertheless, what can be said of crimes and torts in regard to liability without culpability can be predicated of the law in general. Thus, the eminent James Barr Ames, revered by Harvard, writing at the turn of the century, said: "We have seen how in the law of crimes and torts the ethical quality of the defendant's act has become the measure of his liability instead of the mere physical act regardless of the motive or fault of the actor. The history of the law of contracts exhibits a similar transformation in the legal significance of the written or spoken word."[8]

The immediate goal of this special study is to demonstrate that the thesis, liability without culpability, is fundamentally repugnant to the civil law. This objective, however, can best be achieved by establishing the validity of the positive proposition that civil-law liability, to the contrary, is founded on fault. It will be seen that this philosophy of no liability without culpability permeates to the very heart of the civil law. This does not mean, of course, that there will not be many a variance between theory and practice, intention and fulfillment.

The approach to this proposition will be fourfold: (1) The Philosophy at Base, (2) The Philosophy in Application, (3) The Necessary Infirmities of the External Forum, and (4) The Lamentable Aberrations of the External Forum. When the question is viewed from each of these aspects, the total impact should be a reliable impression of the influence of ethical and moral considerations on civil-law liability.

From time to time throughout the positive exposition of this philosophy there will be references, in the nature of explanations, to each of the queries raised by the various merepenalists in the early remarks of this chapter.

### THE PHILOSOPHY AT BASE

Since Oliver Wendell Holmes, Jr., occupies such a respected position in recent common-law history and since he has been adduced in merepenalist support, he could well set the tone for this entire study. It is more to the point, however, that Holmes, in the commentary cited (*The Common Law*), has presented some admirable remarks apropos of this present problem of liability without culpability in the civil law.

> It will be seen that this order of development is not quite consistent with an opinion which has been held, that it was a characteristic of early law not to penetrate beyond the external visible fact, the *damnum corpore corpori datum*. It has been thought that an inquiry into the internal condition of the defendant, his culpability or innocence, implies a refinement of juridical conception equally foreign to Rome before the Lex Aquilia, and to England when trespass took its shape. I do not know any very satisfactory evidence that a man was generally held liable either in Rome or England for the accidental consequences even of his own act. But whatever may have been the early law, the foregoing account shows the starting-point of the system with which we have to deal. Our system of private liability for the consequences of a man's own

acts, that is, for his trespasses, started from the notion of actual intent and actual personal culpability.[9]

This theory of Holmes that the law, especially of torts, originated with liability based upon "actual intent and actual personal culpability" is not, however, the majority doctrine on the matter. "Another, and more generally accepted theory, is that the law began by making a man act at his peril, and gradually developed toward the acceptance of moral standards as the basis of liability."[10]

Later elucidation of this point will indicate that this latter theory is more acceptable. Like the development of the moral consciousness of the child over the years into the maturity of an adult, the law has moved gradually from ill-formed and crude beginnings to the subtleties and nuances of today—to the pervasive philosophy of liability founded on fault.[11]

### An Historical Conspectus

As the law of the Normans under William the Conqueror after 1066 blended with the Anglo-Saxon customary law and slowly matured through the years after Bracton, the thirteenth-century lawyer-priest, primitive, childlike theories of liability gave way to the concept of liability based on guilt.

A milestone in this progress was the King's Bench case of *Weaver v. Ward*.[12] Weaver and Ward were soldiers engaged in war games at the command of the Lords of the Council. In the process Weaver was injured as Ward *"casualiter et per infortunium et contra voluntatem suam"* discharged his musket and "did hurt and wound the plaintiff." The court was firmly faced with a dilemma. Ward was completely blameless. He had neither intended to injure Weaver nor negligently handled his musket. The piece had been discharged "by accident and through an unfortunate happenstance and against his will." Yet it was equally clear that the offending musket had been in the hands and the control of Ward. The issue was clearly drawn.

Who was to bear the loss? The court in handing down its decision enunciated the clear principle of no liability without culpability: "And therefore no man shall be excused of a trespass . . . except it may be judged utterly without his fault." This was in the early 1600s.

As the years passed, the common-law actions became more varied. This progress, in the mid-1800s, "was accompanied by a growing recognition that, regardless of the form of the action, there should be no liability for pure accident, and that the defendant must be found to be at fault, in the sense of being chargeable with a wrongful intent, or with negligence."[13]

By the year 1850 the Supreme Judicial Court of Massachusetts could be heard in a ringing statement of the philosophy:

> We think, as the result of all the authorities, the rule is correctly stated by Mr. Greenleaf, that the plaintiff must come prepared with evidence to show either that the intention was unlawful, or that the defendant was in fault; for if the injury was unavoidable, and the conduct of the defendant was free from blame, he will not be liable. 2 Greenl. Ev. §§ 85 to 92; *Wakeman v. Robinson,* 1 Bing. 213.[14]

This adjudication arose out of an action of trespass for assault and battery. The facts adduced at the trial indicated that two dogs, belonging to Brown and Kendall, were fighting in the presence of their masters. In order to separate the dogs, Kendall secured a long stick and commenced beating them. During these proceedings, Brown stood behind Kendall and the fighting dogs. As Kendall retreated from the fight, laying about as he went, "in raising his stick over his shoulder, in order to strike the dogs, he accidentally hit the plaintiff in the eye, inflicting upon him a severe injury."[15] Since manifestly there was no fault in Kendall's action, the question was reducible to one of liability without blame.

Perhaps there is an unwonted tendency to read too much between the following lines; nonetheless, it is of interest to study this summary statement of the Supreme Court of the United States made in 1921 in *Brown v. United States*:

> The law has grown, and even if historical mistakes have contributed to its growth it has tended in the direction of rules consistent with human nature.[16]

Although a fuller discussion is appropriate for later in this chapter, it is relevant to quote the words of a 1956 case, *Randall v. Shelton*, as indicative of the most modern attitude of the courts on this question. "Plaintiff is entitled to protection from wrongful injury wherever she may lawfully be, and the true question presented is whether or not the defendant committed a culpable act, not the plaintiff's geographical location."[17]

These random examples taken over the years are not meant to be probative but merely illustrative. The proof itself, however, can be found in the scholarly historical studies of men such as Holmes, Wigmore, and Ames.

At the conclusion of his first chapter, "Early Forms of Liability," in *The Common Law*, Holmes summarizes the pertinent philosophy of the civil law. (In so doing, moreover, he casts some light on the true import of those words of his which were earlier advanced as corroborative of the merepenalist position. To refresh the recollection, Holmes wrote: "It remains to be proved that, while the terminology of morals is still retained, and while the law does still and always, in a certain sense, measure legal liability by moral standards, it nevertheless, by the very necessity of its nature, is continually transmuting those moral standards into external or objective ones from which the actual guilt of the party concerned is wholly eliminated."[18]) Further comment should make Holmes's meaning clear. The following preceded immediately the merepenalist quotation.

> But none of the foregoing considerations, nor the purpose of showing the materials for anthropology contained in the history of the law, are the immediate object here. My aim and purpose have been to show that the various forms of liability known to modern

law spring from the common ground of revenge. In the sphere of
contract the fact will hardly be material outside the cases which
have been stated in this Lecture. But in the criminal law and the
law of torts it is of the first importance. It shows that they have
started from a moral basis, from the thought that someone was
to blame.[19]

The esteemed Wigmore, writing in 1894, concludes his
three-article treatment of *Responsibility for Tortious Acts* with
the following three summary statements:

> But to-day we do certainly consider, not merely the sufferer's dam-
> age, but the blamableness of the defendant's conduct; while no
> such distinction was yet made, in the 1300s, even in cases of mere
> "misadventure."[20]

> The evidence seems certain that the rationalization towards the line
> of present standards began at a much earlier period than has been
> supposed. In other words, there has never been a time, in English
> law, since (say) the early 1500s, when the defendant in an action
> for Trespass was not allowed to appeal to some standard of blame
> or fault in addition to and beyond the mere question of his act
> having been voluntary; *i.e.* granting a voluntary act, he might still
> excuse himself (apart from excuses of self-defence, consent, and
> the like).[21]

> The precedents show us, then, that somewhere about 1500 a decided
> sloughing-off of the last stage of the primitive notion took place,
> and a defendant could exempt himself in this sort of an action if
> his act, though voluntary, had been without blame; the standard
> being more indefinite, and perhaps not as liberal, as to-day, but not
> different in kind.[22]

It may be said, in concluding this general statement of the
civil-law philosophy, that the work of Ames in 1908 is the most
rewarding. His conclusion:

> So that today we may say that the old law has been radically
> transformed. The early law asked simply, "Did the defendant do
> the physical act which damaged the plaintiff?" The law of today,
> except in certain cases based upon public policy, asks the further
> question, "Was the act blameworthy?" The ethical standard of rea-

sonable conduct has replaced the unmoral standard of acting at one's peril.[23]

## THE PHILOSOPHY IN APPLICATION

These summary statements and the cases cited in exemplification reflect in a comprehensive way the pervading spirit and the broad philosophy of the Anglo-Saxon common-law system. The overall goal, the aim, the deeply desired objective of the civil law, is liability founded only on fault. This unmistakable philosophy in *ad hoc* application by the legislature, the executive, and the judiciary has many illuminating aspects, all of which conduce to the thorough conviction that punishment without fault is abhorrent to the common law.

The telling insights into this philosophy, however, can only be achieved by specified and exact enunciations of its principles in day-to-day applications to the civil law. (Note well: In these following formal enunciations and their later elucidation, the terms *liability, punishment, penalty,* and *sanction* will be used synonymously and indiscriminately. So, too, will *culpability, guilt, fault,* and *blame*. The refined meanings of *poena* and *poena* and the rest, however, are not irrelevant by any means. In the conclusion to this dissertation on civil-law culpability, the precise natures, particularly of the liability [punishment] and the culpability [fault], will be analyzed. Meantime, no attempt will be made to qualify them each time they are used, even though they are used loosely.)

The formal enunciations of the common-law philosophy of culpability based on fault:

1 In theory: Never should there be liability without corresponding culpability.
2 In practice: Never will there be liability without culpability, unless it be
   a *per accidens,* on the necessary and understandable assumption that the citizen is guilty—never is a person

punished *per se* by a *poena* in the strict sense as a punishment for fault on the assumption of innocence

or

b *per se*, on some erroneous and ill-founded policy,
adopted in spite of, not because of, innocence and for
putatively higher and overriding reasons.

Thus, in neither theory nor practice is liability without culpability ever imposed for innocence alone, without some other presumably prevailing, albeit mistaken, reason. This is an exactly
stated summary of the status of the philosophy of liability without culpability in the civil law. Such status, moreover, is as consonant with the abiding premise of liability founded on fault as
the frailty of the human legal system will permit.

A detailed elaboration of these summary statements will go
far toward defining with precision and filling in the gaps in the
outline of the philosophy of the civil law concerning the punishment of the guiltless.

### The Necessary Infirmities of the External Forum

There are certain intrinsic disabilities and limitations in any
human system of law which give rise to a regrettable but necessary anomaly. The anomaly consists of the two elements of a
seeming contradiction existing side by side. On the one side is
the firm adherence of the civil law to the principle of liability
founded on fault. On the other there is the inevitable persistence
of many instances of the infliction on innocent citizens of what is
ostensibly punishment without fault.

These instances of apparent inequities in the practical application of the philosophy are readily explained. The explanation
lies in the difference between establishing a legal system on a
moral foundation, on the moral principles of no liability without
culpability; and employing legal, not moral, norms in the application of the law once founded and enacted. There is no doubt
that the Anglo-Saxon common law is founded on a moral base.

The law is framed to give the maximum justice to all, to apply the principles of the natural law in every instance.

Ultimately, however, this conflict between theory and practice is referable to the fundamental differences between the internal forum and the external.

In the internal forum there are no such problems in the implementation of the law. In both foundation and application, God (and the priest in the confessional) faces no difficulty in adhering at all times and in every case to His firm philosophy of punishment, in the strict sense, for fault alone. God is successful in this because the forum of the conscience possesses none of the deficiencies of a man-made legal system.

In the external forum, however, the matter is totally otherwise. Although the norm of the foundation of the system is moral, its execution is perforce legal. The exigencies and imperfections of the external forum are fundamentally reducible to the intrinsic limitations of man's legal ability as legislator, executive, and judge, and to the frailty of the system itself— but not to an avowed policy of liability without culpability.

Speaking broadly and pointing up the most obvious difference between the internal forum and the external, man cannot search the heart of man. Said Chief Justice Brian in the mid-1400s: "The thought of man shall not be tried, for the devil himself knoweth not the thought of man."[24] Insofar, therefore, as the heart of man cannot be searched, insofar as legislator, enforcement officer, and judge are fragile human beings, thus far there will be unwitting victims of the system, persons visited with liability without culpability.

Whenever, however, such guiltless citizens are thus afflicted, it is not on the law's assumption that they are not guilty but, to the contrary, that they are. Such sanction is imposed *per accidens* and for several reasons. Mistake not, however. These are valid and necessary reasons—the necessary concessions to any human legal system. (This does not mean that diligent effort should not be expended continually to remove as far as possible these deficiencies from the human legal system. In the absolute end, however, some such defects are essential and hence inevitable. Furthermore, it is most difficult to mark the line between the eradicable and ineradicable in this matter.)

It now remains to explore at each level (legislative, executive, and judicial) the several categories of necessary infirmities of the external forum. Within the sphere of the instant discussion, every instance of an innocent person visited with such a *poena* is attributable to one or another of these inadequacies.

### Legislative

Among the many deficiencies of civil-law legislation which serious meditation would suggest to the analytical mind, two areas are perhaps preeminent: (1) the debility of the legislative intellect and (2) the necessity for an arbitrary rule.

When one contemplates the complexity of present-day life and the multiplicity of laws necessitated by the ingenuity of the modern mind, the wonder is not that the legislative draftsmen incorporate into their laws so many inequities, traps for the innocent, loopholes for the guilty, and even outright injustice, but rather that their legislative product, by and large, does so well in meting out equal justice to all. The regrettable fact, however, remains that as long as legislation must perforce be entrusted to human beings, some innocent persons will suffer as if for fault.

The second category is possibly more prolific of apparent liability without culpability. It is beyond the competence of even the most enlightened legislator to envisage every unusual instance, each exception to the general rule. The law, therefore, must set arbitrary limits and standards, and apply them with as much precision as possible. No statute could feasibly contain every exemption or provide for every emergency. Even were this possible, such legislation would be impractical.

Furthermore, arbitrary proscriptions, for example, against jaywalking, exceeding specified limits of vehicular speed, driving through stop signs, are absolutely necessary. This is because of the general inability of the mass of citizens prudently to determine the time and place for exceptions or, in general, to make valid *ad hoc* interpretations or modifications of a given statute.

In some instances, moreover, such arbitrary proscriptions are founded on the inherent danger in permitting even one justifiable exception. Such one exception could so undermine the inviolability of the law as to threaten its total efficacy. Thus, a legislator in a purely naturalistic (and hence hypothetical) society might conclude to the necessity of the statutory prohibition of any and all divorce of spouses on the assumption that even one arguably justified exception would be the leak that would ruin the dike. Such rigid proscriptions could be considered as necessary to avoid greater evils.

For each of these valid reasons the innocent often suffer.

### Executive

In the execution of the law, the same two types of imperfections are present: (1) the debility of the law-enforcement intellect and (2) the necessity of an arbitrary rule.

The law-enforcement officer is handicapped by a necessary, and even reasonable, lack of time and money. In a high percentage of instances he cannot and should not attempt to inquire into hearts. The intrinsic nature of the civil law has defined his enforcement role as ministerial, not discretionary. Such a civil-law exigency will invariably impose a hardship on some innocent citizens. This is the explanation of the problem raised at the outset of this treatment by the moralist Kelly when he reflected on the "penalties imposed without regard to inadvertence or impossibility to fulfill the law—e.g., parking and some other traffic penalties in some jurisdictions (are they *poenae* or service charges?)." Such penalties are meant to be true *poenae*. They are set up as legitimate sanctions in order to achieve the four-fold purpose of sanction, and they are imposed on the assumption of guilt. The inability, either of the law to cope with a justifiable exception or the ministerial nature of the role of the law-enforcement officer precluding the possibility of an *ad hoc* exception, explains those instances where a truly innocent, albeit apparently guilty, citizen suffers what would be otherwise a true *poena*. This particular situation will be considered in more detail in succeeding pages.

In those cases where even the ministerial law-enforcement officer might legally exercise some discretion in excepting an innocent person from the application of the law, there yet remain the omnipresent and deplorable although understandable inefficiency, laziness, and even stupidity and venality of the police officers. Again, however, the ostensible penalty is leveled on the assumption of culpability.

### Judicial

Even more than the legislative and executive branches, the Anglo-Saxon common-law courts have been—and must continue to be—a source of hardship and even inequity for an innocent few. The highly developed and exactly refined rules of pleading, procedure, and evidence have been the justifiable boast and pride of the common law. While these detailed rules have been a solace and comfort to the many, they have inflicted on a rare occasion a judgment of guilt on an innocent man. Nonetheless, until the judge and jury can read the conscience of the accused or the minds and hearts of the litigants, some very few must suffer for a manifestly greater good.

The extent, however, to which astute legal minds can progress in refining further these rules of pleading, procedure, and evidence is difficult to assay. One thing is certain. The very nature and exigencies of the external forum will always present some regrettable cases.

There has indeed been much improvement, particularly in the area of pleading and procedure. In the earliest days of common-law pleading, the wooden rigidities of the forms of action, the inflexible regulations governing phraseology, the formalities of brief-making, and the mechanics of courtroom procedure left many a plaintiff and defendant bearing a hardship they ill deserved in the light of the merits of their cause but which they were required to undergo, justifiably and necessarily, in consideration of the state of legal reasoning at the time. Fortunately each decade has seen appreciable progress. A high point in this progress came in 1938 with the impeccable new *Federal Rules of Civil and Criminal Procedure*. These Federal rules have brought to the barest minimum the old inequities of the common-law pleading and procedures.

An apt illustration of the necessary infirmities of the external forum is in the vaunted common-law rules of evidence. Among these, the hearsay rule is preeminent.

The hearsay rule in substance, shorn of some collateral and outer-fringe areas of controversy, is indisputably sound. A study of this rule in the celebrated *Donnelly v. United States* could conceivably offer a concrete summary of the entire concept of the *per accidens* imposition of liability without culpability founded on the necessary assumption of guilt.[25]

*Donnelly*, however, has one defect. The particular nuance of the rule which was controlling in *Donnelly* is not absolutely incontrovertible. The analysis by the *Donnelly* court of the rule in general, however, is unimpeachable as illustrative of the present point.

On the Klamath River in the Hoopa Valley Reservation, Chickasaw, a member of the Klamath tribe, was shot through the body and mortally wounded by an assailant who was presumably lurking in the bushes at river's edge. A certain Donnelly, a white man, was in time tried and convicted in the Circuit Court of the United States for the Northern District of

California upon an indictment for murder, and was duly sentenced to life imprisonment. Upon a writ of error the case was heard by the Supreme Court of the United States in 1912. The court found no error appearing in the record and affirmed the judgment of conviction. Three judges, however, did dissent.

For present purposes the chief question, among six presented to the Supreme Court, concerned the hearsay rule.

At his trial, Donnelly offered to introduce testimony of prevailing importance to his case. This testimony the trial judge refused to admit as excluded by the hearsay rule.

Donnelly was prepared to bring forward evidence to the effect that one Joe Dick, an Indian, since deceased, had confessed that it was he who had in fact shot Chickasaw. At the trial, the facts adduced in favor of the Government strongly tended to exclude the theory that more than one person participated in the shooting. Had Joe Dick's confession been admissible, it "would have directly tended to exculpate the plaintiff in error."[26]

Counsel for Donnelly not only showed at the trial that Dick was dead, which would account for his absence as a witness, but brought forward other circumstances which allegedly would point to Joe Dick as the guilty man. Dick lived in the vicinity, and therefore presumably knew the habits of Chickasaw. The footprints upon the sandbar at the scene of the crime led directly to an acorn camp where Dick was stopping at the moment, not toward Donnelly's home. There was, moreover, another imprint on the sand which could be interpreted as the impression made by a person in a sitting position. Since Joe Dick was a victim of consumption, shortness of breath could arguably have impelled him thus to pause for a moment.

All of this notwithstanding, the trial judge excluded the confession of Joe Dick.

In affirming this action of the lower court and the judgment of life imprisonment, the Supreme Court wrote a forceful essay on the underlying rationale of the hearsay rule.

Hearsay evidence, with a few well recognized exceptions, is excluded by courts that adhere to the principles of the common law. The chief grounds of its exclusion are, that the reported declaration (if in fact made) is made without the sanction of an oath, with no responsibility on the part of the declarant for error or falsification, without opportunity for the court, jury, or parties to observe the demeanor and temperament of the witness, and to search his motives and test his accuracy and veracity by cross-examination, these being most important safeguards of the truth, where a witness testifies in person, and of his own knowledge; and, moreover, he who swears in court to the extra-judicial declaration does so (especially where the alleged declarant is dead) free from the embarrassment of present contradiction and with little or no danger of successful prosecution for perjury. It is commonly recognized that this double relaxation of the ordinary safeguards must very greatly multiply the probabilities of error, and that hearsay evidence is an unsafe reliance in a court of justice.[27]

The court continued with a reference to one of the many exceptions to the hearsay rule: declarations of third parties made contrary to their own interest. The court refused to apply this exception since, as it said, it is almost universally held that this interest must be of a pecuniary character. In the instant case, therefore, it was inapplicable. The court proceeded to say that "in this country there is a great and practically unanimous weight of authority in the state courts against admitting evidence of confessions of third parties made out of court and tending to exonerate the accused."[28]

In concluding, Mr. Justice Pitney, speaking for the court, sought the support of the great Chief Justice Marshall, likewise speaking for the Supreme Court of the United States. Marshall adverted to the greater good which the hearsay rule was designed to protect.

These several opinions of the court (meaning the trial court) depend on one general principle. The decision of which determines them all. It is this: that hearsay evidence is incompetent to establish any specific fact, which fact is in its nature susceptible of being

proved by witnesses who speak from their own knowledge. . . .
It was very justly observed by a great judge that "all questions
upon the rules of evidence are of vast importance to all orders and
degrees of men; our lives, our liberty, and our property are all
concerned in the support of these rules, which have been matured
by the wisdom of ages, and are now revered from their antiquity
and the good sense in which they are founded."[29] One of these rules
is that "hearsay" evidence is in its own nature inadmissible. That
this species of testimony supposes some better testimony which
might be adduced in the particular case, is not the sole ground of
its exclusion. Its intrinsic weakness, its incompetency to satisfy the
mind of the existence of the fact, and the frauds which might be
practiced under its cover combine to support the rule that hearsay
evidence is totally inadmissible. . . . The danger of admitting
hearsay evidence is sufficient to admonish courts of justice against
lightly yielding to the introduction of fresh exceptions to an old
and well-established rule; the value of which is felt and acknowledged by all. If the circumstance that the eyewitnesses of any fact
be dead should justify the introduction of testimony to establish
that fact from hearsay, no man could feel safe in any property, a
claim to which might be supported by proof so easily obtained.
. . . This court is not inclined to extend the exceptions further than
they have already been carried.[30]

How different would be the adjudication of the confessor in
the confessional or of God Himself at the last judgment, assuming, of course, the reliability of Joe Dick's confession. It is this
very assumption that the common-law courts cannot make.

It is somewhat unfortunate that the outcome of *Donnelly*
should revolve around a particular exception to the hearsay
rule: declarations of third parties made contrary to their own
interest. One may not agree that such interest must be of a pecuniary character. No matter. This is not essentially relevant to
the present study. There is no doubt that the hearsay rule in
essence is an incontrovertibly necessary apparatus of the Anglo-
Saxon common-law system. In other words, until judge and jury
can divine the hearts of men, the hearsay rule will be an imperative and highly desirable ornament of the rules of evidence.

Although *Donnelly* could be adjudged a close case, it remains an admirable instance of a possibly innocent person suffering at the hands of the justifiable rules of the system—rules which, of course, are totally absent in the internal forum.

It is altogether possible that the analysis thus far, and in particular that of *Donnelly*, might answer the moralist Kelly's third query regarding "other criminal penalties imposed by a court which fails to recognize as excusing the causes which led the defendant to nonobservance."[31]

It is also highly likely that herein lies the explanation of the oft-adverted-to words of Holmes as quoted by the merepenalists. (Again to refresh the recollection: "It remains to be proved that, while the terminology of morals is still retained, and while the law does still and always, in a certain sense, measure legal liability by moral standards, it nevertheless, by the very necessity of its nature, is continually transmuting those moral standards into external or objective ones, from which the actual guilt of the party concerned is wholly eliminated."[32]) What Holmes was simply saying was that the exigencies of the external forum demand rules, such as the instant hearsay rule, which cannot always and everywhere meet with complete success in penetrating to the actual moral guilt or innocence of the parties. He did not mean, however, that liability would be imposed without culpability as an accepted standard. If this is what Holmes did mean, he would apparently be in error.

## The Lamentable Aberrations of the External Forum

In this second major category, the guiltless citizen, subjected to unwarranted liability, has a much more justifiable complaint. Here his unfortunate position is not because of a necessary deficiency of the external forum itself—a deficiency which an infinite amount of wisdom could not remove—but rather because judge, jurist, and jurisprudent (1) have proved unaware of the intricate problems facing the law, (2) have shown a misguided desire to do good or a misunderstanding of what is the truly greater good, (3) have been, which is more likely, ill-trained in the niceties of moral and ethical concepts, or (4) last, which is true in some cases and is certainly the reason for the slow progress forward, have been simply incapable of reasoning through to the heart of an issue and of applying a traditional philosophy to a new and even bizarre fact situation.

The totality of errors, in argument and policy, is exemplified in three subdivisions: (1) The Inability of the Court To Penetrate to Subtleties, (2) So-called Public Policy—the Ability To Pay, (3) So-called Public Policy—the Inability To Pay.

These fallacies are by no means necessary concomitants of the common-law system. They are, in fact, nonessential and nonintrinsic. Enlightened thinking and diligent labor can, and certainly to a great extent will, correct the mistakes. In fact, there has been heartening progress over the last four centuries in eliminating theories and doctrines antagonistic to the philosophy of liability founded only on fault. What yet remains may well be corrected in short years.

It might be argued that some inconcinnities in general policy matters as well as *ad hoc* reasoning will be present as long as a human judge is on the bench and a human jurisprudent is elaborating the doctrine or setting the pattern of argument and rationalization. On the very first page of *The Common Law*, written eighty years ago, Holmes could lead one to conclude that such disabilities will never cease to direct the well-meaning law into inconsistent argumentation and ill-founded policies. "The felt necessities of the time, the prevalent moral and political theories, intuitions of public policy, avowed or unconscious, even the prejudices which judges share with their fellow-men, have had a good deal more to do than the syllogism in determining the rules by which men should be governed."[33]

The imposition of liability without culpability in these three categories is not founded on the assumption that the innocent party is guilty, which was the assumption heretofore. Liability is generally imposed with the court's knowledge of innocence— not, however, because of the innocence but in spite of it. Invariably the court acts for reasons altogether unrelated to innocence or guilt, for some reason certainly ill-advised and often specious and erroneous but which nonetheless induces the court so to act. Never is the blameless person subjected to liability on the theory that virtue should be punished but rather that some other seemingly higher principle should prevail.

Among these reasons could lie the explanation to the moralist Kelly's reference to "tax penalties and even imprisonment imposed by a judge who regards as certain what the defendant regarded as dubious and therefore not binding."[34]

Since the purposes of illustration are adequately achieved without reference to the legislative or executive branches, the following three subdivisions will be confined to the courts' work.

## *The Inability of the Court To Penetrate to Subtleties*

The field of tort law in the sixth decade of the twentieth century offers three fascinating instances of the struggle of the legal mind, alternately successful and unsuccessful, with relatively intricate subtleties revolving around the question of liability without culpability. Although these are only examples, they are undoubtedly outstanding: (1) the concept of trespass, (2) the definition of intent, and (3) the notion of strict liability.

The concept of trespass was probably formulated earliest.

The early Anglo-Saxon feudal system was founded, in its major outlines, upon the importance (and consequently on the inviolability) of the land and its castle. The concept of property tenure and the sanctity of the freehold imparted to the early law of trespass its governing philosophy and major principles. "But it is an elementary principle that every unauthorized, and therefore unlawful, entry into the close of another, is a trespass. From every such entry against the will of the possessor the law infers some damage . . ."[35] From this fundamental principle, embodied in the definition of trespass, arose some interesting conclusions.

Consider the example of *Louisville Railway Co. v. Sweeney.*

Stemming undoubtedly from this sacred character of the land, the rule gradually developed over the years that one who trespassed upon the land of another, even though the trespass was neither intentional nor negligent, was to be held liable for any damage occasioned by his later actions, even though blameless, simply because of the trespass to the land.

The Court of Appeals of Kentucky in the year 1914 founded its decision in the *Louisville Railway Co. v. Sweeney*[36] case on just such grounds.

Jennie Sweeney lived in Louisville at the point where Payne Street begins to make a curve at Charlton. On a June day in 1911, Jennie stood quietly near the gate in her front yard. In the midst of a conversation with a neighbor she looked up, "heard a terrible crash of fire, an awful noise, and looking forth" saw one of the streetcars of the Louisville Railway Company miss the curve, leap the track, collide with a telephone pole, send the pole against the gate of the yard. The result: The gate was thrown full athwart Mrs. Sweeney. With this, she "allowed as how [she] didn't know no more from that."[37]

On these facts the Court of Appeals of Kentucky saw no necessity for inquiring into culpability at all. There was a trespass. That was sufficient. Without investigation either into negligent or intentional misconduct, the action of the lower court, imposing liability on the railway company without proven culpability, was affirmed. Thus a completely blameless, nonnegligent, nonintentional trespass was held, without more, to warrant the imposition of liability for all of the subsequent, equally blameless, damage. This holding was the law of the state of Kentucky until the year 1956.

In 1956, however, the Kentucky court found itself face to face with the stark realities of its position on nonnegligent, nonintentional trespass. Since it seemed quite certain that the Louis-ville Railway Company in the *Sweeney* case was, as a matter of actual fact, guilty of some fault, the court did not blanch at granting recovery to Mrs. Sweeney, founding its judgment on the trespass and foregoing the necessity of some proof of culpa-bility. Because the end was certainly justified, the means did not seem so illogical.

But in *Randall v. Shelton* the principle of liability founded on a nonnegligent, nonintentional trespass was reduced to such a logical absurdity that even the most unenlightened court could reason to the fallacy. What had been a subtlety in previous cases became a monstrosity in *Randall*.[38]

The problem that faced the court was the delicate distinction between the putative damage caused by the trespass and the damage caused by later acts completely unrelated to the tres-pass itself other than in the fact that they occurred on the land of the plaintiff.

The question then resolved itself into this: Is the deeply in-grained conviction of the court that even a blameless, nonnegli-gent, nonintentional trespass carries some wrong sufficient to color every later act, even though innocent, and impart to it such culpability as to result in liability? In *Sweeney* the court said yes. In *Randall* the question was sharply limned.

The young Shelton girl lived on State Highway 92 in Whitley County, Kentucky. On the morning of her injury she was standing in her front yard when a red, dual-wheeled truck owned by Randall passed on the gravel road in front of her home. As the truck sped by, so the girl said, "It throwed the rock out and hit me and broke my leg."[39] In corroboration, Mrs. Shelton testified at the trial: "I seed the rock come out of them double-wheeled red cab truck across the road where she was in the edge of the yard and hit her on the leg and she fell."[40]

"There was no proof whatever of any negligence upon the part of the truck driver. All that was shown was that a rock was thrown from the wheels of the truck as it passed."[41] Thus the court faced the undeniable question of liability without culpability. It was fully conscious that "the *Sweeney* case . . . is a leading one,"[42] but the simplicity of the facts traced the necessary distinctions in bold lines. In spite of *stare decisis* and its former firm position, the Court of Appeals of Kentucky overruled *Sweeney* and reduced the elements of the argumentation to the simplest terms.

> An attempt in this case to apply a strict rule of liability based upon a concept of trespass to land would lead to an incongruous result. The plaintiff contends that she had walked into her front yard from the roadway. The defendant contends that she was not on her property. To say that she could recover for her injuries if she was in her yard but could not recover if she was one step outside of it is a patent absurdity. Plaintiff is entitled to protection from wrongful injury wherever she may lawfully be, and the true question presented is whether or not the defendant committed a culpable act, not plaintiff's geographical location.[43]

The Court of Appeals, therefore, refused to impose liability without culpability. It realized that a nonnegligent, nonintentional trespass was not sufficient, as *Sweeney* had held, to render unlawful every act occurring thereafter, merely because of the blameless trespass itself. "To further point up the absurdity of the situation, suppose the plaintiff had been in her front yard talking to a neighbor and the stone had struck both. Assuming no negligence, would there be any logic in ruling that the plaintiff could recover and the neighbor could not?"[44]

*Randall v. Shelton,* therefore, is an admirable illustration of the progress of the law toward an ideal. Although the courts of Kentucky, until the recent date of 1956, had and would have imposed liability without fault in cases within the purview of *Sweeney,* the realization finally prevailed that the innocent trespasser should not be visited with liability merely because of a nonnegligent, nonintentional entry. Kentucky at last acknowledged by acquiescence that "in other jurisdictions the principle is recognized that unless a trespass is either intentional or negligent, no liability attaches."[45]

In contradistinction there is a fascinating parallel study of the development of liability founded on fault in the homologous field of intentional trespass.

Whereas in *Sweeney* and *Randall v. Shelton* the trespass was blameless, neither negligent nor intentional, in *Kopka v. Bell Telephone Co. of Pennsylvania*,[46] it was undisputedly intentional and, hence, presumably culpable.

Bell proceeded to enter Kopka's land, without his permission, and dug a pole hole some six and a half feet deep and seventeen inches wide, just inside the road on the main farm. When Kopka finally learned that Bell had been on the property, he headed out to investigate. It was in the gloaming of a cloudy day. While walking around in his search, Kopka's left leg slipped into the hole, with the result that he suffered specified personal injuries. The case was not tried on the issue of any wrongful act by the telephone company, either negligent or intentional, committed after the entry onto the property. It was a question solely of whether the intentional trespass itself rendered the telephone company liable for any injuries to Kopka, without reference to any other later negligent or intentional and, hence, wrongful act.

Thus, *Kopka* was on all fours with *Sweeney* and *Randall v. Shelton* in its reliance on the inviolability of the land and the rules of the law of trespass, with the sole and outstanding difference being that the trespass of *Sweeney* and *Randall v. Shelton* was nonnegligent and nonintentional, whereas in *Kopka* it was intentional. In no one of the three cases was there a blameworthy act after the actual trespass itself.

Philosophically, therefore, the ultimate question here was whether the wrongful element in the intentional trespass was sufficient to render any later nonnegligent and nonintentional (and, hence, blameless) act the trespasser's legal responsibility.

In the *Randall v. Shelton* case the Court of Appeals of Kentucky concluded that the nonculpable striking of young Shelton could not be rendered culpable merely because the stone entered the land of the injured party, with the realization, of course, that the entry itself was nonnegligent and nonintentional.

In *Kopka*, however, the Supreme Court of Pennsylvania felt that the rule was otherwise when the trespass was intentional:

> The authorities are clear to the effect that where the complaint is for trespass to land the trespasser becomes liable not only for personal injuries resulting directly and proximately from the trespass but also for those which are indirect and consequential.[47]

In effect the intentional trespass itself so colors the situation as to render the trespasser liable for actions he later performs for which he would not be otherwise liable were he not a trespasser. The *Restatement of the Law of Torts*, in Comment c to Paragraph 380, was cited by *Kopka* in support of its stand:

> It is, therefore, not necessary to the liability of the trespasser that his conduct should be intentionally wrongful or recklessly or negligently disregardful of the interest of the possessor. . . . Thus, one who trespasses upon the land of another incurs the risk of becoming liable for any bodily harm which is caused to the possessor of the land . . . by any conduct of the trespasser during the continuance of his trespass no matter how otherwise innocent such conduct may be.[48]

In other words, does an act otherwise completely blameless, neither negligent nor intentional, become blameworthy by the adding of the fact that it was performed on the land of another after an entry that was intentional and without permission?

Further to highlight the issue, the court in *Randall v. Shelton* answered this question in the negative when the entry was nonnegligent and nonintentional, and the court in *Kopka* answered the question in the affirmative when the entry was intentional.

Juxtapose *Randall v. Shelton* and *Kopka*, therefore, and ask: Is the culpability in an intentional trespass of such gravity, compared to a nonnegligent, nonintentional trespass, as to render subsequent acts culpable which would not be so were it not for the intent to enter? Both the Pennsylvania court and the *Restatement of the Law of Torts* hold that the culpability of an intentional trespass does so operate.

One might reasonably conjecture that the thirty years since *Kopka* (1932) and the *Restatement* (1934) would see a reappraisal and a consequent change of the law, as was witnessed in the transition from *Sweeney* to *Randall v. Shelton*. The *Restatement of the Law, Second, Torts, Tentative Draft No. 2*, released in March 1958, puts to rest any such thoughts. It restated *Kopka*, although it did remark that the section "was the subject of a prolonged debate on the floor of the Institute meeting in 1930. (See Proceedings for that year, page 210.) Judge Biggs challenged the Section . . . as going beyond all of the cases and unsound in principle."[49]

The slow maturation of the primitive legal mind and the philosophy of liability founded on fault can be traced grade by grade in the evolution of the notion of intent. To define an intentional act is to enumerate the essential elements of moral culpability in it. The elaboration of the definition of intent could be said to be an epitome of the parallel growth of the whole Anglo-Saxon common-law philosophy of fault.

In the decades after William, the courts were faced with the most elemental kinds of crimes and torts—assault, battery, trespass upon the close, conversion of a cow, and the like—and responded with the most elemental definition of intent.

Medieval jurisprudence seemed unable to distinguish the various types of causes and correspondingly to place the blame upon the morally responsible ultimate, efficient cause rather than upon an accidental, immediate, instrumental cause.

> Another peculiarity to be noticed is, that the liability seems to have been regarded as attached to the body doing the damage, in an almost physical sense. An untrained intelligence only imper-

fectly performs the analysis by which jurists carry responsibility back to the beginning of a chain of causation. The hatred for anything giving us pain, which wreaks itself on the manifest cause, and which leads even civilized man to kick a door when it pinches his finger, is embodied in the *noxae deditio* and other kindred doctrines of early Roman law.[50]

This inability to distinguish and this predisposition to place liability on the last visible instrumental cause in the long series of causation led the early Anglo-Saxon courts into some absurdities in the law of intent. If a tree was to fall upon a man and kill him, vengeance was visited on the tree. It was carried away and chopped into many pieces. In the years *circa* 1100, if a man stabbed another with a knife in a completely blameless act of self-defense, he was nonetheless cast into prison and treated as guilty of a felony. After all, it was his knife, he held it, and he had control of it. Once in prison the hapless man was dependent on the pardon of the king. Slow realization of the underlying injustice led first to the royal pardon as a matter of course and ultimately to self-defense as a defense to the criminal prosecution for the killing. By 1400, self-defense was a complete bar to any action for battery.

The fundamental confusion, however, between efficient and instrumental causes has manifested itself in the most modern times. Even as late as 1891, the Wisconsin court in *Vosburg v. Putney*[51] perpetuated this confusion in a simple litigation for battery.

An eleven-year-old boy, seated at his desk in the classroom, extended his leg across the aisle and mildly tapped the ankle of a fellow student. The result, because of an abnormal condition caused by a previous injury, was a serious lameness and prolonged pain. The Wisconsin court reasoned much in the manner of the 1200s. The boy had intended the kick. The kick was unlawful as violative of classroom regulations. Had there been no kick, there would have been no lameness. Unable to distinguish between the mere occasion for the operation of a completely independent cause, the previous latent condition, and a true cause, the court found the eleven-year-old liable not merely for the momentary discomfort in the ankle (which should have been the maximum damages referable to the kick itself) but for the subsequent lameness and all of the attendant pain, discomfort, and expenses. This holding reflected the general thesis that the person who places an intentional act is liable for all of the consequences which can in any way be related to that act, even though they be unforeseen and not the moral responsibility of the actor.

This inflexible attitude persisted for many years after the turn into the twentieth century. Liability, regardless of fault, was imposed upon the actor once it was proven that the initial act was intentional. The parallel with the philosophy of the law of intentional trespass is striking.

Over the first half of the twentieth century, however, legal scholars slowly refined their understanding of the nature of intent. They realized the essential differences among the intent (1) to kick the ankle, although unsuccessfully, (2) to kick the ankle in order to make contact but not to hurt, (3) to kick the ankle in order to cause a normal degree of pain, or (4) to kick the ankle in order to arouse a latent wound. This progress in the analysis of the nature of intent reached a point of considerable development (although, it is maintained, by no means perfection) in the *Restatement of the Law, Second, Torts, Tentative Draft No. 1*,[52] of April 1957, when the American Law Institute submitted its revision of the definition of intent. This revision would cure the injustice of the old attitudes surrounding the law of intent, remedy the evils of *Vosburg*, and found the notion of intent firmly on the philosophy of no liability without culpability. The new "§ 8A. INTENT" fully recognized this philosophy.

> The word "intent" is used throughout the restatement of this subject to denote that the actor desires to cause the consequences

of his act, or that he knows that the consequences are substantially certain to result from it.

Moral responsibility can attach only when the intellect has knowledge of the consequences of the act. The *Tentative Draft* refuses to permit liability unless the actor either evidenced a direct desire to bring about the consequences or placed the act with "substantial certainty" of the results. Needless to say, the eleven-year-old in *Vosburg* had no such substantial certainty. Under 8A he would not have been liable.

Although justifiable criticism may yet be leveled at the exact accuracy of "substantial certainty" (better: "reasonable certainty"), nonetheless it cannot be denied that the revision of the *Tentative Draft* is based substantially on the theory of liability founded on fault.

This history of the development of the definition of intent gives heartening assurance that the common-law courts are striving toward perfection and gives gratifying promise of some success. It could perhaps be expected that innocents such as Putney, who are yet today the victims of the courts' inability to penetrate to subtleties, will be the happy recipients tomorrow of the enlightened efforts of the present. The current, perhaps permanent, inability to solve every problem immediately should not, however, be equated with a desire or a policy of imposing liability without fault.

The last of the three examples is the notion of strict liability.

At regular stages in the history of the law of torts, the courts and the commentators have been faced, seemingly by surprise, with new and unusual (even bizarre to the times) fact situations, generally the result of the advance of an increasingly sophisticated society. Each such sudden step forward, more often than not, has found the court and commentator floundering for a solution. They have seemed unable to push away the accidentals in order to reach the essential question, to which they would have been able, then, to apply the law.

The earliest technological advance which thus caught the court unawares was the animal, wild, domesticated, and in-between. Another instance in this progress was the entire category of so-called ultrahazardous activities, which took various forms in the mid-1800s—unusual collections of water, a steam engine driven along the highway, a heavy steamroller, even the spread of fire. Next came dynamite, TNT, and other such explosives. Some decades later the airplane became a source of legal bewilderment. Artificial insemination today is taxing the legal mind. Most recently there are atomic energy, reaction, and fallout, and the multitude of ramifications in the wake of the fission of the atom.

In many of these instances, and there are many more of a similar nature, the courts in their bewilderment rushed head-long to the conclusion of strict liability, liability without fault. This was understandable. Even an untrained mind could reason correctly to the conclusion that in ninety-nine out of a hundred instances the owner and keeper of such animals, steam engines, airplanes, or atoms was in actual fact seriously at fault if such an instrumentality caused injury to someone or something. With such odds, the most facile and apparently surest solution was to lay down the blanket rule that every such keeper-defendant was liable, no matter what. This explanation answers the vast majority of areas within the law where strict liability is applied.

Furthermore, perhaps more to the point in this discussion, the limited field of strict liability is the chief source of the remaining examples in the law of the imposition of liability without culpability. A satisfactory explanation, therefore, of this doctrine would contribute substantially toward an understanding of the common-law approach to liability founded on fault.

There are several discernible causes underlying the common applications of strict liability, none of which could be attributed to an avowed theory of, or a preference for, liability without culpability.

By far the most valid explanation for the existence of the doctrine lies in the court's realization that there is in truth some fault in the ninety-nine out of a hundred cases involving such instrumentalities. There is, therefore, little fear on the part of the courts either of harming the innocent or of reaching an incorrect decision.

The second cause, almost a corollary of the first, is the surprising incapability of the court to detect the one case in a hundred where there was in fact no fault in the keeper-owner. In such areas, it may take successive courts many generations to reason through to the proper rule, especially if the initial error was stated forcefully or was the product of a respected court.

In the third place, some courts have reasoned erroneously that liability should rest on the basis of negligence in the very keeping of such a dangerous force. Such courts are oblivious of the isolated exceptions, forgetting that it might not be negligent or unreasonable to keep, for example, a tiger or a lion in a zoo.

A fourth class of jurisdictions holds rather indiscriminately that there is some kind of fault in even exposing the community to the risk of such dangerous things.

The point in all of these various explanations is important. Close discernment will indicate what few advert to, or would even admit, that the application of strict liability, although the term is loosely considered synonymous with liability without fault, is ultimately founded on some underlying notion of fundamental culpability. The assumption really is that there is fault, somewhere, somehow, of some kind. In deepest essence, therefore, it could be cogently argued that strict liability is only apparently liability without fault and that in rigid logic it should not be so described. Where it would seem that this is not the case, the courts impose liability not because the owner-keeper is innocent but in spite of this fact or simply because of their ineptitude and inability to penetrate to the proper solution of a very delicate and complex fact situation.

Whenever the human intellect is faced with an extremely complex problem, it requires, perforce, some considerable time to assimilate all of the facts, factors, and principles involved. This is exemplified in lesser human affairs. What appears to be an insurmountably difficult question at the beginning of the week can become absurdly simple by the end of the week. So, too, has it been historically with some of the areas of strict liability. It is submitted, moreover, that this pattern will recur repeatedly over the coming years. For example, the early vexation with the question of dangerous animals found its outlet in the imposition of strict liability. As the days pass, however, one instance after another seems to be leading the courts to a conviction that there is no fault in the keeping itself. Hence, either negligence or intent, culpability, should be a prerequisite to liability. Thus, the Supreme Court of Appeals of West Virginia in 1930[53] rejects the doctrine of strict liability for the keeping of animals and quotes Thompson, writing sixty years ago, in support of its stand:

> Latterly, however, there seems to be a disposition upon the part of authorities to hold the more reasonable rule, that all that should be required of the keeper of such animals is that he should take that superior caution to prevent their doing mischief which their propensities in that direction justly demand of him.[54]

The most felicitous study of this historical pattern—first a precipitous imposition of strict liability, and then the slow, tortured retrenchment—is *Rylands v. Fletcher* and the long series of cases following it.

In 1868 the House of Lords imposed strict liability on "the person who has brought on his land and kept there something dangerous, and failed to keep it in."[55] By ruling thus, the court held the defendant liable "for all the natural consequences of its escape."[56]

The defendants were the owners of a mill. In order to supply it with water they constructed a reservoir on nearby land.

Plaintiff on his part was working a certain coal mine under lands close to, but not adjoining, the premises on which the reservoir was constructed. He worked the mine in the direction of the reservoir until he came upon certain old workings, abandoned at a time beyond living memory. Short days later one of the shafts of the deserted mine, met during the excavation of the reservoir, gave way and burst downward. Water rushed into the old abandoned workings, flowed on through the new communications joining the old mine to the new mine. The result was a flooded mine. The mineowner sued for damages. The court found that the defendant had been completely free of fault in constructing the reservoir.

The court summarized its rule of strict liability: "We think that the true rule of law is that the person who for his own purposes brings on his land, collects and keeps there anything likely to do mischief if it escapes, must keep it at his peril, and if he does not do so is *prima facie* answerable for all the damage which is the natural consequence of its escape."[57]

As the years passed, the doctrine of strict liability set down so firmly in *Rylands v. Fletcher* was slowly eroded. The first eroding distinction confined the applicability of the case to non-natural use of the land. Fault was a prerequisite for liability if the use was natural. In *Golden v. Amory*[58] the owner-keeper was not held liable for the intervention of a *vis major* or an act of God. In *Reed v. Lyons & Co., Ltd.*,[59] an English court held that the doctrine of *Rylands v. Fletcher* would apply only where there was an escape. Injury from an explosion of shells was, therefore, not covered by the doctrine, since the requisite escape was not present. Although an early case applied *Rylands v. Fletcher* to personal injuries, this application was later eliminated on the grounds that *Rylands v. Fletcher* applied only to property damage.

Prosser summarizes the status of the *Rylands v. Fletcher* case: "Almost immediately after the decision in *Rylands v.*

*Fletcher*, it was considered and rejected in three American jurisdictions. . . . Following these decisions, the great majority of
courts in the United States rejected *Rylands v. Fletcher* insofar
as it applies to activities not inherently dangerous."[60]

In the United States today strict liability yet persists in two
areas: the keeping of animals and ultrahazardous activities not
commonly engaged in. As is clear, *Rylands v. Fletcher* has been
virtually emasculated. How long it will take the remaining areas
of strict liability to follow the course charted by *Rylands v.
Fletcher* is matter for conjecture.

When all of the nonessentials are stripped away and the philosophy underlying strict liability is laid bare, one cannot help
but conclude that the courts were, in actuality, founding the liability, which they nonetheless considered strict, upon the principle of culpability.

> A man has an animal of known ferocious habits, which escapes
> and does his neighbor damage. He can prove that the animal es-
> caped through no negligence of his, but still he is held liable.
> Why? It is, says the analytical jurist, because, although he was not
> negligent at the moment of escape, he was guilty of remote heed-
> lessness, or negligence, or fault, in having such a creature at all.
> And one by whose fault damage is done ought to pay for it.[61]

Note that Holmes has concluded his analysis with a second reason, the ability to pay, essentially distinct from the first. Thus,
he introduces a second principal aberration in the philosophy
of the external forum.

### So-called Public Policy—the Ability To Pay

Stand far above this civil-law question of liability without
culpability and ask: What single example can best lead to an
understanding of those rare aberrations of the common law
when the courts depart from their traditional philosophy of liability founded on fault? The answer would undoubtedly be:
those instances where the Robin Hood, bleeding-heart impulse

of the emotions is too strong for the cold-morning, light-of-day reasoning of the intellect. It is then that the court gives way to its pity for the poor and the hapless, and determines to let him who can pay, pay. It is then that the court confuses liability with the ability to pay.

In such instances, however, it must be strongly noted that the court is not motivated by the principle that an innocent man should pay because he is innocent but by the totally unrelated doctrine that a poor man should be helped by a richer. The court does subscribe to the principle of liability founded only on fault, but at the moment the emotions have concluded that a higher principle must prevail over a lower. Not that the former principle is not good, but rather that the latter is better.

A second factor joined to the ability to pay adds respectability to this particular judicial deviation.

Since someone has been injured someone must pay. This conclusion is not concerned with financial ability but leaves little doubt in the court's mind when such ability is also present. In 1681: "If a man assault me, and I lift up my staff to defend myself, and in lifting it up hit another, an action lies by that person, and yet I did a lawful thing. And the reason of all these cases is that he that is damaged ought to be recompensed."[62] This vice is an excess of the virtue of charity. When charity is not tempered by reason it can become vicious.

Add another error and the explanation of the aberration is complete. It has always been difficult for a court to distinguish between an ultimate, responsible, efficient cause and an immediate, physical, instrumental one. "The early law asked simply, 'Did the defendant do the physical act which damaged the plaintiff?' . . . These decisions must be regarded as survivals of the ancient rule that where a loss must be borne by one of two innocent persons, it shall be borne by him who acted."[63]

In the Massachusetts case of *McGuire v. Almy,*[64] handed down in 1937, one finds these fallacies aptly blended to reach

a multiply erroneous decision. *McGuire v. Almy* joins the sur-
render of reason to emotion—pity the poor, and let the rich
pay—to the inability of the judicial intellect to distinguish between a merely physical and a morally responsible cause. Latent, of course, is the conviction that, since someone suffered,
someone should pay.

McGuire, a registered nurse, was in the employ of Almy, an
insane person. McGuire had been informed that Almy was a
"mental case and was in good physical condition"[65] and that for
some time two nurses had been in attendance. Almy slept next
door to McGuire. The patient's room was kept locked, and a
wire grating covered the window.

In April 1932, Almy, while locked in her room, had a violent attack. McGuire heard the crashing furniture and then
knew that Almy was "ugly, violent, and dangerous."[66] With this,
Almy announced in clear terms that if McGuire came into her
room she would kill her. Thereupon, McGuire stepped into the
room, walked toward Almy, and tried to take hold of her hand,
which held the leg of a lowboy. As threatened, Almy struck
McGuire's head and caused the injury which brought about the
later litigation.

The Supreme Judicial Court of Massachusetts confirmed the
judgment in favor of the nurse McGuire against Almy. Its opinion in support of this decision is a masterpiece of contradictions.

After holding simply that an insane person is liable for his
torts, the Massachusetts court threw up its hands and added:
"Nor do the courts discuss the effect of different kinds of insanity or of varying degrees of capacity as bearing upon the ability
of the defendant to understand the particular act in question or
to make a reasoned decision with respect to it."[67]

The court next stated clearly the grounds for its decision:

These decisions are rested more upon grounds of public policy and
upon what might be called a popular view of the requirements of
essential justice than upon any attempt to apply logically the un-

derlying principles of civil liability to the special instance of the mentally deranged. Thus it is said that a rule imposing liability tends to make more watchful those persons who have charge of the defendant and who may be supposed to have some interest in preserving his property; that as an insane person must pay for his support, if he is financially able, so he ought also to pay for the damage which he does; that an insane person with abundant wealth ought not to continue in unimpaired enjoyment of the comfort which it brings while his victim bears the burden unaided; and there is also a suggestion that courts are loath to introduce into the great body of civil litigation the difficulties in determining mental capacity which it has been found impossible to avoid in the criminal field.[68]

It should not be thought that the Massachusetts court was oblivious of the implications. To the contrary.

> The rule established in these cases has been criticized severely by certain eminent text writers both in this country and in England, principally on the ground that it is an archaic survival of the rigid and formal mediaeval conception of liability for acts done, without regard to fault, as opposed to what is said to be the general modern theory that liability in tort should rest upon fault.[69]

For the reasons indicated above, however, the Massachusetts court determined that it would not be moved from the traditional position.

> Notwithstanding these criticisms, we think, that as a practical matter, there is strong force in the reasons underlying these decisions. . . . Fault is by no means at the present day a universal prerequisite to liability, and the theory that it should be such has been obliged very recently to yield at several points to what have been thought to be paramount considerations of public good.[70]

The concluding relevant statement of the Massachusetts court indicates the extent to which it has abandoned all attempts to penetrate to the real issues of the case: "But the law will not inquire further into his peculiar mental condition with a view to excusing him if it should appear that delusion or other consequence of his affliction has caused him to entertain that intent or that a normal person would not have entertained it."[71]

*McGuire v. Almy* is a relatively recent case. The law is indeed slow to correct errors. Writing over fifty years ago, James Barr Ames expressed hopes for the future, yet much remains unchanged in mid-century.

> The law of today, except in certain cases based upon public policy, asks the further question, "Was the act blameworthy?" The ethical standard of reasonable conduct has replaced the unmoral standard of acting at one's peril. Nor is the modern ethical doctrine applied even now to all cases logically within its scope. Under this doctrine a lunatic unable to appreciate the nature or consequences of his act ought not to be responsible for the damage he has inflicted upon another. . . . Inasmuch as nearly all the English writers upon torts, and many of the American writers also, express the opinion that the lunatic, not being culpable, should not be held responsible, it is not unreasonable to anticipate that the English courts and the American courts, not already committed to the contrary doctrine, will sooner or later apply to the lunatic the ethical principle of no liability without fault. The continental law upon this point is instructive. By the early French and German law the lunatic was liable as in England for damage that he caused to another. In France today the lunatic is absolutely exempt from liability. The new German Code has a general provision to the same effect.[72]

### So-called Public Policy—the Inability To Pay

As might be expected, the legal mind which would find difficulty in distinguishing liability from the ability to pay, would also be hesitant to visit liability upon one unable to pay and thereby let the innocent party again bear the loss. Since this is an indirect imposition of liability without fault, one brief example and its subsequent history should suffice.

In the year 1854 in the city of Syracuse, the New York Central Railroad "by the careless management, or through the insufficient condition, of one of their engines, set fire to their wood-shed, and a large quantity of wood therein."[73] The home of Mr. Ryan, situated at a distance of 130 feet from the shed, soon took fire from the heat and sparks and was entirely consumed, notwithstanding diligent efforts to save it. A number of other houses were also burned by the spreading of the fire. Mr. Ryan brought an action to recover from the New York Central the value of his building thus destroyed. The lower court denied recovery, and the Court of Appeals affirmed the judgment.

The reasoning of the court is succinct, prescinds completely from fault, and founds the decision somewhat wondrously on the inability to pay—of the New York Central.

> To sustain such a claim as the present, and to follow the same to its legitimate consequences, would subject to a liability against which no prudence could guard, and to meet which no private fortune would be adequate. . . . To hold that the owner must not only meet his own loss by fire, but that he must guaranty the security of his neighbors on both sides, and to an unlimited extent, would be to create a liability which would be the destruction of all civilized society. No community could long exist under the operation of such a principle.[74]

The court could not quite understand that the solution to the problem of the inability to pay was not a declaration of nonliability (which is completely related to fault and not at all to finances) but a declaration of bankruptcy (which is completely related to the inability to pay and not at all to fault).

Amidst this dark holding of liability without fault, there shines through some evidence that the court was cognizant of the force of the correct principle: "To neglect such precaution, and to call upon his neighbor on whose premises a fire originated, to indemnify him instead, would be to award a punishment quite beyond the offence committed."[75] Even here, therefore, the court itself thought its decision was founded on culpability. Its only error lay in locating and estimating the fault.

Although the full impact of this rule has not yet been fully eliminated, it should be said that the New York legislature rose partially to the occasion by the passage of a statute establishing liability for negligence in starting a forest fire. The liability, contrary to *Ryan*, extended to other properties, "however distant from the place where the fire was set or started and notwithstanding the same may have burned over and across several separate, and intervening and distinct tracts, parcels or ownerships of land."[76]

\* \* \*

When one takes the view from the housetop, there seems to be one inevitable conclusion: The common law is firmly founded on the premise of no liability without fault. Any desertion of this principle is explicable by two factors: (1) the inevitable debilities of the human legal system in the application of theory to *ad hoc* practice and (2) weakness of intellect joined to strength of emotions in both the formulation of policy and the adjudication of cases. In broadest summary, so spoke the 1843 case of *Harvey v. Dunlop*:

> No case or principle can be found, or if found can be maintained, subjecting an individual to liability for an act done without fault on his part . . . All the cases concede that an injury arising from an inevitable accident, or, which in law or reason is the same thing, from an act that ordinary human care and foresight are unable to guard against, is but the misfortune of the sufferer, and lays no foundation for legal responsibility.[77]

This, then, is the state of the common law. It offers good reason for pride—it is basically sound and moral—and for vigorous effort—it leaves much to be done.

> It is obvious that the spirit of reform which during the last six hundred years has been bringing our system of law more and more into harmony with moral principles has not yet achieved its perfect work. It is worth while to realize the great ethical advance of the English law in the past, if only as an encouragement to effort for future improvement.[78]

*Relevant Implications*

The chapter's conclusion should relate the civil-law attitude toward liability without culpability to the merepenalist position on the imposition of a penalty on a blameless citizen.

The crux of the entire matter lies in the purpose and nature of the penalty imposed.

The purely penal system imposes the sanction, not for some extraneous reason, but to save the verity of the law itself. It is imposed because of a violation of the law and is always related to that violation. The merepenalist penalty is leveled consistently without fault and on the assumption of innocence. The freedom from guilt of the person punished is a postulate of the system. The imposition of the sanction is an essential policy precription. In this purpose and nature of the sanction lies the night-and-day difference between the common-law and penal-law systems.

Whenever in the common law, to the contrary, liability happens to fall on the guiltless, this liability is not because of the violation but is in fact unrelated to it. The common law has tried manfully to adhere rigidly to the principle that there never should be liability without culpability. In practice, the common law has been unsuccessful in two areas: the external forum's (1) necessary infirmities and (2) lamentable aberrations.

In the former, the sinless citizen suffered without fault on the assumption of guilt. With the penal system, he suffered on the assumption of innocence. In the second, his innocence was known, but he suffered for other higher, although misguided, prevailing reasons (for example, public policy)—not because of but in spite of, even reluctantly in spite of, innocence. The merepenalist lays on the penalty for no other reason than the innocent act.

The point is, moreover, that in neither common-law case was the *poena* a punishment in the strict sense. It was, in fact, unconnected with guilt. In the first category, the *poena* is clearly an inconvenience, hardship, *incommodum* of the external forum. The particular citizen pays the price for the intrinsic frailty of the legal system. These hardships will, of necessity, remain. They are exactly of a piece with the many examples so often cited, *poenae* in the wide sense, totally foreign to fault (any visitation from God, the loss of the pastorate by the leprous priest, the denial of sacred orders to the "bigamous" ordinand or the judge-would-be-cleric, the demotion of the episcopal see, the loss of the treasonous inheritance, the demotion of the See of Alexandria).

In the second common-law class, the *poena* is much more a visitation of God. The former suffering could not be avoided. This could have been. Here, the hapless citizen suffers without fault because of the debility of the instant judge or some high-minded, but ill-conceived, public policy. These hardships can be—some will be—removed, but none are true *poenae* in the strict sense.

The merepenalists, in their attempt to buttress their theory of the imposition of a sanction on a blameless citizen, have apparently misconceived the true nature of the common-law liability without culpability. They have observed the instances where the common law has seemingly endorsed their system and have reasoned from these *ad hoc* exceptions (where *poena* in the wide sense was suffered *per accidens*, not imposed directly *per se*) to a policy of imposing a *poena* in the strict sense, always and as a rule, where there is no *culpa*.

Justice Holmes can now be understood as saying nothing at odds with the reasoning of this chapter:

> While the terminology of morals is still retained, and while the law does still and always, in a certain sense, measure legal liability by moral standards, it nevertheless, by the very necessity of its nature, is continually transmuting those moral standards into external or objective ones, from which the actual guilt of the party concerned is wholly eliminated.[79]

In the light of this exposition of the civil-law philosophy of liability founded on fault, it would seem that the merepenalist position can in fact find little solace in the Anglo-Saxon common law.

# PART FOUR

# A Collateral Attack toward Solution

*Reflections in Mitigation of the Conscience Obligation*

## CHAPTER IX

# A Counterproposal toward Solution

One of the reasons compelling the penal-law lawyers to such strong espousal of the doctrine has been the purported onerousness[1] of the multitude of positive-law mandates, all binding in conscience and, as it were, multiplying guilt in the citizenry through constant violation.

In the reply to this particular thesis, there is implicit another extrinsic argument—the absence of an impelling need for the penal-law system. As a theory advanced in alleviation of a burdensome situation, it can be justified with difficulty. Even were it intrinsically sound, it could be rejected as unnecessary, pursuant to the maxim *Entia non sunt multiplicanda sine necessitate.* The answer to the problem and the lack of necessity of the system lie in this: In every instance within the area of alleged applicability of the doctrine, the same result, freedom from obligation to a law, can be achieved (where, of course, the freedom is justified) by resort to other standards of law, moral theology, and ethics. Elsewhere it must be admitted that the general rule prevails: The civil law binds in conscience.

This does not mean that there are not some, perhaps not many, cases in which the penal-law doctrine would and does condone disobedience to the law where it should not, where right reason would order obedience. In this lies the chief threat to the right order of society. The correct conclusion is that the citizen should either obey the law, bound in conscience, or that he should not obey it for one of several valid reasons, expressed historically in aphorisms and succinct principles, none of which is the doctrine of *lex pure poenalis*.

These moral principles have received acceptance over the centuries, contain no questionable, intrinsic contradictions, and adequately supply the answer to the questioning citizen without the violence of the inherent illogic of the penal law.

Herewith is submitted, therefore, a counterproposal in solution of the problem posed by the elimination of *lex pure poenalis*. There are two distinct fields in the area now allegedly covered by the penal law: (1) those laws which should bind in conscience, where the penal law improperly permits disobedience, where no excusing principle of any kind should apply, and (2) those laws which should not bind in conscience in any event, irrespective completely of any penal law. The counterproposal: (1) Obey the law where it properly binds in conscience. (2) Where it should not so bind, do not obey—but for the legitimate and acceptable reasons of traditional law, jurisprudence, ethics, and morality.

## THE TRADITIONAL SOLUTION

Law shall be virtuous, just, possible to nature, according to the custom of the country, suitable to time and place, necessary, useful, clearly expressed lest by obscurity it lead to misunderstanding, framed for no private benefit but for the common good.[2]

Thus does the eminent Spaniard Isidore of Seville (*circa* 560-636), the last of the great Latin Fathers, summarize generally the body of customary maxims and principles designed

to temper the harshness, where warranted, of certain positive-
law legislation. A commentary on Isidore offers some suitable
instances of the traditional approach. These maxims and principles are not exhaustive of their kind but are merely advanced
as examples of the manner in which the accepted reasoning of
the centuries is able to solve the problems which the penal-law
doctrine was purportedly designed to meet.

(In most cases, these moral principles and aphorisms are as
old as the law itself and do not permit of specific documenta-
tion. The *passim* references merely instance their use in an
actual context or indicate a fuller explanation of that context.)

### The Law Must Foster Religion

When Isidore describes the law as "virtuous," he is indicating that a positive law must conduce to the development of the
religious life of the community. This principle is highly consonant with the First Amendment to the Constitution of the United
States: "Congress shall make no law . . . prohibiting the free
exercise" of religion. As the Supreme Court of the United States
expressed it, "We are a religious people." These words of Mr.
Justice Douglas speaking for the court will serve as a suitable
expression of this first maxim. He elaborates the philosophy underlying the principle:

> We are a religious people whose institutions presuppose a Supreme
> Being. We guarantee the freedom to worship as one chooses. We
> make room for as wide a variety of beliefs and creeds as the spir-
> itual needs of man deem necessary. We sponsor an attitude on the
> part of government that shows no partiality to any one group and
> that lets each flourish according to the zeal of its adherents and the
> appeal of its dogma. When the state encourages religious instruc-
> tion or cooperates with religious authorities by adjusting the sched-
> ule of events to sectarian needs, it follows the best of our traditions.
> For then it respects the religious nature of our people and accom-
> modates the public service to their spiritual needs. To hold that it
> may not would be to find in the Constitution a requirement that the

government show a callous indifference to religious groups. That would be preferring those who believe in no religion over those who do believe.[3]

The positive law, says Thomas, must be and "is called virtuous because it fosters religion."[4] This reference is not to laws patently invalid, contrary to divine law, and directly concerned with worship and religion (for example, legislation which would encourage idolatry, abolish all religious worship, establish an atheistic state) but rather regards laws which simply do not in their broad purpose advance the cause of religion.

In the instance of the so-called Sunday "blue laws," a competent moralist could well submit the "probable opinion" (reflecting sufficient competent authoritative support) which would permit conscientious Jewish merchants to engage in business on Sunday in spite of, for example, the Pennsylvania Sunday Closing Law: "Whoever does or performs any worldly employment or business whatsoever on the Lord's day, commonly called Sunday (works of necessity, and charity and wholesome recreation only excepted), shall, upon conviction thereof in a summary proceeding, be sentenced to pay a fine of four dollars."[5]—or the Massachusetts "Lord's day" statute: "Whoever on the Lord's day keeps open his shop, warehouse or workhouse, or does any manner of labor, business or work, except works of necessity or charity, shall be punished by a fine of not more than fifty dollars."[6] The soundness of this moral judgment would be supported not only by the split of the federal courts but also by the dissents within them. The three-judge United States District Court for the District of Massachusetts held the Massachusetts "Lord's day" statute unconstitutional in *Crown Kosher Super Market of Massachusetts, Inc. v. Gallagher*.[7] Magruder, C.J., wrote the opinion for the majority, with a dissent by McCarthy, D.J. To the contrary, the statutory three-judge United States District Court for the Eastern District of Pennsylvania held the Pennsylvania Sunday Closing Law not violative of the Federal

Constitution. Hastie, C.J., wrote the opinion for the majority in *Two Guys from Harrison-Allentown, Inc. v. McGinley* with a dissent in part by Welsh, Sr. D.J.[8]

Probable jurisdiction was noted in April 1960 by the Supreme Court of the United States in appeals from both lower federal courts.[9] On the appeals, both cases[10] were argued over the same period, December 7 and 8, 1960, and were decided May 29, 1961. Third and fourth cases involving the same question, one on appeal from the Maryland Court of Appeals (*McGowan v. Maryland*),[11] and the other a companion case to *Two Guys from Harrison-Allentown, Inc.* (*Braunfeld v. Brown*),[12] were also argued and decided at the same time.[13] The four opinions reached one conclusion: The laws did not conflict with constitutional guarantees as to religion. The federal opinion, *Moss v. Hornig*, in early 1963 reiterated this position.[14]

Even though the Supreme Court of the United States agreed with the Pennsylvania Federal Court that such legislation was constitutional, there remains competent authority to the contrary, concluding that

> What Massachusetts has done in this statute is to furnish special protection to the dominant Christian sects . . . without furnishing such protection . . . to Orthodox and Conservative Jews who observe Saturday as the Sabbath, and to the prejudice of the latter group. . . . The rabbi-plaintiffs would be hindered in their function of supervising the food to be eaten by the members of their congregations, and they would also suffer great detriment in their efforts to preserve, in these circumstances, due observance of the Jewish Sabbath and of the dietary laws by them.[15]

In his dissent to the majority opinion of the Supreme Court of the United States on the appeal, written by Chief Justice Warren, Mr. Justice Douglas might well be conceived to be speaking as a moralist as well as a jurist and lawyer:

> The issue of these cases would therefore be in better focus if we imagined that a state legislature, controlled by orthodox Jews

and Seventh Day-Adventists [*sic*], passed a law making it a crime to keep a shop open on Saturdays. Would a Baptist, Catholic, Methodist, or Presbyterian be compelled to obey that law or go to jail or pay a fine? Or suppose Moslems grew in political strength here and got a law through a state legislature making it a crime to keep a shop open on Fridays. Would the rest of us have to submit under the fear of criminal sanctions?[16]

Although Justice Douglas repeats his celebrated statement from *Zorach*—"For these reasons we stated in Zorach v. Clauson . . . 'We are a religious people whose institutions presuppose a Supreme Being.' "[17]—he himself cannot be thought to be espousing completely and wholeheartedly, if at all, the instant maxim under discussion. He takes merely a negative attitude of non-interference with religion. He would not permit affirmative fostering of religion. Though he maintains, "The First Amendment . . . admonishes government to be interested in allowing religious freedom to flourish," Mr. Justice Douglas is as prepared to allow atheism and agnosticism to flourish—which is scarcely compatible with Isidore's mandate and Thomas' positive assertion that the law must affirmatively foster religion.

Nonetheless the dissent of Douglas, joined with the deep conflict among and within the federal courts, leaves the religious Jew firm in his conviction that he has no moral obligation to obey the cited Sunday closing laws. To add support to this stand are the dissents of Mr. Justice Brennan and Mr. Justice Stewart in both the *Crown Kosher Super Market* and the *Braunfeld* cases. Says Mr. Justice Brennan: "But their effect is that appellants may not simultaneously practice their religion and their trade, without being hampered by a substantial competitive disadvantage. Their effect is that no one may at one and the same time be an Orthodox Jew and compete effectively with his Sunday-observing fellow tradesmen."[18] Mr. Justice Stewart added

I agree with substantially all that Mr. Justice Brennan has written. Pennsylvania has passed a law which compels an Orthodox

Jew to choose between his religious faith and his economic survival. That is a cruel choice. It is a choice which I think no State can constitutionally demand. For me this is not something that can be swept under the rug and forgotten in the interest of enforced Sunday togetherness. I think the impact of this law upon these appellants grossly violates their constitutional right to the free exercise of their religion.[19]

Exactly the same spirit in both majority and dissent was reflected in the Supreme Court of the United States in mid-1963 in *Sherbert v. Verner.*[20] There the fundamental issue was reducibly the same. The litigation concerned unemployment compensation to a Seventh-day Adventist unable to find five-day-a-week employment. The Supreme Court, through Mr. Justice Brennan, found that the ruling of the South Carolina administrative agency "forces her to choose between following the precepts of her religion and forfeiting benefits, on the one hand, and abandoning one of the precepts of her religion in order to accept work, on the other hand."[21] "For . . . 'If the purpose or effect of a law is to impede the observance of one or all religions or is to discriminate invidiously between religions, that law is constitutionally invalid . . .' *Braunfeld v. Brown.*"[22]

In *Sherbert* as in prior cases, the Supreme Court founded its holding on mere noninterference with the practice of religion and not on a positive encouragement of all religion.[23] "In Mr. Justice Rutledge's words, adopted by the Court today in *Schempp, ante,* p. 217, the Establishment Clause forbids every form of public aid or support for religion. 330 U.S., at 32."[24]

Justice Stewart, however, concurring in the result, would seem to adopt the fullness of Isidore's position. He believes the Constitution "affirmatively requires government to create an atmosphere of hospitality and accommodation to individual belief or disbelief. In short, I think our Constitution commands the positive protection by government of religious freedom—not only for a minority, however small—not only for the majority, however large—but for each of us."[25] (Justice Stewart agreed with the conclusion in *Sherbert* that denial of compensation would violate the Constitution but was also convinced that in so concluding the Supreme Court must overrule the long line of church-state cases and found the holding on a duty to foster positively all religion.)

Mr. Justice Stewart, indeed, takes a very vigorous stand against the court's past holdings on church-state. He inveighs strongly against the plaguing dictum of Justice Jackson in *Everson*[26] which forbids the states to aid one religion or all religions equally. His forthright stand should and could well become the law: "I think the Court's mechanistic concept of the Establishment clause is historically unsound and constitutionally wrong."[27] It was logical, of course, for Justice Stewart to maintain that "the *Braunfeld* case was wrongly decided and should be overruled."[28]

In a word, there is no justification for a law which places a burden even indirectly on religious Jews (that is, the necessity of closing their shops for two days a week) or on Seventh-day Adventists (that is, the denial of unemployment compensation). Without doubt, this renders the practice of their religion difficult or in some cases even impossible. Certainly such a law does not foster religion.

Consider next one hypothetical example of the relatively widespread problem facing boards of education of school districts across the nation. Representatives of the various religious sects within a given district have, for instance, approached the school board for permission to utilize the classrooms in public-school buildings during released time for classes in religion. All groups are represented, and there is an ample number of classrooms to afford each sect equal facilities.

The chairman and the board are convinced that these facts are verified in *McCollum*[29] and that such permission therefore would be illegal. They quote the conclusion of the court through Mr. Justice Black.

This is beyond all question a utilization of a tax-established and tax-supported public school system to aid religious groups to spread their faith. And it falls squarely under the ban of the First Amendment (made applicable to the states by the Fourteenth) as we interpreted it in *Everson v. Board of Education*, 330 U.S. 1. There we said: "Neither a state nor the Federal Government can set up a church. Neither can pass laws which aid one religion, aid all religions, or prefer one religion over another."[30]

To the contrary, (1) the masterful dissent in *McCollum* of Mr. Justice Reed[31] expressing his strong views of the tradition of the nation, (2) the later opinion and holding of the Supreme Court of the United States in *Zorach*,[32] and (3) the realization that the facts point up an equal aid to all religions, to religion in general—all these considerations would lead an able moralist to the solidly probable opinion that acquiescence would entail no violation of a conscience obligation.

Such a response would likewise be applicable to chaplains in the armed services, in veterans' hospitals, and the like, in point of equal aid to all religions in supplying the facilities and materials for divine worship (for example, wines and bread for the Lord's Supper in a Protestant service; phylacteries, prayer shawls, and Talmud for a Jewish assembly; chalice and vestments for the sacrifice of the Mass).

### The Law Must Be Reasonable

A law is no law and, hence, commands no obedience if it is not founded on right reason. Aquinas wrote:

> I answer that . . . as Augustine says . . . "That which is not just seems to be no law at all." Hence the force of a law depends on the extent of its justice. Now in human affairs a thing is said to be just from being right according to the rule of reason.[33]

Speaking on this same point, Leo XIII is more directly outspoken: "Where the power to command is wanting, or where a law is enacted contrary to reason, or to the eternal law, or to

some ordinance of God, obedience is unlawful, lest while obey-
ing man we become disobedient to God."[34]

Reasonableness goes to the essence of a statute (prescinding
from the question of severability) and, hence, its validity. The
invalidity resultant on essential unreasonableness would affect
all subjects covered by the law in every application at all times
everywhere. This is in contradistinction to special circumstances
which would permit exceptions in specific cases, thus exempting
specified persons from an otherwise reasonable law.

Consider the following provisions of the Eighteenth Amendment to the Constitution of the United States: "Section 1. . . .
the manufacture, sale, or transportation of intoxicating liquors
within, the importation thereof into, or the exportation thereof
from the United States . . . for beverage purposes is hereby prohibited." During the years immediately following World War I,
respected moral authority adjudged these provisions of the
Eighteenth Amendment to be unreasonable, hence not binding
in conscience on the citizenry.

> Some features of our Prohibition legislation may really be harmful
> or unjust. I believe that to be the case. For example, the require-
> ment that no person may make intoxicating liquor of any sort on
> his own premises for his own use, or to give to his friends; and the
> article which forbids a person to carry liquor for his own use from
> one place to another—are tyrannical and unjust interferences with
> the liberty and rights of the citizen. They are not essential to the
> main object of the law, which is to abolish the commercial manu-
> facture and sale of intoxicating liquors.[35]

Such a law would be deemed an incursion on the right of a citizen to make even moderate use of a legitimate product of the
land provided by the Creator. Ryan was opposed to the penal-
law doctrine and maintained, moreover, that the Eighteenth
Amendment in its main features was binding in conscience.

Subject to the same invalidity would be statutes passed by
various jurisdictions prohibiting the use of alcoholic beverages

by minors even in the privacy of the home under parental supervision. Such would be the categorical provision of the 1959 Missouri statute prohibiting even the possession of intoxicating beer (which is defined as a beverage which exceeds in its alcoholic content 3.2 percent by weight) by a young man under twenty-one years of age: "an act relating to the purchase or possession of intoxicating liquor or nonintoxicating beer by a minor, with a penalty provision for violation thereof."[36]

It is not likely that the municipal ordinances creating the so-called "speed traps" would in the extreme cases bind in conscience (for example, the instance in extremely small towns of a one-block, ten-mile-per-hour zone located in the heart of a thirty-five-mile-per-hour area).

Reliable moralists would probably hesitate to hold a citizen to the moral obligation of obedience to statutes or ordinances prohibiting small wagers in social gambling in the home. The ludicrous instance in the city of Detroit highlights the unreasonableness of such laws:

Vice Must Go
"Gambling Ring" Broken by Belle Isle Police
Police arrested 14 old men on Belle Isle Tuesday and booked them for investigation of engaging in an illegal occupation.
Police confiscated three decks of playing cards and a little more than $1.
The men, aged from 65 to 73, were arrested on orders of Sgt. Donald Kreuger, of the Harbormaster Bureau. . . . Two patrolmen had warned the men they were violating a City ordinance which prohibits card playing in public. . . . There were two penny ante poker tables and one rummy table, Sgt. Kreuger said. . . . Later Police Superintendent Louis J. Berg ordered the prisoners released and ordered all charges against the 14 dropped.[37]

The arrest was made pursuant to the ordinance providing: "No person or persons shall play any games whatever in or upon any park, public place or boulevard. . . . Gambling and other games of chance are strictly forbidden."[38]

### Nemo Tenetur ad Impossibile[39]

When the maxim states that "no one is held to the impossible," and Isidore of Seville requires that a law be "possible to nature," both are saying that the citizen cannot be held in conscience to something that is *grave incommodum*, to a law whose onerousness is out of proportion to the good to be gained by its objective.[40] A hunting party embarking at Banff and journeying some sixty or seventy miles into the Canadian Rockies would not be bound in conscience to forego the two-week vacation in order to return to register and pay the fee for the licenses they had unwittingly neglected to obtain before leaving.

This same principle carried beyond application to isolated individuals is properly referable to a law intrinsically impossible of observance.

> Secondly, it depends on the ability of the agent; because discipline should be adapted to each one according to his ability, taking into account also the ability of nature, for the same burdens should not be laid on children as on adults.[41]

If it is therefore without the competence of all or substantially all of the people to measure up to the exactitude of the law, the law is clearly invalid and not binding in conscience. Isidore's phrase "adapted to time and place" carries with it substantially this concept.

### Consuetudo Contra Legem[42]

The notorious conduct of the people, of which the legislator is substantially cognizant, over many uninterrupted years, uniformly and openly violative of the express wording of a statute, effectively abrogates the law and thereby removes any conscience obligation which might otherwise have been present. Ultimately the invalidating efficacy of this "custom against the law" is founded on the assumption of a tacit revocation of the law as evidenced by the lawmaker's continued toleration and inaction joined with his undoubted knowledge of the widespread and persistent violation. This failure on the part of the legislator to employ the usual means of law enforcement is a valid expression of a legislative intent to withdraw the statute from operation. Under such conditions as these desuetude has the power of nullifying a law.[43]

It is understandable that the operation of this principle could be confused with the application of the penal-law *"indicium of the will of the legislator"* founded on the customary attitude of the people. The maxim *consuetudo contra legem* is determinative of the intent to legislate—it negatives the law altogether—whereas the *indicium* of so-called customary attitude is presumably indicative of a legislative intent not to oblige. Habitual violation, therefore, with the knowledge of the legislature is not an index of the will to pass a purely penal law but rather of the intent to revoke the law completely. In the former, the legislator desires a true law (but with no obligation to obey). In the latter, he does not.

> Customary attitude of the public, that it is not wrong to violate a law, does not signify that the law is "merely penal." Well-established and tolerated custom of non-observance is merely an indication of the mind of the lawgiver that the law is a "dead letter."[44]

—that is, that the intent to legislate, not the intent to oblige, has been withdrawn.

There are several cautions appropriate to the application of this maxim: (1) The nonobservance must be continuous, open, general, and widespread. (2) It must be of sufficient duration reasonably (3) to apprise the legislator of the situation. (4) Finally, the failure to enforce the law must be attributable to intentional toleration rather than to a temporary breakdown of the law-enforcement agency, lack of vigilance, inefficiency, or the like.

One outstanding example of the operation of *consuetudo contra legem* should suffice to illustrate the essence of the principle.

Within the field of taxation one of the most disregarded laws on the books of the various states is the personal-property tax, an *ad valorem* assessment against the personal property of individuals. The tax is generally based on the fair market value of the personalty in the possession of the taxpayer on a particular date designated in the tax-return form. (In Illinois, for example, the critical date is April 1 of each year; in Missouri, January 1.) The taxpayer is expected to list the various taxable items with his honest estimate of the current market value.

In Missouri, where the violation is uniformly flagrant, Taxpayer X, anonymous at his request but nonetheless real and identifiable, who has insured his household furniture and furnishings at an estimated value of $8,000, regularly files his Tangible Personal Property Tax showing a fair market value of $100 for these household appurtenances. Taxpayer X is merely reflecting the operation of the maxim *consuetudo contra legem* and is acceding to the "custom and usage" prevalent among all of the citizens in the Missouri community. Should some citizen conceive doubts as to the universality of this practice, he may, for example, in St. Louis (which has county status) and St. Louis County call at the Assessor's Office, request to inspect the Personal Property Tax Returns submitted and signed by his close neighbors and thereby convince himself that this indeed is a legitimate instance of a "custom against the law."

Further indication of the desuetude of this law would be gained by a study of the tax-return form itself. The second category of tangible personalty lists the following items, neither more nor less:

Horses, mares and geldings, all ages,
Asses and genets, all ages,
Mules, all ages,
Neat cattle, all ages,
Swine, all ages,
Sheep, all ages,
Goats, all ages,

Poultry,
Domesticated small animals,
Bee colonies and other livestock.[45]

This listing would not be so remarkable were it not for the fact that this tax-return form is designated for the special use of the citizens of St. Louis which has been exclusively residential, industrial, and commercial for decades.

In Illinois, where the practice is equally prevalent, a local expression of the disregard for the personal-property-tax law finds certain trust companies customarily sending money by check in the amount of millions of dollars to New York banks on the day preceding the critical date of the personal-property tax, in this case, April 1. The New York banks return the money with their own checks on the day subsequent to the tax date. This recognized procedure is justified by the phrase "custom and usage," which is nothing else than the manner in which the financial community couches *consuetudo contra legem.*

In Highland Park, Illinois, the law provides that the assessed value for both the personal-property tax and the real-estate tax be published in the local newspaper, which affords all of the taxpayers the opportunity of gauging the least amount acceptable to the taxing authorities.

Apropos of this, a longtime Chicago attorney writes relevant to the general attitude of the residents of Cook County toward the state-levied personal-property tax: "This tax is almost universally ignored in Cook County. Those who do make a return and pay are advised by the assessors to declare all personal property at a fraction of its value. In fact, automobiles are taxed on a prepared schedule of valuation which drops to 0 after four years."[46]

Until the manifest legislative intent in such cases has been expressed to be otherwise, the taxpayer could not be justifiably held in conscience to more than the minimum amount established by the community.

### Lex Dubia Non Obligat

"A doubtful law does not oblige."[47] It is of the essence of obligation that the person obligated have complete knowledge of that to which he is bound.[48] If there is a justifiable question as to the meaning of the law, if the terms are so vague and ill-defined as to confuse well-intentioned persons, the obligatory effect of the law ceases. This is the requisite posited by Isidore: The law must be "clearly expressed lest by obscurity it lead to misunderstanding."

Relevant to this maxim, moreover, is the fundamental rule of statutory interpretation, valid in both civil and moral law, that all statutes containing strictures are to be construed strictly against the statute and in favor of freedom. This rule of construction joined with the instant maxim will, therefore, in appropriate application, relieve the aggrieved subject of obligation.

The more technical the field of law the more prolific of doubt does it become. The history of Taft-Hartley since its inception has been one of judicial interpretation, congressional amendment, and academic commentary. So, too, in varying degrees has it been of SEC, ICC, and antitrust legislation. More egregious in this regard has been the Internal Revenue Code which, because of changes and confusing phraseology, has kept Congress and the courts (and tax attorney, accountant, and tax-payer) in a constant state of uncertainty.

During the years of unresolved conflict over the meaning of, for example, a muddled tax law, the conscientious citizen would not be bound (1) to take means (such as counsel fees, time, energy) extraordinary or even burdensome in relation to the taxable amount involved in order to resolve doubts that even the courts have left unresolved nor (2) to pay a sum questionable because of vagueness or obscurity.

It would be reasonable to say that the taxpayer at any time during the long ten-to-twenty-year period of chaos would have had understandable difficulty in interpreting with any success the Estate Tax provisions of Section 2036 (Transfers with Retained Life Estate) of the Internal Revenue Code. The pertinent part reads:

> The value of the gross estate shall include the value of all property . . . to the extent of any interest therein of which the decedent has at any time made a transfer . . . by trust or otherwise, under which he has retained for his life or for any period not ascertainable without reference to his death or for any period which does not in fact end before his death—(1) the possession or enjoyment of, or the right to income from, the property, or (2) the right, either alone or in conjunction with any person, to designate the persons who shall possess or enjoy the property or the income therefrom.[49]

As Rabkin and Johnson summarized this chaos:

> This statute has had a tangled judicial history, especially with respect to trusts created before its enactment. The Supreme Court reversed itself, and was in turn overruled by Congress.[50]

When this "tangled judicial history" is joined with a correspondingly tangled legislative history, it is a legitimate conclusion that the section was for some time prior to the resolution of the problem by the Supreme Court of the United States beyond the ability of either taxpayer or tax counsel to fathom.

The total history has ebbed and flowed through seven distinct tides: (1) "Inter vivos transfers (without adequate consideration in money or money's worth) which are 'intended to take effect in possession or enjoyment at or after [the transferor's] death' have been expressly includible in the transferor decedent's gross estate since the original enactment of the estate tax in 1916. Revenue Act of 1916, sec. 202(b)."[51] "It would seem that the same court [the Supreme Court of the United States] would at least hold that where a decedent has reserved a life estate, the statute was applicable."[52] Yet in *May v. Heiner*,[53] the Supreme Court held otherwise and amplified its meaning by *per curiam* decisions in three later cases handed down March 2, 1931: *Burnet v. Northern Trust Co.*;[54] *Morsman v. Burnet*;[55]

*McCormick v. Burnet.*[56] "The decision of the Supreme Court came almost like a bombshell because nobody ever anticipated such a decision."[57] (2) On the very next day, March 3, 1931, Congress acted to correct this situation. The Joint Resolution of March 3, 1931, signed by the president on the same day, amended the statute to provide for the taxation of retained life interests and incorporated the amendment into the Revenue Act of 1926. (3) In 1932 another amendment, Revenue Act of 1932 § 803(a), included the provision "not ascertainable without reference to his death." (4) Neither of these amendments contained any provision concerning retroactive application. These amendments were later held inapplicable to interests created prior to March 3, 1931, even in the case of decedents dying thereafter (*Hassett v. Welch*).[58] This was in 1938. (5) In 1949 the Supreme Court held that the 1930 decision in *May v. Heiner* was wrong and that the "possession or enjoyment" phrase of § 811 (c) as it existed before 1931 was sufficient to impose tax where the decedent has retained the life income. Therefore, such a trust was held taxable, whether created before or after 1931. Thus it was in *Commissioner v. Estate of Church.*[59] (6) It was at this stage that Congress intervened again. A 1949 amendment went part way in overruling the *Church* decision, by providing that no estate tax was created by the retention of a life estate where the transfer was made before March 4, 1931 and where the decedent died before January 1, 1951. Moreover, where the transfer was made after March 3, 1931 and before June 7, 1932, and where the decedent died before January 1, 1951, there was no tax if the property was taxable solely by reason of the retention rights for a period "not ascertainable without reference to his death."[60] (7) Then, in 1953, Congress completed the overruling of the *Church* case. If the trust had been created before March 4, 1931, estate tax might not be predicated upon a reserved life estate, no matter when the death occurred. Similarly, if the trust was created before June 7, 1932, the tax might not be predicated upon the 1932 amendment. This 1953 amendment applied to any death after February 10, 1939.[61] As to deaths before February 11, 1939, see Technical Changes Act of 1953, Section 207(b). The 1953 amendment has been carried into the 1954 Code.[62]

Conservative moralists would undoubtedly conclude that the taxpayer would have been permitted during the days of this doubt and confusion the most self-serving interpretation possible, even though against the prevailing holdings of the Supreme Court, without fear of moral culpability.

Taxpayer is married, has two children, is living in a modest apartment which is too small for the needs of his family. He desires to acquire a reasonable suburban residence but lacks the requisite down payment. When apprised of these facts, his employer graciously proffers the $2,500 necessary, remarking that he has for some time desired to show his respect and affection for Taxpayer "in the form of some kind of gift or other."

In his April returns, after consultation with his tax counsel and moralist, Taxpayer determines not to list the $2,500 as income, upon the conviction that the moneys received were not compensation (were they, they would as taxable income move Taxpayer from the thirty-four-percent to the thirty-eight-percent bracket) but rather a gift from a devoted friend.

On his part, the employer has not shown the $2,500 as income on Taxpayer-employee's W-2 Information Return of compensation paid to employee but has assumed with Taxpayer that what he has given has been a gift.

Is Taxpayer morally culpable in refusing to pay approximately $1,000 in income tax pursuant to the statute? The law categorically states that the tax is to be paid on "all income from whatever source derived, including . . . compensation for services, including fees, commissions, and similar items."[63]

Resort to the courts for the answer to taxpayer's moral quandary leaves him in various stages of doubt during various periods of time. Adjudicated cases are at best nebulous on this question of what is compensation and what is a gift in specific reference to transfers from an employer to an employee. Intent is apparently considered to be the main criterion.

For instance, in the *LoBue* case,[64] the Supreme Court of the United States in May of 1956 reversed the decision of the distinguished Third Circuit Court of Appeals[65] and held that an employee's stock option was not a gift but resulted in compensation to the employee at the time of the exercise of the option. It was not such as to qualify as a restricted stock option under the Internal Revenue Code.

In May of 1960, the Supreme Court faced two cases involving the same question. In *Commissioner v. Duberstein*,[66] the Supreme Court determined that a Cadillac automobile received from a business friend by Duberstein for furnishing names of potential customers to the donor was compensation for past services or an inducement to further service rather than a gift. The court held that in determining whether a transfer was a nontaxable gift or taxable compensation the proper norm is one that inquires into the basic motive for the transferor's conduct—the dominant reason, in fact, that explains his action in making the transfer. This, the court continued, is not to be measured by a specific test for determining when a transfer is a gift or not, as urged by the government, but it is to be "based ultimately on the application of the fact-finding tribunal's experience with the mainsprings of human conduct to the totality of the facts of each case."[67]

Short days after *Duberstein* in June 1960, the Supreme Court of the United States in *Kaiser v. United States*[68] affirmed the Court of Appeals for the Seventh Circuit[69] which had in its turn reversed the District Court for the Eastern District of Wisconsin.[70] A jury in the district court had held that strike-benefit payments made by a union to the taxpayer were gifts and not taxable income. The facts indicated that the benefits were

(1) given to both member and nonmember strikers, (2) governed by individual need, (3) dependent upon the unavailability of unemployment compensation, and (4) that no conditions were attached to the assistance. This verdict of the jury the federal district court set aside.

After appropriate appeals, both the Court of Appeals for the Seventh Circuit and the Supreme Court of the United States held that the district court had improperly set aside the jury's findings and that, in fact, the assistance of the union given to the strikers was a gift and not, as a matter of law, income.

A capitulation finds these recent federal opinions in such sharp conflict that it is inconceivable that a taxpayer would be bound in conscience under these conditions to follow the income-tax statute, in spite of the holdings of the Supreme Court of the United States in *LoBue* and *Duberstein*.

These instances of *lex dubia* are but two of many and illustrate forcefully the application of the principle throughout the entire field of the civil law. Study, for further example, the doubt enveloping the statement embodied in Form 870-AS, which the taxpayer is required to sign in the settlement of a dispute with the Internal Revenue Service. The leading case on this subject is *Botany Worsted Mills v. United States*.[71] There is, on the other hand, in conflict a Court of Claims case, *Guggenheim v. United States*,[72] and a decision of the Court of Appeals of the Eighth Circuit, *Cane v. United States*.[73]

It should be apparent that many of the moral questions which arise from day to day can find their solutions in one, two, or more of the principles here delineated. The attempt has been to select examples which are more peculiarly or properly referable to the maxim or principle under consideration.

### The Law Must Further the Common Good

"It is an essential of the law that it should be directed to the common good."[74] Thomas concludes his commentary on Isidore relevant to this moral principle: The remaining words "meant that the law should further the common welfare; so that necessity refers to the removal of evils, usefulness to the attainment of good . . . The law is ordained to the common good."[75] In another place, Thomas expatiates on the concept:

> On the other hand, laws may be unjust . . . by being contrary to human good, through being opposed to the things mentioned above; either in respect to the end, as when an authority imposes upon his subjects burdensome laws conducive not to the common good but rather to his own cupidity or vainglory . . . or in respect to the form, as when burdens are imposed unequally on the community, although with a view to the common good. . . . Wherefore such laws do not bind in conscience.[76]

It is true that the broad concepts of justice, reasonableness, equity, and the promotion of the common good are manifestly not mutually exclusive. When considered in their broadest applicability, they could cover a multitude of situations and be justifiably adduced as the fundamental and ultimately governing principle for the solution of most of the cases heretofore presented. They do not, therefore, permit of individual treatment based on a perfectly logical norm of separation, but each does have its peculiar differentiating nature and its especial point of emphasis. One such specification of the general principle of the common good warrants some particular attention: A law to be just must apply equally to all.

Vermeersch elaborates this principle, insisting that a law must be "just, that is, hew to the line of equality and infringe on the right of no one."[77] More specifically—

> For the very binding force of the law itself it is necessary . . . that it be just, that is, insofar as the common good will permit, it must adhere to the requirement of distributive justice in apportioning equally the benefits and the burdens.[78]

This sixth of the traditional tenets of moral theology has been admirably paraphrased in the Fourteenth Amendment to the Constitution of the United States: "nor shall any state . . . deny to any person within its jurisdiction the equal protection of the laws." This principle prohibits "discriminating and partial legislation . . . in favor of particular persons as against others in like condition."[79] But it also has reference to the manner in which the law is administered:

> Though the law itself be fair on its face and impartial in appearance, yet, if it is applied and administered by public authority with an evil eye and an unequal hand, so as practically to make unjust and illegal discriminations between persons in similar circumstances, material to their rights, the denial of equal justice is still within the prohibition.[80]

The areas of applicability of this principle are many and varied—labor legislation, the field of civil rights, taxation. Two pellucid instances should serve as adequate illustrations.

In May of the year 1880 the City of San Francisco enacted into law an ordinance providing that

> It shall be unlawful, from and after the passage of this order, for any person or persons to establish, maintain, or carry on a laundry within the corporate limits of the city and county of San Francisco without first having obtained the consent of the board of supervisors, except the same be located in a building constructed either of brick or stone.[81]

Yick Wo, a native of China and a subject of the Emperor of China, had been engaged in the laundry business in San Francisco for twenty-two years. His establishment had been licensed after an inspection by the Board of Fire Wardens and pronounced safe for the business purposes of a laundry.

The nub of the litigation came in the petition (concededly true) of Yick Wo:

> Your petitioner and more than one hundred and fifty of his countrymen have been arrested upon the charge of carrying on business without having such special consent, while those who are not subjects of China, and who are conducting eighty-odd laundries under

similar conditions, are left unmolested and free to enjoy the enhanced trade and profits arising from this hurtful and unfair discrimination. The business of your petitioner, and of those of his countrymen similarly situated, is greatly impaired, and in many cases practically ruined by this system of oppression to one kind of men and favoritism to all others.[82]

This posed a disturbing moral problem for the many Chinese of good intentions who found themselves in like circumstances and yet who were neither apprehended nor before the courts. This was particularly true inasmuch as the Supreme Court of California as well as the Circuit Court of the United States for the District of California in separate litigations had upheld the validity of the ordinance in question.

A conscientious moralist would assuredly hesitate to advise Yick Wo and his compatriots that they had a moral obligation to observe the orders of the law-enforcement officers of the City of San Francisco. In this particular instance, the Supreme Court corroborated this moral judgment. The court concluded that the provisions of the Fourteenth Amendment

> . . . are universal in their application, to all persons within the territorial jurisdiction, without regard to any differences of race, of color, or of nationality; and the equal protection of the laws is a pledge of the protection of equal laws.[83] . . . the facts shown establish an administration directed so exclusively against a particular class of persons as to warrant and require the conclusion, that, whatever may have been the intent of the ordinances as adopted, they are applied by the public authorities charged with their administration, and thus representing the State itself, with a mind so unequal and oppressive as to amount to a practical denial by the State of that equal protection of the laws which is secured . . . by the broad and benign provisions of the Fourteenth Amendment to the Constitution of the United States.[84]

Law-abiding citizens in the city of New Orleans were faced in mid-1960 with a well-defined moral problem: whether or not as members of the Orleans Parish School Board they were

bound in conscience to obey various statutes of the state of
Louisiana which "directly or indirectly, require or promote segregation of the races in the Orleans Parish public schools":[85]
(1) The right to reclassify schools on a racially integrated basis
is reserved solely to the legislature.[86] (2) The governor shall
supersede a school board which is under a court order to deseg-
regate and shall take over the exclusive control, management,
and administration of public schools.[87] (3) The right to close
all schools if one school is integrated and the right to close any
school threatened with violence or disorder are within the pow-
ers of the governor.[88] (4) The races shall be segregated in the
public schools of Louisiana, and supplies and funds shall be
withheld from integrated schools.[89]

The Federal District Court in *Bush v. Orleans Parish School
Board* made it clear that the inequality of treatment of the
Negro citizens rendered the law invalid as violative of the com-
mon good. It would be a rare theologian who would not concur.

> "In short, the constitutional rights of children not to be discrimi-
> nated against in school admission on grounds of race or color de-
> clared by this Court in the Brown case[90] can neither be nullified
> openly and directly by state legislators or state executive or judi-
> cial officers, nor nullified indirectly by them through evasive
> schemes for segregation whether attempted 'ingeniously or ingenu-
> ously' " (*Cooper v. Aaron*, 358 U.S. 1, 17, 78 S.Ct. 1401, 1409,
> 3 L.Ed.2d 5).[91]

The federal court found that the cumulative effect of these statutes and acts was continued segregation in the public schools.
"They are but additional weapons in the arsenal of the State for
use in the fight on integration."[92]

The district court was particularly grieved at some of the
financial advantages afforded the segregationists by certain of
the statutes.

> These acts specifically provide for segregation of the races in
> the public schools and withhold, under penalty of criminal sanc-

tions, free school books, supplies, lunch, and all state funds from integrated schools. They are, of course, unconstitutional on their face.[93]

This unconstitutionality was founded on the denial to Negro citizens of equal protection of the laws. In 1885 Mr. Justice Fields in the famous *Barbier v. Connolly*, speaking for the Supreme Court of the United States, presented a memorable summary of this sixth maxim. The Fourteenth Amendment requires that

> equal protection and security should be given to all under like circumstances in the enjoyment of their personal and civil rights; that all persons should be equally entitled to pursue their happiness and acquire and enjoy property; that they should have like access to the courts of the country for the protection of their persons and property, the prevention and redress of wrongs, and the enforcement of contracts; that no impediment should be interposed to the pursuits of anyone except as applied to the same pursuits by others under like circumstances; that no greater burdens should be laid upon one than are laid upon others in the same calling and condition, and that in the administration of criminal justice no different or higher punishment should be imposed upon one than such as is prescribed to all for like offences.[94]

## De Minimis Non Curat Lex

"Wherefore D. [*sic*] Renard himself,[95] who seems to reject completely the entire doctrine of merely penal laws, hastens to embrace the opinion of D'Hulst according to which the celebrated maxim '*De minimis non curat praetor*' has applicability to many of the lesser statutes of the nation."[96]

The usual layman unversed in the technicalities of the civil and moral law is forcefully impelled to embrace the penal law when he contemplates the multitude of daily instances in which the citizen violates, but only to a minute degree, the strict letter of the law. With the innate ethical sense of right and wrong that is common to most of mankind, he is absolutely convinced that there is no moral culpability in driving a motor vehicle at a rate of speed of thirty-two miles per hour, perhaps even thirty-three, in a commercial district where the speed of automobile traffic is regulated by an ordinance setting a maximum limit of thirty, or to drive seventy-five miles per hour in a zone on the Pennsylvania Turnpike where the limit is established at seventy, or to catch fifty-four bass when an ordinance placed the legal limit during the fishing season at fifty. And the layman would be perfectly correct in this conviction, since "the law does not concern itself with trivialities." Neither the civil nor the moral law will bind the subject in conscience to insubstantial deficiencies in his obedience of positive-law enactments.

> The second maxim of principles on which his action is based ("the law pays no attention to trifles") is a well-recognized principle when properly applied. It is generally used when very small or infinitesimal errors are urged, as in a $1,000 judgment was [sic] excessive by $15 or some such illustration.[97]

Thus, an appreciable area of concern characteristically attributed to the penal law is more properly the preserve of the *de minimis* principle. Although the majority of instances of applicability of the maxim are understandably to be found in the more pedestrian and picayune day-to-day brushes with the law, its application is perhaps better illustrated by resort to the adjudicated cases.

Wilson and Company was a national meat-packing company of prominence. Among the four thousand persons employed at Wilson's sprawling Chicago plant were 276 members of the mechanical and maintenance division. Evidence adduced at the trial indicated that the employment contract between union and corporation provided that "employees who are required to work over 8 hours in any one day . . . be paid one and one-half times their regular rate for all such overtime hours."[98] It also appeared on trial that many of the maintenance division employees were required by the rule of the company to be dressed for work and "punched in" by 7:55 A.M. Finally, it was conceded that the corporation had treated the five minutes in excess of the eight regular hours on each such day as noncompensable.

Some 149 aggrieved maintenance men instituted litigation under Section 16(b) of the Fair Labor Standards Act[99] for the period from July 15, 1941, to July 18, 1945.

Defendant Wilson and Company alleged as its principal defense the doctrine of *de minimis*. The trial court overruled this defense but did state that the amount of claimed working time "comes very close, I think, to coming within the rule of which you talked, your de minimis rule."[100] The Circuit Court of Appeals, however, in reversing the District Court applied *de minimis* and relied on the *Mt. Clemens Pottery Co.* case[101] in which the Supreme Court of the United States had resorted to *de minimis*. Mr. Justice Murphy spoke for a divided court:

> We do not, of course, preclude the application of a *de minimis* rule where the minimum walking time is such as to be negligible. . . . When the matter in issue concerns only a few seconds or minutes of work beyond the scheduled working hours, such trifles may be disregarded. Split-second absurdities are not justified by the actualities of working conditions or by the policy of the Fair Labor Standards Act. It is only when an employee is required to give up a substantial measure of his time and effort that compensable working time is involved. The *de minimis* rule can doubtless be applied to much of the walking time involved in this case, but the precise scope of that application can be determined only after the trier of facts makes more definite findings as to the amount of walking time in issue.[102]

In its comments on *de minimis* the circuit court remarked

> It is thus apparent that no rigid rule can be laid down with mathematical certainty as to when the de minimis rule applies. Each situation presented must be examined in the light of what is "substantial" and "reasonable" in view of all the factors present. Here, not more than five minutes a day is involved. The checking in at the time clock, the receiving of instructions from supervisory personnel, the obtaining of tools from tool chests and cabinets, and the walking to the place plaintiffs were required to be are similar

to the preliminary activities which were held governed by de minimis in the Mt. Clemens case.[103]

It would seem worthy of remark that *de minimis* was applied by
the circuit court even in the face of the fact that the damages
stretched over a four-year period presumably five days a week.

Although *Wilson & Co.* is manifestly a civil litigation to recover unpaid overtime compensation, the general reasoning of
the court would be applicable in criminal statutory situations
and would also be operative as a norm for the far greater number of occasions which would never reach litigation.

It is incumbent to comment, however, that the instant decision could well be repudiated by competent moralists as it was
by the lower federal court. In support of the rejection of this
conclusion of the circuit court it should be emphasized that
(1) the total amount claimed by some could reach the figure of
$175, as it did in the case of one specific plaintiff, and (2) since
the daily exclusion of each five-minute period in the capitulation for compensation was a formal policy of Wilson and Company, it seems doubtless that all the repeated instances would
coalesce into a moral unit, even though they extended over a
four-year span. Query, therefore, whether the $175 was in fact
*de minimis* even though prorated over one thousand workdays.
The crux of the decision, of course, rests in the question whether
the thousand days conjoin into a single totality. One would move
gingerly in pronouncing this corporate policy of noncompensa-
tion as anything other than one prolonged moral act. Were this
so, it would be difficult to apply *de minimis*. (It is doubtful,
however, if the withholdings of all employees would be lumped
to form one act, although even that is arguable.) The case is
close in both civil and moral law but aptly illustrates the principle of *de minimis*.

In *Bristol-Myers Co. v. Lit Brothers, Inc.*,[104] E. R. Squibb
and Sons and Lambert Pharmaceutical Company combined with
Bristol-Myers in a bill in equity to restrain by injunction an al-

leged violation of the Pennsylvania Fair Trade Act which provided that

> Willfully and knowingly advertising, offering for sale, or selling any commodity at less than the price stipulated in any contract entered into pursuant to the provisions of section one of this act, whether the person so advertising, offering for sale, or selling is, or is not, a party to such contract, is unfair competition and is actionable at the suit of any person damaged thereby.[105]

The practice reprobated by Bristol-Myers consisted in the issuing of trading stamps for each ten cents of the purchase price of two of Bristol-Myers' trademarked products: "Sal Hepatica" and "Ipana" toothpaste. The trading stamps were redeemable for premiums on articles of value, but only after nine hundred and ninety of the stamps had been pasted in a stamp book furnished for the purpose. Upon presentation to the stamp company of a completed book of stamps, the customer received an article of merchandise worth at retail $1.75, for which Lit Brothers paid the stamp company $1.40. As the court said: "In other words, the customer qualifies himself to receive a bonus worth $1.75 when he has paid Lit Brothers $99 for purchases."[106]

In holding for the defendant the court commented that ninety-nine dollars worth of Ipana toothpaste would purchase 396 tubes—a supply adequate for a long lifetime.[107] The court stated that

> There is also a time-honored maxim of the law which applies to this case to wit: "De minimis non curat lex." As Broom says in his "Legal Maxims": "Courts of justice generally do not take trifling and immaterial matters into account." In "The Reward," 2 Dods, Adm. R. 269, 270, Sir W. Scott observed that "the court is not bound to a strictness at once harsh and pedantic in the application of statutes. The law permits the qualification implied in the ancient maxim, de minimis non curat lex. Where there are irregularities of very slight consequence, it does not intend that the infliction of penalties should be inflexibly severe. If the deviation were a mere trifle, which, if continued in practice, would weigh

little or nothing in the public interest, it might properly be over-looked.[108]

## Epikeia

Of all the traditional principles of moral theology advanced in mitigation of the law, that of *epikeia* has the broadest applicability. In essence, *epikeia* is the interpretation of the true intent of the legislature. Without doubt, the legislative intent must always be followed.[109]

Ultimately the word is from ἐπιείκεια ("reasonable or likely"). It is commonly equated with *equitas*, the equity of the English system administered originally by the chaplain to the king and later the priest-lawyers of the chancery. This is not accurate, but the subject is an historical one which has been treated elsewhere.[110]

Again, do not confuse the lawmaker's intent to legislate or not, to legislate this way or that, binding in conscience, with the Suarezian intent to oblige or not. The concern of *epikeia* is with the intent to legislate or not, to legislate this way or that. The doctrine of *epikeia* operates on the assumption that the legislation if it exists, or the legislation once interpreted according to the lawgiver's intent or mind, binds the subject in conscience. The intent, in short, does not concern obligation but either (1) the existence itself or (2) the meaning or content of the law.

Riley in his extensive treatment of the subject remarks on the multiplicity of definitions but adheres to one:

> A correction or emendation of a law which in its expression is deficient by reason of its universality, a correction made by a subject who deviates from the clear words of the law, basing his action upon the presumption at least probable, that the legislator intended not to include in his law the case at hand.[111]

The doctrine treats not of obligation but of obligation to what.

Thomas approaches *epikeia* in his question: "Whether he who is under a law may act beside the letter of the law."[112]

I answer . . . that . . . every law is ordered to the common weal of men, and derives the force and nature of law accordingly. Insofar, moreover, as it departs from this does it cease to have binding force. Hence the Jurist says: "By no reason of law or favor of equity are we allowed to interpret harshly and render burdensome those useful measures which have been enacted for the welfare of man." Now it happens often that the observance of some point of law conduces to the common weal in the majority of instances, yet in some cases is very hurtful. Since the lawgiver cannot have in view every single case, he shapes the law according to what happens most frequently, by directing his intentions to the common good. Wherefore if a case were to arise wherein the observance of that law would be hurtful to the general welfare, it should not be observed. For instance, suppose that in a besieged city it be an established law that the gates of the city are to be kept closed. This is good for the public welfare as a general rule, but if it were to happen that the enemy are in pursuit of certain citizens who are defenders of the city it would be a great loss to the city if the gates were not open to them. And so in that case, the gates ought to be opened, contrary to the letter of the law, in order to maintain the common weal which the lawgiver had in view.[113]

The doctrine of *epikeia* performs to a substantial degree the tasks assigned to the penal law. *Epikeia* is universally held.[114]

The question naturally arises: Who is to interpret the intent of the legislator? In the application of *epikeia*, as with all other moral principles (and with legal problems in the civil law as well), prudent persons should seek the counsel of experts in the field. Where this is impossible, each individual, consonant with his intellectual abilities, must reason to a considered conclusion in the specific instance. It behooves him afterwards to inquire of reliable authority in the interests of his future conduct and toward his own education. Aquinas answers the question with the following observation:

Nevertheless, it must be noted that if the observance of the law according to the letter does not involve any sudden risk needing instant remedy, not everyone is competent to expound what is useful and what is not useful to the state. Those alone can do this who are in authority and who on account of such like cases, have the power to dispense from the laws. If, however, the peril be so sudden as not to allow the delay involved by referring the matter to authority, the mere necessity brings with it a dispensation, since necessity knows no law.[115]

Occasions for the application of *epikeia* in the daily life of the citizen are frequent and manifold. The automobile driver proceeding through the countryside at midnight, observing the regulations for vehicular speed applicable for the general area, will understandably not be held in conscience to observe the lower limit posted for a school zone located in a completely rural section. The same reasoning would lead to a like conclusion in the case of special speed regulations established for the protection of construction workers, when it is manifest that operations have ceased for the weekend.

Because of the importance of *epikeia* and as further illustration of its use, it would seem imperative to consider the manner in which it is applied by the civil-law courts of the United States. In the well-known case of *Tedla v. Ellman,*[116] brother and sister violated the unmistakable words of the New York statute by walking in the wrong direction on the highway, with traffic passing to their left, instead of right:

> Pedestrians walking or remaining on the paved portion, or travelled part of a roadway shall . . . keep to the left of the center line thereof, and turn to their left instead of right side thereof, so as to permit all vehicles passing them in either direction to pass on their right.[117]

In the event, the brother was killed. In tort litigation for recovery the defendant motorist alleged the violation of the statute by the pedestrian plaintiff as contributory negligence as a matter of law, which would thereby bar recovery for the death. Testimony at the trial indicated that "there were very few cars going east" at the time of the accident but that there was "very heavy Sunday night traffic"[118] proceeding to the west.

It is true that this is not a criminal matter, but the force of the court's reasoning would have perfect pertinence in reference to the question of the binding force of the statute: Did the brother and sister commit a moral wrong in walking with the light traffic when the statute commanded the opposite?

The court in rejecting counsel's argument declared that the legislature had certainly not intended that pedestrians should observe the general rule of conduct even under circumstances where observance would subject them to an unusual risk. Judge Lehman speaking for the majority of the Court of Appeals of New York introduced an excellent dissertation on the proper interpretation of legislative intent with a statement of the broad philosophical base of *epikeia*:

> It is unreasonable to ascribe to the Legislature an intention that the statute should have so extraordinary a result, and the courts may not give to a statute an effect not intended by the Legislature.[119]

The equitable approach of the court in the *Tedla* case is on all fours with the traditional Roman *equitas*,[120] the ἐπιείκεια of the Greeks and of course with the *epikeia* of moral theology.

To Aristotle ἐπιείκεια was a rectification or emendation of the law in instances where obligatory observance would be manifestly in violation of justice or natural equity.[121] Suarez adds his authority in support of the doctrine of *epikeia* and gives further insight into its nature:

> It is advisable to distinguish between the interpretation of a law and true *epikeia* or equity. For interpretation of a law is a much broader concept than *epikeia*, inasmuch as the relationship between the two is that of a superior to an inferior, since every instance of *epikeia* is an interpretation of law, whereas not every interpretation of law is, conversely, *epikeia*. Cajetan has noted this distinction . . . he says that often, or rather always, laws require interpretation because of the obscurity or ambiguity of their terms or for other similar causes. Yet not every interpretation of this kind is *epikeia*, but only that interpretation in which we consider a law as failing in some particular instance, owing to its universal character, that is,

owing to the fact that it was established for all cases, and in some specific instance it is so deficient that it cannot justly be observed in those conditions.[122]

Thus does the New York court in *Tedla* formulate a concise statement of *epikeia*:

A general rule of conduct—and, specifically, a rule of the road—may accomplish its intended purpose under usual conditions, but, when the unusual occurs, strict observance may defeat the purpose of the rule and produce catastrophic results.[123]

Later, the court amplifies the concept, remarking

Nor should it be construed as an inflexible command that the general rule of conduct intended to prevent accidents must be followed even under conditions when observance might cause accidents . . . We cannot assume reasonably that the Legislature intended that a statute enacted for the preservation of the life and limb of pedestrians must be observed when observance would subject them to more imminent danger.[124]

These words of the New York court might have been spoken by Lehmkuhl, the German Jesuit moralist: *Epikeia* "is therefore an application of the law according to what is equitable and good in accordance with which it is presumed that the legislator would not wish his law in these extraordinary circumstances (which he did not foresee) to remain in force and that he himself would have made provision for just this exception if such a case had originally arisen in his mind."[125]

Of far greater cogency in illustrating the general endorsement and adoption of *epikeia* by the Anglo-Saxon jurisprudence is the enunciation of the doctrine in the *Restatement of the Law of Torts*. The distinguished authors of the *Restatement* express succinctly the generally accepted rule and the reasons therefor:

Many statutes and ordinances are so worded as apparently to express a universally obligatory rule of conduct. Such enactments, however, may in view of their purpose and spirit be properly construed as intended to apply only to ordinary situations and to be subject to the qualification that the conduct prohibited thereby is not wrongful if, because of an emergency or the like, the circumstances justify an apparent disobedience to the letter of the enactment.[126]

This would be a reliable expression of the American common-law definition of *epikeia*, as well as of moral theology.

\* \* \*

These are some—and it is emphasized that they are only samplings—of the more common maxims and principles of moral theology that adequately fill the role proposed for the penal law. These, then, are such as comprise the substance of the counterproposal toward a solution.

Somewhat surprisingly, authors have seemingly not come forward heretofore with such a proposal as a solution. Herron certainly advocates it in general and does make one or two specific suggestions. "One does not have to cling to the penal law theory in order to avoid overburdening the conscience of the faithful; the general norms, which moral theology provides for the guidance of men, are sufficient."[127]

Other commentators have attempted to meet the need by approaches less broad and generally less acceptable. Woroniecki proposes a form of self-dispensation in certain cases.[128] He has however been contemned in many quarters, even by opponents of penal law,[129] albeit somewhat hastily. It would seem that much would depend on Woroniecki's understanding of "self-dispensation." Is it *epikeia*? Thus Dunn states: "In order to mitigate the severity of his anti-penal-law position, Woroniecki asserts that in certain circumstances the subject could dispense himself from a given law. Evidently our judges and police officers have not heard everything yet."[130] Nor Dunn read either *Tedla v. Ellman* or the *Restatement of the Law of Torts*. Or Thomas: "If, however, the peril be so sudden as not to allow of the delay involved by referring the matter to authority, the mere necessity brings with it a dispensation, since necessity knows no law."[131] Herron specifies his suggested solution and instances some of the traditional principles as ameliorative, such as *Nemo tenetur ad impossibile* and the requisites of justice, reasonableness, and utility.

But most antimerepenalists have been content in the main with a rebuttal and rejection of the system, relying, it would seem, on the conviction that the elimination of an unnecessary entity left no gap to fill.

## CHAPTER X

# A Supplemental Brief in Conclusion

Although much apparent severity is softened by an enlightened and rational utilization of traditional theology, the conclusion is nonetheless inexorable: The civil law is binding in conscience. All of the qualifications, exceptions, and mitigations will not change this general principle of jurisprudence. This has been the central thesis of this book.

Once all the logical arguments *contra* have been advanced and all the inherent unreasonableness has been exposed, even a solution submitted, there yet remain, however, certain psychological and emotional obstacles—the residue of centuries of misconception and partial understanding—to a thorough rejection of the penal-law doctrine. Two final observations might remove these psychological blocks and provide insight for the attempt at a solution.

## GRAVITY DETERMINES CULPABILITY

It is altogether possible that the principal cause for the concern of most—from simple citizen to intuitive jurisprudent and moralist—with the doctrine of the moral obligatoriness of the civil law lies in a failure to understand and perhaps emotionally savor the nature and the gravity (or, more properly, the lack of gravity) of the culpability involved in violating such positive laws. The average person, whether he be layman or expert, generally does not quail at attaching moral obligation not to evade taxes in the amount, say, of two million dollars. But he might become a bit queasy when told that he is bound in conscience to pay a customs levy of two dollars. With many, the resentment is not toward the principle of moral obligation but rather with the appellation "sin" affixed, for example, to the failure to obey a parking regulation or observe a stop sign.

This uneasiness could conceivably evanesce were one to realize that culpability—sin—ranges in gravity from the most serious mortal sin (for example, matricide, incest, double adultery) on through less serious but nonetheless mortal sins (for example, theft of a hundred dollars from a wealthy person) and finally on down into a category different in kind, to an infinity of grades of venial sins.

If it is understood that culpability consequent on a violation of a civil law is perfectly proportioned to the gravity of the law, perhaps much of the emotional opposition to the proposition will disappear. For example, violation of the municipal ordinance of Grosse Pointe, Michigan, limiting the time during which an automobile may park on the streets of the municipality carries a fine of twenty-five cents.[1] If the gravity of this offense were expressed in terms of moral obligation, it would seem that the ingrained reluctance to embrace the thesis would be removed. "He was culpable in the amount of twenty-five cents." "He sinned a quarter's worth."

Another way to express this difficulty would be this: Because the customary manner of designating culpability has been in terms of only two clear-cut categories (that is, mortal or venial sin) and because the span of gravity in each of these two categories is virtually infinite, the mind untrained to subtle distinction equates the sin involved in overtime parking with the sin in incest. The difference is one of kind.

Even more subtle, and hence more difficult to make, and hence more repugnant if not made, is the distinction of degree between two venial sins. The average person resents being accused of a venial sin for failure to secure a hunting license when he knows that in some certain circumstances it would only be a venial sin to steal eighty dollars. The cure for this would be to make the terminology fit the crime and to excogitate a much more specified and appropriate series of gradations. It might be propitious to categorize the infinite grades of venial sin into the fourfold division of descending gravity of (1) minor delinquency, (2) lesser dereliction, (3) slight deficiency, and (4) mere inadequacy. These could well suffice as designations for all venial violations of the positive law. The term "inadequacy"—or perhaps, better, "deficiency"—could describe the most minor offense, with the understanding that the violation does in fact carry culpability, albeit the lowest grade, and is a breach of the moral obligation of the civil law, being, therefore, a species of venial sin. Just as each person describes the moral binding force of the civil law in different terminology ("should," "ought," "bound in duty," "what a good citizen would do"), so too ought we to describe variously the consequent culpability (venial sin, minor delinquency, dereliction, deficiency, inadequacy, imperfection [if properly defined], shortcoming, something a good citizen should not do, a breach of honor, or the like).

## The Culpability of Minor Deficiencies

Closely akin to these thoughts is another, a fallacy common to the common-law jurisprudence: An act which might entail culpability, if sufficiently serious, will eventually cease to be a sin when the gravity becomes only minor, unless, of course, it becomes so negligible as to satisfy the requirements of *de minimis*. All are able to visualize the moral turpitude in the refusal of a controlling stockholder to mail his proxy if it is manifest that his vote will save the corporation from a million-dollar fraud. But it is difficult to appreciate the culpability of the holder of ten shares of a giant corporation who neglects to take steps proportioned to his ownership to obstruct a similar fraud. Although the guilt may be slight, it is nonetheless neither nothing nor nonexistent. It is at worst the barest inadequacy or, if one would prefer, the most venial of venial sins; but it is, nonetheless, something.

### Probabilism

A caution is here in order for the day-to-day counsel of the people. As long as *lex pure poenalis* can list so much competent authority in its support, the citizenry can be advised that the doctrine of probabilism ("one may follow the opinion that favors liberty as long as he is certain that it is well-founded, even though contrary opinion be more probable"[2]) will permit them to follow the theory in certain of their practical daily affairs.

### The Last Word

Now that everything has been said that must be said, it must be disconcertingly pointed out that Dunn approaches parlously near the truth when he says: "The extrinsic evidence [the number of proponents] is overwhelming on the side of the penal law."[3] Unless the legal scholars of the world, moral and civil, address themselves to a mature and intensive reappraisal of this influential theory, Dunn's prognosis will be realized: The penal law "probably will continue to remain in 'possession.' "[4]

Nonetheless, it was the sanguine objective of this study that the doctrine of the moral binding power of the civil law hereby and herewith be firmly established and that the theory of the purely penal law on its part be laid to rest at last, these long four centuries since its genesis. Whatever the event, perhaps at least the spread of the penal-law doctrine will be somewhat arrested by it.

The last word must be this: As commendable as its objective —and no one can doubt that its purpose is praiseworthy—the doctrine of *lex pure poenalis* is not only unnecessary and historically ill-founded but inherently untenable. Although its end is often justified, the end as yet does not justify the means. The system remains founded on intrinsic illogic. As laudable as its goal may be, it must be said with Thomas to the Tempters:

> The last temptation is the greatest treason:
> To do the right deed for the wrong reason.

But the rejection of the penal-law system was only a by-product of this study. The principal purpose was the delineation of the philosophy of the civil law—a philosophy founded on the eternal and natural laws, dependent on the authority of a duly-constituted state and elaborated from the central thesis that the civil law binds in conscience. Onto this structure the complete edifice of the civil law can be erected.

---

The rules of form for two kinds of citation are observed in the following notes. Literary citation follows standard literary style. Legal citation (such as to cases, statutes, and articles in legal periodicals) follows the special style generally accepted in legal writing.

## CHAPTER I

1 William Blackstone, *Commentaries on the Laws of England* (4 vols. 8th ed. Oxford: Clarendon Press, 1778), I, 57-58. [Italics in original.]

2 John Calvin, *Institutes of the Christian Religion*, Bk. IV, Chap. X, Sec. 5; translated by Henry Beveridge (2 vols. London: J. Clarke, 1953), II, 417.

3 Oliver Wendell Holmes, Jr., *Book Review*, 6 AM. L. REV. 723 (1872) ; reprinted in 44 HARV. L. REV. 788 (1931).

4 Matthew Herron, T.O.R.; in "The Problem of Penal Law," *Proceedings of the Tenth Annual Convention of the Catholic Theological Society of America* (New York: Catholic Theological Society of America, 1955), pp. 277, 271.

5 Edwin F. Healy, S.J., *Moral Guidance* (Chicago: Loyola Univ. Press, 1942), p. 26.

6 Author's neologism for a *lex pure poenalis* proponent.

7 "Inter scriptores recentes vix est moralista et canonista alicuius nominis qui leges mere poenales rejiciat" (José Nemesio Güenechea, *Principia Juris Politici* [2 vols. Rome: Gregorian Univ. Press, 1938-1939], II, 244).

8 Edward T. Dunn, S.J., "In Defense of the Penal Law," *Theological Studies*, 18 (1957), 59.

9 Author's neologism for a *lex pure poenalis* proponent.

10 From *Moral and Pastoral Theology* by Henry Davis, S.J., Published in Four Volumes by Sheed & Ward Inc., New York; II, 339.

11 *Ibid.*, 338.

12 "Imo juxta nonnullos auctores omnes leges tributariae possunt esse mere poenales" (Joseph Aertnys and Cornelius A. Damen, *Theologia Moralis* [2 vols. 15th ed. Turin: Marietti, 1947], I, 616).

13 "Probabilius leges tributorum, quales hodie vigent in plerisque regionibus, ex se sunt mere poenales. Quare obligant tantum vel ad solvendum ab initio tributum, vel ad poenam seu multam quae fraudantibus imponatur, non violenter eludendam" (Eduard Genicot, S.J., and Joseph Salsmans, S.J., *Institutiones*

*Theologiae Moralis* [2 vols. 17th ed. Bruges: Desclée de Brouwer, 1952],
I, 498).

[14] Healy, *Moral Guidance*, p. 247.

[15] "Case of Conscience," *American Ecclesiastical Review*, 70 (1924), 199.

[16] Philip S. Land, S.J., *Tax Obligations According to Natural Law*, 4 St. Louis
U.L.J. 129, 143 (1956). See also "Evading Taxes—Can't Be Justified in Conscience," *Social Order*, 5 (1955), 121.

[17] Int. Rev. Code of 1939, ch. 10, §§ 1710-11, 53 Stat. 192 (now Int. Rev. Code
of 1954, § 4241).

[18] Int. Rev. Code of 1939, ch. 10, § 1712, 53 Stat. 192 (now Int. Rev. Code of 1954,
§ 4242).

[19] U.S.D.C., E.D. La.

[20] *Vitter v. United States*, 279 F.2d 445, 449 (5th Cir.), *cert. denied*, 364 U.S. 929
(1960).

[21] *Munn v. Bowers*, 47 F.2d 204 (2d Cir.), *cert. denied*, 283 U.S. 845 (1931);
*Knollwood Club v. United States*, 48 F.2d 971 (Ct. Cl. 1931); *Wild Wing
Lodge v. Blacklidge*, 59 F.2d 421 (7th Cir. 1932).

[22] *Billings v. Campbell*, 188 F. Supp. 261 (N.D. Tex. 1960).

[23] *Down Town Ass'n. of the City of N.Y. v. United States*, 278 F.2d 313, 314
(2d Cir. 1960), *affirming* 4 Am. Fed. Tax R. 6133 (S.D.N.Y. June 3, 1959),
*cert. denied*, 364 U.S. 836 (1960).

[24] *Id.* at 315.

[25] *Ibid.* The reference was to U.S. Treasury Regulation 43, §§ 101.24-.25, 26 C.F.R.
§§ 101.24-.25.

[26] For a few among many: *United States v. McIntyre*, 253 F.2d 728 (4th Cir.
1958); *Downtown Club of Dallas v. United States*, 240 F.2d 159 (5th Cir.
1957); *Rockefeller Center Luncheon Club v. Johnson*, 131 F. Supp. 703
(S.D.N.Y. 1955); *Yondotega Club* (Detroit, Mich.) *v. United States*, 22 Am.
Fed. Tax R. 1246, 38-1 U.S. Tax Cas. ¶ 9134 (E.D. Mich. Jan. 28, 1938);
*Detroit Club v. United States*, 22 F. Supp. 424 (Ct. Cl. 1938); *Quinnipiack
Club* (New Haven, Conn.) *v. United States*, 4 F. Supp. 996 (Ct. Cl. 1933).
Further instances: *Hulette v. United States*, 202 F. Supp. 330 (W.D. Ky.
1962), *aff'd*, 315 F.2d 826 (6th Cir. 1963); *Edgewood Country Club v. United
States*, 310 F.2d 379 (4th Cir.), *affirming per curiam* 204 F. Supp. 508 (S.D.
W.Va. 1962); *Scott v. United States*, 300 F.2d 141 (6th Cir. 1960); *Louisville
Country Club, Inc. v. Gray*, 285 F.2d 532 (6th Cir. 1960); *Abbott v. United
States*, 62-2 U.S. Tax Cas. ¶ 15,437 (S.D. Tex. July 13, 1962).

[27] Int. Rev. Code of 1939, c. 27A, § 3285, 65 Stat. 529 (now Int. Rev. Code of
1954, §§ 4401, 4421).

[28] *Merou Grotto, Inc. v. United States*, 5 Am. Fed. Tax R.2d 1996, 1999, 60-1 U.S.
Tax Cas. ¶ 15,283 (N.D. Ind. Jan. 6, 1960).

[29] *Edgewood American Legion Post No. 448, Inc. v. United States*, 246 F.2d 1
(7th Cir. 1957); *Woodard v. Campbell*, 235 F.2d 268 (7th Cir. 1956);
*Bohemian Gymnastic Ass'n Sokol of City of N.Y. v. Higgins*, 147 F.2d 774
(2d Cir. 1945); *West Side Tennis Club v. Commissioner*, 111 F.2d 6
(2d Cir.), *cert. denied*, 311 U.S. 674 (1940); *Jockey Club v. Helvering*,

76 F.2d 597 (2d Cir. 1935); *Hessman v. Campbell*, 134 F. Supp. 416 (S.D. Ind. 1955).

[30] E.g., *Voiture No. 364, etc. v. United States*, 5 Am. Fed. Tax R.2d 2000, 60-1 U.S. Tax Cas. ¶ 15,275 (N.D. Ind. Jan. 6, 1960).

[31] *United States v. $1,058.00 in U.S. Currency*, 323 F.2d 211 (3d Cir. 1963) (wagering tax); *Magnesium Casting Co. v. United States*, 323 F.2d 952 (1st Cir. 1963) (manufacturers tax); *Waterman-Bic Pen Corp. v. United States*, 1963-2 U.S. Tax Cas. ¶ 15,530; 12 Am. Fed. Tax R.2d 6374 (S.D. N.Y. Oct. 22, 1963) (cabaret tax); *Zekind v. United States*, 1963-2 U.S. Tax Cas. ¶ 15,525; 12 Am. Fed. Tax R.2d 6366 (E.D. Mo. Sept. 12, 1963) (swimming club); *"The Benedicts" v. United States*, 1964-2 U.S. Tax Cas. ¶ 15,585 (W.D. N.C. Aug. 17, 1964) (social club); *United States v. Ruth*, 1964-2 U.S. Tax Cas. ¶ 15,586 (E.D. S.C. Aug. 3, 1964) (cabaret tax); *United States v. Russo*, 1964-2 U.S. Tax Cas. ¶ 15,584 (7th Cir. Aug. 6, 1964) (wagering tax).

CHAPTER II

[1] For an exposition of these postulates preparatory to the specific subject of this study, see David C. Bayne, S.J., *The Natural Law for Lawyers—A Primer*, 5 DE PAUL L. REV. 159 (1956).

[2] Jacques Maritain, *The Rights of Man and Natural Law*, translated by Doris C. Anson (New York: Scribner, 1943), pp. 60-61. [Italics in original.]

[3] ". . . rationis ordinatio ad bonum commune, et ab eo qui curam communitatis habet, promulgata" (Thomas Aquinas, O.P., Saint, *Opera Omnia* [25 vols. Parma: Fiaccadori, 1852-1873], Vols. I-IV: *Summa Theologica*, I-II, q. 90, a. 4). All citations from Thomas follow the standard format without page references and hence may be found in any of the multitude of editions either in original or translation. Translations throughout are the author's unless otherwise noted. The three parts of the *Summa Theologica* are found in the following volumes of Fiaccadori's *Opera Omnia*: S.T., I, in Vol. I; S.T., I-II, in Vol. II; S.T., II-II, in Vol. III; S.T., III, in Vol. IV. Henceforward, these citations to the *Opera Omnia* will not be repeated.

[4] "Lex est ordinatio rationis ad bonum commune ab eo qui curam communitatis habet, promulgata" ["Law is an ordinance of reason for the common good, promulgated by him who has the care of the community"] (Francis Suarez, S.J., *Opera Omnia* [28 vols. Paris: Vives, 1856-1878], Vols. V-VI: *De Legibus*, Lib. I, Cap. XII, Sec. 3). Suarez was quoting from Aquinas, S.T., I-II, q. 90, a. 4. The ten books of *De Legibus* are found in the following volumes of Vives's *Opera Omnia*: Lib. I-V, in Vol. V; Lib. VI-X, in Xol. VI. Henceforward, these citations to the *Opera Omnia* will not be repeated.

[5] "Revera tamen lex dicenda est omnis norma qua legislator, utens sua potestate regendi societatem, i.e. sua iurisdictione, normam efficaciter suis subditis praescribere intendit" (Arthur Vermeersch, S.J., *Theologia Moralis* [3 vols. 4th ed. Rome: Gregorian Univ. Press, 1947], I, 148).

[6] "In omni lege quaedam ordinatio subditorum ad bonum commune habetur. Legislator determinat aliquem ordinem secundum quem sive actiones faciendae, sive res disponendae sunt ad finem societatis. "Huiusmodi ordinationem vult efficacem" (*ibid.*, 145).

[7] Henry de Bracton, *De Consuetudinibus et Legibus Angliae*, edited by George E. Woodbine (New Haven: Yale Univ. Press, 1915).

[8] Miriam T. Rooney, *Borrowings in Roman Law and Christian Thought*, 6 THE JURIST 457 (1946).

[9] Blackstone, *Commentaries*, I, 44.

[10] "Itaque sanctio est coactio poenalis quae ad firmandam legem vel ad compensandum sociale detrimentum, legis violatione effectum, ad legem est addita" (Vermeersch, *Theologia Moralis*, I, 146).

[11] *Jenkins v. State*, 14 Ga. App. 276, 80 S.E. 688, 690 (1914).

[12] *State v. U.S. Express Co.*, 164 Iowa 112, 145 N.W. 451, 455 (1914).

[13] "De lege autem propria et respectu rationalis creaturae, cum constet non inducere illam necessitatem simpliciter, dubium est an inducat moralem, quae obligatio dicitur" (Suarez, *De Legibus*, Lib. I, Cap. XIV, Sec. 1).

[14] "Nihilominus dicendum est primo nullam esse propriam legem quae obligationem non inducat, id est, necessitatem quamdam operandi, vel non operandi" (*ibid.*, 4).

[15] Ben W. Palmer, *Hobbes, Holmes and Hitler*, 31 A.B.A.J. 569 (1945).

[16] Thomas E. Holland, *The Elements of Jurisprudence* (10th ed. New York: Oxford, 1906), p. 79.

[17] John C. Ford, S.J., *The Fundamentals of Holmes' Juristic Philosophy*, 11 FORDHAM L. REV. 255 (1942).

[18] Jerome N. Frank, *Mr. Justice Holmes and Non-Euclidean Legal Thinking*, 17 CORNELL L.Q. 568, 570-71, 572-79 (1932).

[19] Harry C. Shriver, editor, *Holmes: His Book Notices and Uncollected Letters and Papers* (New York: Central Bk. Co., 1936), p. 157.

[20] Mark De Wolfe, editor, *Holmes-Pollock Letters* (2 vols. Cambridge: Harvard Univ. Press, 1941), II, 252.

[21] *Ibid.*, 200.

[22] *Oliver Wendell Holmes: Collected Legal Papers* (New York: Harcourt, 1920), p. 167.

[23] Holmes, 44 HARV. L. REV. 788 (1931).

[24] *Holmes: Collected Legal Papers*, p. 310.

[25] Shriver, *Holmes: Uncollected Papers*, p. 187.

[26] Francis E. Lucey, S.J., *Natural Law and American Legal Realism: Their Respective Contributions to a Theory of Law in a Democratic Society*, 30 GEO. L.J. 493, 513 (1942).

[27] John T. Schuett, S.J., *A Study of the Legal Philosophy of Jerome N. Frank*, 35 U. DET. L.J. 28, 49 (1957).

[28] "Lex quaedam regula est et mensura actuum, secundum quam inducitur aliquis ad agendum vel ab agendo retrahitur: dicitur enim lex a ligando, quia obligat ad agendum" (Aquinas, *S.T.*, I-II, q. 90, a. 1).

[29] ". . . leges positae humanitus vel sunt iustae vel iniustae. Si quidem iusate sint, habent vim obligandi in foro conscientiae a lege aeterna, a qua derivantur,

secundum illud Prov. 8:15: 'Per me reges regnant, et legum conditores justa decernunt' " (*ibid.*, q. 96, a. 4).

30 Augustinus Lehmkuhl, S.J., *Theologia Moralis* (2 vols. 11th ed. Friburgi Brisgoviae: Herder & Co., 1910), I, 145.

31 Suarez, *De Legibus*, Lib. III, Cap. XXI, Sec. 5. See also Lib. I, Cap. XIV, Sec. 4.

32 Blackstone, *Commentaries*, I, 57.

33 Frederick Pollock, *Essays in Jurisprudence and Ethics* (London: Macmillan, 1882), p. 25.

34 John A. McHugh, O.P., and Charles J. Callan, O.P., *Moral Theology* (2 vols. New York: J. F. Wagner, 1958), I, 135.

35 Vermeersch, *Theologia Moralis*, I, 145.

36 Aloysius Sabetti, S.J., and Timothy Barrett, S.J., *Compendium Theologiae Moralis* (34th ed. New York: Pustet, 1939), p. 75. This work is the lineal descendant of the original by John Peter Gury, S.J., annotated by Antonius Ballerini, S.J.

37 Joseph D'Annibale, *Summula Theologiae Moralis* (3 vols. 5th ed. Rome: Desclée de Brouwer, 1908), I, 199; Thomas Joseph Bouquillon, *Theologia Moralis Fundamentalis* (3rd ed. Bruges: Beyaert, 1903), pp. 353, 467; Lehmkuhl, *Theologia Moralis*, I, 145. For a fuller treatment, see Victor Vangheluwe, "De ortu atque profectu sententiae disjunctivae in explicanda lege pure poenali," *Miscellanea Moralia* (Louvain: Nauwelaerts, 1948), pp. 209-24.

38 "Sententia ista hodie merito deseritur; quia nullus legislator legis observationem et poenam aequali modo amat et vult, sed efficaciter, saltem per poenam, ordinationem suam urgere intendit" (Vermeersch, *Theologia Moralis*, I, 147).

39 Dunn, *Theological Studies*, 18 (1957), 42.

40 *Ibid.*, 44.

41 Suarez, *De Legibus*, Lib. V, Cap. IV, Sec. 2, 7. For other adherents to this theory, see Dominicus M. Prümmer, O.P., *Manuale Theologiae Moralis* (3 vols. 11th ed. Friburgi Brisgoviae: Herder & Co., 1953), I, 140-41; Dominic Viva, S.J., *Cursus Theologico-Moralis* (4 vols. Patavii: Manfré, 1723), Vol. I: *De Legibus*, q. 4, a. 2, n. 2; Martinus Becanus, S.J., *Summa Theologiae Scholasticae*, Pars II, Tract. III, Cap. 7, q. 2 (Paris: Quesnel, 1658), pp. 325-26; A. Van Hove, "Quelques publications récentes au sujet des lois purement pénales," *Miscellanea Moralia*, pp. 252-53; Gommar Michiels, *Normae Generales Juris Canonici* (2 vols. Lublin: Lublin Catholic Univ. Press, 1929), I, 260-66; Philip Maroto, *Institutiones Juris Canonici* (2 vols. 3rd ed. Rome, 1921), Vol. I, Sec. 221; Güenechea, *Principia Juris Politici*, II, 246.

42 Dunn, *Theological Studies*, 18 (1957), 42-43.

43 James Brown Scott, *The Catholic Conception of International Law* (Washington: Georgetown Univ. Press, 1934), p. 138.

44 Blackstone, *Commentaries*, I, 57-58. [Italics in original.]

45 "Lex mere poenalis . . . tota quanta conscientiam non obligat . . ." (Vermeersch, *Theologia Moralis*, I, 148).

46 ". . . tota quanta se continet in ordine iuridico seu fori exterioris" (*ibid.*).

47 *Ibid.*

48 Lucius Rodrigo, S.J., *Praelectiones Theologico-Morales Comillenses* (4 vols. Sal Terrae: Santander, 1944), II: *Tractatus De Legibus*, 182.

[49] *Ibid.,* 251-53.

[50] ". . . non vi legis humanae sed legis divinae quae oboedientiam iustis legibus imponit" (Vermeersch, *Theologia Moralis,* I, 148).

[51] John J. Lynch, S.J., summary of remarks of Ford; in "The Problem of Penal Law ('Digest of the Discussion')," *Proceedings,* pp. 283-84.

[52] Rodrigo, *Praelectiones,* II, 251-53.


CHAPTER III

[1] Hieronymus Noldin, S.J., *Summa Theologiae Moralis* (3 vols. 31st ed. Oeniponte: Rauch, 1956), I, 158.

[2] "In Iure ecclesiastico leges *vix ullae mere poenales* reperiuntur" (Genicot-Salsmans, *Institutiones Theologiae Moralis,* I, 92).

[3] Antonius M. Arregui, S.J., *Summarium Theologiae Moralis* (18th ed. Bilbao: El Mensajero del Corazón de Jesús, 1948), p. 46.

[4] Prümmer, *Manuale Theologiae Moralis,* I, 140; Rodrigo, *Praelectiones,* II, 260.

[5] Benedict Henry Merkelbach, O.P., *Summa Theologiae Moralis* (3 vols. 5th ed. Paris: Desclée de Brouwer, 1946), I, 259.

[6] Herron; in *Proceedings,* p. 275.

[7] Robertus Bellarminus, S.J., Saint, *Disputationes de Controversiis Christianae Fidei,* Tom. I, "Quinta Controversia Generalis—De Membris Ecclesiae Militantis," Lib. III: *De Laicis sive Saecularibus,* Cap. XI: "Lex civilis non minus obligat in conscientia, quam lex divina . . ." (9 vols. Ingolstadt: Sartorius, Vols. I-VI, 1599; Vols. VII-IX, 1593), III, 466. Henceforward, all citations of Bellarmine will be to Liber III: *De Laicis.* Therefore only the chapter and Sartorius' pages will be cited. This treatise can be found in translation by Kathleen E. Murphy, as *De Laicis; or, The Treatise on Civil Government* (New York: Fordham Univ. Press, 1928).

[8] Dunn, *Theological Studies,* 18 (1957), 53.

[9] Suarez, *De Legibus,* Lib. V, Cap. IV, Sec. 8-12.

[10] *Ibid.*

[11] Thomas Slater, S.J., *A Manual of Moral Theology* (2 vols. 5th ed. New York: Benziger, 1925), I, 59.

[12] Vermeersch, *Theologia Moralis,* I, 150; Suarez, *De Legibus,* Lib. V, Cap. IV, Sec. 8; Rodrigo, *Praelectiones,* II, 257-60.

[13] Juan Bautista Ferreres, *Compendium Theologiae Moralis* (2 vols. 17th ed. Barcelona: Subirana, 1953), I, 125; Bouquillon, *Theologia Moralis Fundamentalis,* pp. 468, 454; A. Janssen, "Les lois Pénales ('Existence')," *Nouvelle Revue Théologique,* 50 (1923), 295.

[14] ". . . criterium directum mere poenalis generatim non est nec esse potest declaratio expressa voluntatis legislatoris . . . Hic enim ageret contra suum finem, declarando legem suam non obligare in conscientia" (F. Claeys-Boúúaert, "De lege mere poenali," *Collationes Gandavenses,* 12 [1925], 24).

[15] Vermeersch, *Theologia Moralis,* I, 150-51.

[16] Suarez, *De Legibus,* Lib. V, Cap. IV, Sec. 8; Rodrigo, *Praelectiones,* II, 185.

[17] Suarez, *De Legibus,* Lib. V, Cap. IV, Sec. 8; Noldin, *Summa Theologiae Moralis,* I, 170.

18 Thomas A. Iorio, S.J., *Theologia Moralis* (3 vols. 3rd ed. Naples: D'Auria, 1946), I, 116; Vermeersch, *Theologia Moralis*, I, 151.
19 See Holmes's works cited in Chapter II, notes 15-24, *supra*.
20 Suarez, *De Legibus*, Lib. V, Cap. IV, Sec. 10; Merkelbach, *Summa Theologiae Moralis*, I, 259.
21 Suarez, *De Legibus*, Lib. V, Cap. IV, Sec. 9; Iorio, *Theologia Moralis*, I, 117.

CHAPTER IV

1 In the elaboration of the Suarezian psychology, there was notable reliance on the competent, albeit unpublished, work of John Erwin Naus, S.J., "The Foundation of Obligation in Suarez" (M.A. thesis, Dept. of phil., Saint Louis Univ., 1949). See also the study of Frank Bernard Higgins, S.J., "The Penal Law Theory of Suarez" (unpublished M.A. thesis, Dept. of phil., Saint Louis Univ., 1957).
2 Suarez, *De Legibus*, Lib. I, Cap. IV, Sec. 6.
3 ". . . in intellectu non datur imperium respectu voluntatis, quod non sit per modum judicii. Neque aliter potest intellectus impellere, seu movere voluntatem, nisi per cognitionem, vel judicium" (Suarez, *O.O.*, Vol. II: *De Angelis*, Lib. VII, Cap. VI, Sec. 26).
4 ". . . consensus proprie significat applicationem illam voluntatis ad aliquod medium, quae sequitur ex praemissa consultatione intellectus, quae acceptatio si sit efficax, et separans unum medium ab aliis, illudque praeferens, dicitur electio: facta autem electione necessarium est, ut id medium executioni mandetur, cui deservit usus . . ." (Suarez, *O.O.*, Vol. III: *De Anima*, Lib. V, Cap. VII, Sec. 4).
5 Suarez, *De Legibus*, Lib. I, Cap. IV, Sec. 11-12.
6 *Ibid.*, Sec. 12.
7 *Ibid.*
8 *Ibid.*
9 *Ibid.*, Sec. 8.
10 ". . . potest voluntas non solum contradictorie non velle, quod sic judicatum est, sed etiam contrarie velle oppositum; ergo manet libera quoad exercitium, et specificationem" (Suarez, *De Angelis*, Lib. VII, Cap. VI, Sec. 15).
11 ". . . si judicet intellectus hoc medium esse utile, vel eligibile, etiamsi simul judicet aliud esse utile, potest voluntas unum eligere, neque est necesse ut intellectus prius de altero determinate judicet esse eligendum, imo neque esse eligibilius alio" (Suarez, *O.O.*, Vols. XXV-XXVI: *Disputationes Metaphysicae*, Disp. XIX, Sec. VI, para. 11). The 54 *Disputationes Metaphysicae* are found in the following volumes of Vives's *Opera Omnia*: Disp. I-XXVII, in Vol. XXV; Disp. XXVIII-LIV, in Vol. XXVI. Henceforward, these citations to the *Opera Omnia* will not be repeated.
12 *Ibid.*, para. 12.
13 *Ibid.*, Sec. IV, para. 4.
14 *Ibid.*, Sec. V, para. 13.
15 *Ibid.*, para. 21.

## 240   Conscience, Obligation, and the Law

[16] "Hac vero doctrina supposita circa imperium uniuscujusque ad seipsum, de imperio unius ad alium necessario dicendum est, post actum voluntatis legislatoris . . . solum requiri ac necessarium esse ut legislator illud suum decretum et judicium insinuet, manifestet, seu intimet subditis, ad quos lex ipsa refertur. . . . Quod autem hoc sufficiat, patet, quia voluntas principis est ex se efficax: nam est ex sufficienti potestate, et cum absoluto decreto obligandi, ut supponitur: ergo si illa sufficienter proponatur subdito, operatur quod vult: inducit ergo obligationem: ergo consummata est lex: ergo nihil aliud necessarium est" (Suarez, De Legibus, Lib. I, Cap. IV, Sec. 12).

[17] Ibid., Cap. V, Sec. 8.

[18] " . . . praecepta utriusque juris divini et humani positivi non habent per se intrinsecam necessitatem, sed ex voluntate extrinseca . . ." (ibid., Lib. III, introd., Sec. 1).

[19] ". . . sine dubio lex obligat in conscientia, quia vera lex natura sua habet hunc effectum, si non excludatur . . ." (ibid., Cap. XXVII, Sec. 1).

[20] Ibid., Sec. 2.

[21] "Mixta vero dicitur, quae simul moralis est et poenalis, et duo praecepta virtute includit, unum, faciendi vel vitandi talem actum; aliud, sustinendi talem poenam si id non fiat . . . Lex autem pure poenalis dicitur, quae solum habet unum praeceptum quasi hypotheticum sustinendi talem poenam, vel incommodum, si hoc vel illud fiat, etiamsi de actu substrato tali conditioni praeceptum non imponatur" (ibid., Lib. V, Cap. IV, Sec. 2).

[22] "Dicendum est ergo legem, quae in verbis suis, et modo quo fertur, praeceptum continet, etiamsi poenam adjiciat, obligare in conscientia, vel sub mortali, vel sub veniali culpa, juxta qualitatem materiae, et alia signa . . . nisi aliunde constet de expressa mente legislatoris" (ibid., Cap. III, Sec. 6).

[23] ". . . illa intentio mutationem facit in materia legis, quae mutatio est in potestate legislatoris: nam potest hanc vel illam materiam, aut determinate, aut disjunctim, aut absolute, aut sub conditione praecipere, licet non possit a tota materia omnem obligationem in conscientia excludere, si veram legem ferre vult. Quando ergo dicitur intendere non obligare in conscientia, sed ad puram poenam, hoc intelligitur respectu actus immediate praecepti, vel prohibiti; tamen eo ipso talis actus non est adaequata materia illius legis, sed vel hoc disjunctum, aut facere tale opus, aut sustinere, vel exequi talem poenam, vel (et in idem redit) est lex conditionata solvendi talem poenam, si hoc fiat, et tunc a toto disjuncto non excluditur obligatio in conscientia" (ibid., Lib. III, Cap. XXVII, Sec. 3).

[24] "Quod autem illi transgressores, per se loquendo, non peccent, probatur, quia prudenter conformant dictamen suae conscientiae intentioni sui legislatoris: ille autem declaravit in illa transgressione non esse culpam ex vi illius legis; ergo prudenter subditi formant judicium conscientiae, quod nullum ibi interveniat peccatum; ergo re vera non peccant, quia quod est ex legitima conscientia peccatum non est" (ibid., Cap. XXII, Sec. 6).

[25] Aquinas, S.T., II-II, q. 186, a. 9, ad 2. This reliance on Thomas will be studied in more detail later.

[26] Suarez, De Legibus, Lib. V, Cap. IV, Sec. 7.

[27] Ibid., Lib. III, Cap. XXII, Sec. 2-3.

²⁸ "Tertio, licet obligatio aliqua sit de ratione legis, modus tamen obligationis pendet ex intentione praecipientis. Unde fit, ut licet materia legis gravis sit, possit legislator nolle obligare sub mortali; ergo eadem ratione potest nolle obligare in conscientia, sed tantum sub alio modo necessitatis, seu coactionis" (*ibid.*, Sec. 3).

²⁹ ". . . legem poenalem resolvi in aliquam conscientiae obligationem solvendi, vel sustinendi poenam, et hoc satis esse ut sit vera lex, etiamsi ad conditionem, sub qua poenam comminatur, in conscientia non obliget, respectu cujus conditionis dicitur pure poenalis, licet respectu ipsius poenae efficaciam habeat obligandi . . ." (*ibid.*, Lib. V, Cap. IV, Sec. 13).

³⁰ "Omnis autem poena si justa est, peccati poena est, et supplicium nominatur . . ." (Augustine, *De Libero Arbitrio* [Paris: Migne, 1877], Lib. III, Cap. XVIII, Sec. 51; P.L. 32:1296).

³¹ Suarez, *De Legibus*, Lib. III, Cap. XXII, Sec. 5.

³² The citation in Suarez is to Aquinas, *S.T.*, II-II, q. 186, a. 9, ad 2.

³³ "Caput IV. An dentur vel dari possint leges poenales non obligantes in conscientia, sed tantum sub poena, sine interventu culpae" (Suarez, *De Legibus*, Lib. V, Cap. IV).

³⁴ "Regulae religiosorum saepe obligant ad poenam ubi non ad culpam" (*ibid.*, Sec. 4).

³⁵ "Interdictum et irregularitas saepe incurruntur sine culpa. . . . poena interdum incurritur sine culpa, quamvis non sine causa, ut etiam dixit D. Thomas 2.2, quaest. 108, art. 4, ad 2, afferens exempla . . ." (*ibid.*, Sec. 5).

³⁶ ". . . aliquae sunt leges pure poenales, et in conscientia non obligantes, nisi ad poenam . . . tum quia, cum possibiles sint, et saepe possint esse aptiores ad regimen subditorum cum minori periculo et gravamine in aliquibus materiis in quibus majus onus necessarium non est, videtur per se credibile saepe ferri hoc modo leges poenales; tum etiam quia in religionibus sunt clara exempla harum legum . . . et in legibus humanis, pure poenalis censetur illa, quae poenam imponit fugienti de carcere, scindenti ligna in sylva communi, etc." (*ibid.*, Sec. 7).

³⁷ *Ibid.*, Sec. 13.

³⁸ Vermeersch, *Theologia Moralis*, I, 148; Dunn, *Theological Studies*, 18 (1957), 42.

³⁹ ". . . licet inferat poenam (id est gravamen aliquod, seu malum) sine culpa, non tamen sine causa; vel, licet illud inferat sine culpa morali, non tamen sine culpa civili, seu politica, et hoc sufficit" (Suarez, *De Legibus*, Lib. V, Cap. IV, Sec. 13).

⁴⁰ Dunn, *Theological Studies*, 18 (1957), 46.

⁴¹ "Nam, ut dicitur Deut. 25: *Secundum mensuram delicti erit plagarum modus, et significatur in cap. 1 de Constit., in 6, et in cap. Non afferamus,* 24, quaest. 1; unde August. 1. Retract., cap. 9: *Omnis poena, si justa est, peccati poena est, et supplicium nominatur;* et ideo culpam et poenam correlativa esse dixit Gerson. tract. de Vita spirit., lect. 1, et insinuat D. Thomas 1. 2, quaest. 87, art. 7; et quaest. 108, art. 8; ergo, cum lex poenalis juste puniat, supponit culpam in transgressione ejus. Verumtamen etiam haec ratio non urget; nam, licet poena in quadam significatione rigorosa dicat ordinem ad culpam,

tamen latius sumpta pro quocumque supplicio, vel damno aut incommodo potest juste inferri propter justam causam sine culpa, ut late ostendit Navarr. in dicto cap. *Fraternitas*, num. 10 usque ad 14. Vel etiam dici potest, licet omnis poena sit propter culpam, non tamen semper esse propter culpam contra Deum, sed interdum sufficere culpam quasi civilem et humanam" (Suarez, *De Legibus*, Lib. V, Cap. III, Sec. 7).

42 *Ibid.*, Lib. III, Cap. XXVII, Sec. 3. See Chapter IV, note 23, *supra*, for text of citation.

43 ". . . non possit a tota materia omnem obligationem in conscientia excludere, si veram legem ferre vult" (*ibid.*).

44 "Quando ergo dicitur intendere non obligare in conscientia, sed ad puram poenam, hoc intelligitur respectu actus immediate praecepti, vel prohibiti; tamen eo ipso talis actus non est adaequata materia illius legis, sed vel hoc disjunctum, aut facere tale opus, aut sustinere, vel exequi talem poenam, vel (et in idem redit) est lex conditionata solvendi talem poenam, si hoc fiat, et tunc a toto disjuncto non excluditur obligatio in conscientia" (*ibid.*).

45 "Secundo, lex poenalis est vera lex, ut constat, et tamen potest non obligare in conscientia; ergo non est de ratione legis ut obliget in conscientia. Minor patet, tum quia, ut sit lex, satis est ut aliquo modo cogat: tum etiam quia ita videbimus observari in multis regionibus, in quibus verae leges, seu statuta feruntur, et in eis declaratur non obligare ad culpam, sed ad poenam" (*ibid.*, Cap. XXII, Sec. 3).

46 "Tertio, licet obligatio aliqua sit de ratione legis, modus tamen obligationis pendet ex intentione praecipientis. Unde fit, ut licet materia legis gravis sit, possit legislator nolle obligare sub mortali; ergo eadem ratione potest nolle obligare in conscientia, sed tantum sub alio modo necessitatis, seu coactionis" (*ibid.*).

47 ". . . legem poenalem resolvi in aliquam conscientiae obligationem solvendi, vel sustinendi poenam, et hoc satis esse ut sit vera lex, etiamsi ad conditionem, sub qua poenam comminatur, in conscientia non obliget, respectu cujus conditionis dicitur pure poenalis, licet respectu ipsius poenae efficaciam habeat obligandi . . ." (*ibid.*, Lib. V, Cap. IV, Sec. 13).

48 Vermeersch, *Theologia Moralis*, I, 149.

49 Lynch, summary of remarks of Joseph Duhamel, S.J.; in *Proceedings*, p. 283.

50 Vermeersch, *Theologia Moralis*, I, 149.

51 Herron; in *Proceedings*, p. 272.

52 Blackstone, *Commentaries*, I, 57-58.

53 Dunn, *Theological Studies*, 18 (1957), 49-50.

54 ". . . tam multa esse hodie statuta civilia, ut si omnibus vel plurimis ex istis statutis in conscientia esset oboediendum, onus intolerabile sequeretur" (Vermeersch, *Theologia Moralis*, I, 151).


CHAPTER V

1 "Hic enim ageret contra suum finem, declarando legem suam non obligare in conscientia" (Claeys-Boúúaert, *Collationes Gandavenses*, 12 [1925], 24).

2 This point is treated in Chapter IX: A Counterproposal toward Solution, *infra*.

3 Thomas M. Cooley, editor, Blackstone's *Commentaries*, with notes (2 vols. 3rd ed. Chicago: Callaghan, 1884), I, 57, n. 12.

4 For a treatment of one aspect of this tradition, see Bayne, *The Supreme Court and the Natural Law*, 1 DE PAUL L. REV. 216 (1952).

5 *Illinois ex rel. McCollum v. Board of Education*, 333 U.S. 203, 238 et seq. (1948).

6 *Id.* at 239.

7 *Id.* at 253.

8 *Id.* at 254.

9 Francis J. McGarrigle, S.J., "It's All Right, If You Can Get Away with It," *American Ecclesiastical Review*, 127 (1952), 443.

10 John A. Ryan, "Are Our Prohibition Laws 'Purely Penal'?" A Letter to the Editor, *American Ecclesiastical Review*, 70 (1924), 408.

11 Michael Noonan, S.M.; in *Proceedings*, p. 270.

12 18 U.S.C. § 794, as amended.

13 E.g., Merkelbach, *Summa Theologiae Moralis*, I, 259; Prümmer, *Manuale Theologiae Moralis*, I, 140.

14 Suarez, *De Legibus*, Lib. V, Cap. IV, Sec. 8-9.

15 Herron; in *Proceedings*, pp. 276-77.

16 Merkelbach, *Summa Theologiae Moralis*, I, 260; Aertnys-Damen, *Theologia Moralis*, I, 151.

17 Sabetti-Barrett, *Compendium Theologiae Moralis*, p. 116.

18 "Quidquid sit, praestat omnino hac de re numquam verba facere apud populum praesertim rudiorem, illumque suaviter adducere ad leges omnes adimplendas" (*ibid.*).

CHAPTER VI

1 This study of the history of the doctrine is in substantial debt to Vangheluwe, "De Lege Mere Poenali, Inquisitio Historica de Origine Doctrinae Ejusque Evolutione usque ad Medium Saeculum XVIum," *Ephemerides Theologicae Lovanienses*, 16 (1939), 383-429. This is probably the most thorough and scholarly treatment of the subject. Vangheluwe covers the origin of the doctrine in the early thirteenth century and its development to the mid-1500s.

2 An intensive investigation of the history of the nonlegal concept in Italy can offer some insights: Robert J. Kelly, S.J., "Criteria and Examples of Purely Penal Obligation in Italian Writers Down to Angelo and Trovamala" (unpublished doctoral dissertation, Rome: Pontifical Gregorian Univ., 1957).

3 Cf. P. Denifle, O.P., "Die Constitutionen des Predigerordens in der Redaction Raimunds von Peñafort," Archiv für Literatur und Kirchengeschichte des Mittelalters, V (1889), 534.

4 "Ut igitur unitati et paci totius Ordinis provideamus, volumus et declaramus ut Regula nostra et Constitutiones nostre non obligent nos ad culpam, sed ad penam, nisi propter preceptum vel contemptum" (*ibid.*).

5 Georges Renard, *La théorie des "Leges mere poenales"* (Paris: Recueil Sirey, 1929), p. 20; P. Gismondi, "Le Leggi Puramente Penali e le leggi Puramente Morali per la Chiesa e per lo Stato," *Revista Italiana per le Scienze Giuridiche*, 11 (1936), 237, 246.

[6] Vangheluwe, *Ephemerides Theologicae Lovanienses*, 16 (1939), 385.

[7] A. Teetaert, "La 'Summa de Poenitentia' de S. Raymond de Pennafort," *Ephemerides Theologicae Lovanienses*, 5 (1928), 49-72.

[8] Raymond of Penafort, *Summa de Poenitentia*, Lib. II, Titulus: De Pedagiis; from the parchment manuscript: Biblioteca Vaticana, cod. Borghese 78, fol. 39vb.

[9] "Nota etiam hic propter continuationem materiae sex casus in quibus aliquis quotodie punitur juste ac licite [sine] culpa, sed non sine causa. Unde . . . Paupertas, odium, favor et vitium, scelus, ordo—personas spoliant et loca jure suo" (*ibid.*, Lib. III, Titulus: De Poenis; fol. 91va). The omission of *sine* is patently a slip of the scribe.

[10] Heinrich Joseph Denziger and Iohannes Bapt. Umberg, S.J., *Enchiridion Symbolorum Definitionum et Declarationum* (26th ed. Friburgi Brisgoviae: Herder & Co., 1947), n. 341, p. 167.

[11] "C. VI. Constantinopolitana ecclesia secundum a Romana obtinet locum. . . . Renouantes sancti Constantinopolitani concilii decreta, petimus, ut Constantinopolitana sedes similia priuilegia, que superior Roma habet, accipiat, non tamen ecclesiasticis rebus magnificetur, ut illa; ut hec secunda post illam existens, prius quam Alexandrina sedes numeratur; deinde Antiocena, et post eam Ierosolimitana" (Gratian, *Decretum*, Dist. XXII, Canon VI; from the best critical edition: Corpus Iuris Canonici, edited by Aemilius Friedberg [2 vols. 2 editio Lipsiensis. Graz: Druck, 1959], Vol. I: *Decretum Magistri Gratiani*, col. 76).

[12] Vangheluwe, *Ephemerides Theologicae Lovanienses*, 16 (1939), 410.

[13] "Prius quam. Sic ergo aliqua ecclesia privatur jure suo sine culpa sua et hoc fit quandoque propter favorem, quandoque propter odium . . . Alias regulare est, quod nemo sine culpa sua privandus est jure suo. . . . Et nota quod licet quis sine culpa perdat privilegium numquam tamen sine causa. Unde versus: Paupertas etc." (this gloss, as noted by the opening words, was on the words *prius quam* in Distinction XXII of the *Decretum Gratiani, Glossa Ordinaria Joannis Teutonici* [editio Venetiis, 1672] p. 67). Although this Venetian gloss is printed, it is not a critical edition. Hence, the exact limits of Teutonicus' commentary are less than certain. A parchment manuscript copy, transcribed by estimate of paleographic evidence *circa* 1350, was identical to the Venetian edition but omitted the final, direct reference to the hexameter (*Decretum Gratiani cum Glossa Joannis [Teutonici], cum Additionibus Bartholomaei [Brixiensis]*, Biblioteca Vaticana, cod. Vat. Lat. 2493, fol. 25rb). Another parchment manuscript (transcribed *circa* 1250) stopped short of "*Et nota quod . . .*" (*Decretum Gratiani cum glossis Io[hannis Teutonici]*, Biblioteca Vaticana, cod. Pal. Vat. 624, fol. 16rb). So also with a third, *circa* 1350 (*Decretum Gratiani cum Glossis Bartholomaei Brixiensis et Iohannis Teutonici*, Biblioteca Vaticana, cod. Vat. Lat. 1367, fol. 15rb) ; and a fourth, *circa* 1250 (*Decretum Gratiani cum glossa ordinaria Iohannis Teutonici et additionibus Bartholomaei Brixiensis aliisque glossulis marginalibus siglatis et anonymis*, Biblioteca Vaticana, cod. Pal. Vat. 625, fol. 15vb).

[14] ". . . ubi quis sine culpa privatur. Hoc autem scias quod multociens privatur quis sine culpa sed non sine causa" (gloss on Distinction LVI, *Decretum Gratiani cum Glossis Bartholomaei Brixiensis et Iohannis Teutonici*, Biblioteca Vati-

cana, cod. Vat. Lat. 1367, fol. 43rb). A scribe's reference sign appended to *privatur* connects that word to the sentence beginning *Hoc autem*, which is written lower on the page.

15 ". . . quoniam in coniugio multi casus occurrunt, in quibus coniuges sine culpa, sed non sine causa continere coguntur" (Gregory IX, *Decretales*, Lib. II, Titulus VI: Ut Lite non Cont., Cap. V, Sec. 4; Corpus Iuris Canonici, Friedberg, editor, II: *Decretalium Collectiones*, Decretalium Gregorii IX, col. 264).

16 ". . . poenalis afflictio suscepta in auxilium spiritus" (Bellarminus, *De Laicis*, Cap. XI, p. 469).

17 Harper's Latin Dictionary (New York: Am. Bk., 1907).

18 *Ibid.*

19 *Ibid.*

20 *Ibid.*

21 Dunn, *Theological Studies*, 18 (1957), 50.

22 "Utrum religiosus semper peccet mortaliter transgrediendo ea quae sunt in regula" (Aquinas, *S.T.*, II-II, q. 186, a. 9).

23 ". . . regula imponitur religioso sicut lex quaedam" (*ibid.*, Obj. 2).

24 "In aliqua tamen religione, scilicet Ordinis Fratrum Praedicatorum, transgressio talis, vel omissio ex suo genere non obligat ad culpam neque mortalem, neque venialem, sed solum ad poenam taxatam sustinendam, quia per hunc modum ad talia observanda obligantur. Qui tamen possent venialiter vel mortaliter peccare ex negligentia, vel libidine seu contemptu" (*ibid.*, ad 1).

25 "Praeterea, regula imponitur religioso sicut lex quaedam. Sed ille qui transgreditur praeceptum legis peccat mortaliter. Ergo videtur quod monachus transgrediens ea quae sunt in regula, peccet mortaliter" (*ibid.*, Obj. 2).

26 "Ad secundum dicendum, quod non omnia quae continentur in lege, traduntur per modum praecepti; sed quaedam proponuntur per modum ordinationis cujusdam, vel statuti obligantis ad certam poenam. Sicut ergo in lege civili non facit semper dignum poena mortis corporalis transgressio legalis statuti; ita nec in lege Ecclesiae omnes ordinationes vel publica statuta obligant ad mortale; et similiter nec omnia statuta regulae" (*ibid.*, ad 2).

27 One of the fullest treatments of the subject is that by Cándido Mazón, S.J., *Las reglas de los religiosos: su obligación y naturaleza jurídica* ("Analecta Gregoriana," no. 24, Rome: Gregorian Univ. Press, 1940).

28 "Neque dicant de facto statuta complurium institutorum religiosorum esse talia . . . potius deberent dici huiusmodi statuta non-leges simpliciter, quam leges pure poenales" (M. C. Gonzalez, O.P., "De Imperfectione Morali," *Théologie* ["Etudes et Recherches Publiées par le Collège Dominicain d'Ottawa," IV-V, Ottawa: Lévrier, 1944], Cahiers II-III, p. 323, n. 1.

29 Bellarminus, *De Laicis*, Cap. X, p. 469.

30 ". . . poenalis afflictio suscepta in auxilium spiritus" (*ibid.*).

31 "Nec illa est proprie poena . . ." (*ibid.*).

32 McGarrigle, *American Ecclesiastical Review*, 127 (1952), 447.

33 ". . . an talis ordinatio, si detur, vocanda sit lex necne" (Suarez, *De Legibus*, Lib. III, Cap. XXII, Sec. 5).

34 "Respondent aliqui illas non esse leges, sed vel consilia, vel conventiones quasdam, et quasi pacti. Sed hoc gratis dicitur . . ." (*ibid.*, Lib. V, Cap. IV, Sec. 4).

35 Thus does Noldin, *Summa Theologiae Moralis*, I, 128.

36 A fuller and excellent treatment of the question can be found in F. Litt, "Les Lois Dites Purement Pénales," *Revue Ecclésiastique de Liége*, 30 (1938-1939), 368-72. See also 142.

37 Thomas E. Davitt, S.J., analyzes the positions of several of the great theologians on this question in *The Nature of Law* (St. Louis: Herder, 1951).

38 ". . . vindicatio fit per aliquod poenale malum inflictum peccanti" (Aquinas, *S.T.*, II-II, q. 108, a. 1).

39 ". . . dicendum, quod ille qui secundum gradum sui ordinis vindictam exercet in malos, non usurpat sibi quod Dei est, sed utitur potestate sibi divinitus concessa . . ." (*ibid.*, ad 1).

40 ". . . et secundum hoc, aliquis interdum punitur sine culpa, non tamen sine causa" (*ibid.*, a. 4).

41 Dunn, *Theological Studies*, 18 (1957), 50.

42 ". . . poena dupliciter potest considerari: uno modo secundum rationem poenae, et secundum hoc poena non debetur nisi peccato, quia per poenam reparatur aequalitas justitiae, inquantum ille qui peccando nimis secutus est suam voluntatem, aliquid contra suam voluntatem patitur. Unde cum omne peccatum sit voluntarium . . . consequens est quod nullus punitur hoc modo, nisi pro eo quod voluntarie factum est" (Aquinas, *S.T.*, II-II, q. 108, a. 4).

43 "Utrum omnis poena sit propter aliquam culpam" (*ibid.*, I-II, q. 87, a. 7).

44 "Si vero loquamur de poena simpliciter, secundum quod habet rationem poenae, sic semper habet ordinem ad culpam propriam . . ." (*ibid.*).

45 "Alio modo potest considerari poena, inquantum est medicina non solum sanativa peccati praeteriti, sed etiam praeservativa a peccato futuro, vel etiam promotiva in aliquod bonum; et secundum hoc aliquis interdum punitur sine culpa, non tamen sine causa" (*ibid.*, II-II, q. 108, a. 4).

46 ". . . ideo quandoque punitur aliquis in temporalibus bonis absque culpa; cujusmodi sunt plures poenae praesentis vitae divinitus inflictae ad humiliationem vel probationem . . ." (*ibid.*).

47 "Ad secundum. . . . Et ideo numquam secundum humanum judicium aliquis debet puniri sine culpa poena flagelli, ut occidatur, vel mutiletur, vel verberetur. Poena autem damni punitur aliquis etiam secundum humanum judicium, etiam sine culpa, sed non sine causa; et hoc tripliciter: uno modo, ex hoc quod aliquis ineptus redditur sine sua culpa ad aliquod bonum habendum vel consequendum; sicut propter vitium leprae aliquis removetur ab administratione Ecclesiae; et propter bigamiam, vel judicium sanguinis aliquis impeditur a sacris ordinibus" (*ibid.*, ad 2).

48 Codex Juris Canonici, Canon 984, 4°.

49 "Secundo, quia bonum in quo damnificatur, non est proprium bonum, sed commune; sicut quod aliqua Ecclesia habeat Episcopatum pertinet ad bonum totius civitatis, non autem ad bonum clericorum tantum" (Aquinas, *S.T.*, II-II, q. 108, a. 4, ad 2).

50 ". . . et propter pravitatem aut malitiam civium Ecclesia perdit cathedram episcopalem. Ergo non solum pro peccato voluntario vindicta infertur" (*ibid.*, a. 4, obj. 2).

51 "Tertio, quia bonum unius dependet ex bono alterius; sicut in crimine laesae majestatis filius amittit haereditatem pro peccato parentis" (*ibid.*, ad 2).

52 "I. Quod transgressiones constitutionum provincialium, non ad culpam, sed ad poenam tantum obligent transgressores" (Joannes Dominicus Mansi, *Sacrorum Conciliorum nova, et amplissima collectio* [Venice: Zatta, 1784], Tom. XXVI, col. 412).

53 "In jure ecclesiastico de facto non dantur . . ." (Arregui, *Summarium Theologiae Moralis*, p. 46).

54 Thus avers Vangheluwe, *Ephemerides Theologicae Lovanienses*, 16 (1939), 400.

55 Kelly, "Criteria," p. 63 *et seq.*

56 *Ibid.*, p. 63.

57 ". . . etsi in hoc casu sustinet sine culpa, non tamen sine causa" (Henry of Ghent, *Aurea Quodlibeta*, Quod. III, Quaest. XXII [Venice: Jacobus de Franciscis, 1613], fol. 130r., col. 2).

58 Through a misunderstanding of his doctrine, according to Kelly, "Criteria," pp. 63-64.

59 Vangheluwe, *Ephemerides Theologicae Lovanienses*, 16 (1939), 425, 429.

60 "At poena . . . non necessario dependet a culpa. Quoniam etsi poena nunquam alicui imponatur sine culpa, frequenter tamen alicui imponitur sine culpa sua . . ." (Alfonso de Castro, *De Potestate Legis Poenalis*, Lib. I, Cap. IX [2 vols. Louvain: Bergagne, 1557], fol. 49b).

CHAPTER VII

1 Suarez, *De Legibus*, Lib. III, Cap. XXII.

2 D'Annibale, *Summula Theologiae Moralis*, I, 199.

3 Lehmkuhl, *Theologia Moralis*, I, 145.

4 R. Billuart, *Summa Sancti Thomae, sive Cursus Theologiae juxta Mentem Divi Thomae* (13 vols. Paris: Mequignon, 1827), Vol. VIII: *De Peccatis et Legibus*, Dis. IV, a. 4.

5 Janssens, *Nouvelle Revue Théologique*, 50 (1923), 121, 232, 292.

6 Vermeersch, *Theologiae Moralis.*

7 Dunn, *Theological Studies*, 18 (1957).

8 Rodrigo, *Praelectiones*, II, 243-67.

9 Calvin, *Institutes*, Bk. IV, Chap. X, Sec. 5; II, 417.

10 "Der menschliche Gesetzgeber hat auf dem ihm eigenen Gebiete die Befugnis, die Willen unter Sünde oder unter Sünde und Strafe oder auch überhaupt nicht zu verpflichten, es ist deshalb nicht einzusehen, warum er nicht zugleich die geringere Kompetenz besitzen sollte, lediglich in unvollkommener, in *indirekter* Weise, nämlich nur unter Strafe zu verpflichten, falls dies im Hinblick auf das Gemeinwohl genügte" (Otto Schilling, *Handbuch der Moraltheologie* [2 vols. 2nd ed. Stuttgart: Schwabenverlag, 1954, 1952], I, 119).

11 "Ses adversaires déclarés et connus pourraient presque se compter sur les doigts de la main . . ." (Litt, *Revue Ecclésiastique*, 30 [1938-1939], 143).

[12] [Sylvestro (de Prierio) Mazzolini, O.P.,] *Summa Sylvestrina* (Rome, 1516). Sylvester lived 1456?-1523.

[13] Dominic Soto, O.P., *De Justitia et Jure*, Lib. I, Quaest. VI: De potestate legis humanae, a. 5 (Antwerp: Nutium, 1567), fol. 19b.

[14] Anton Koch, "Zur Lehre von den sogenannten Ponälgesetzen," *Theologische Quartalschrift*, 81 (1900), 204-81.

[15] G. Renard, *La Valeur de la Loi* (Paris: Recueil Sirey, 1928); *La théorie des "Leges mere poenales."*

[16] Ulpianus Lopez, S.J., "Theoria legis mere poenalis et hodiernae leges civiles," *Periodica De Re Morali, Canonica, Liturgica*, 27 (1938), 203-16; 29 (1940), 23-33.

[17] Litt, *Revue Ecclésiastique*, 30 (1938-1939).

[18] Hyacinthus Woroniecki, O.P., "De Legis Sic Dictae Poenalis Obligatione," *Angelicum*, 18 (1941), 379-86. Woroniecki's view seems to be a slight modification of that of Lopez.

[19] Davitt, *The Nature of Law*, passim.

[20] McGarrigle, *American Ecclesiastical Review*, 127 (1952).

[21] Bernard Häring, C.SS.R., *The Law of Christ* (3 vols. Westminster: Newman, 1961, 1963), I (translated by Edwin G. Kaiser, C.PP.S., from *Das Gesetz Christi* [5th ed. Freiburg: Wewel, 1959]), 271. See also P. Harmignie, "Ordonnances humaines et obligation de conscience," *Revue Néo-Scholastique de Philosophie*, 32 (1930), 276-320.

[22] *America*, 88 (Jan. 17, 1953), 415.

[23] McGarrigle, *American Ecclesiastical Review*, 127 (1952).

[24] John R. Connery, S.J., "Shall We Scrap the Purely Penal Law?" *American Ecclesiastical Review*, 129 (1953), 244-53.

[25] Aquinas, *S.T.*, I-II, q. 91, aa. 1, 2.

[26] ". . . sicut in quolibet artifice praeexistit ratio eorum quae constituuntur per artem, ita etiam in quolibet gubernante oportet quod praeexistat ratio ordinis eorum quae agenda sunt per eos qui gubernationi subduntur. . . . Deus autem per suam sapientiam conditor est universarum rerum, ad quas comparatur sicut artifex ad artificiata. . . . Est etiam gubernator omnium actuum et motionum quae inveniuntur in singulis creaturis . . . ita ratio divinae sapientiae moventis omnia ad debitum finem obtinet rationem legis. Et secundum hoc lex aeterna nihil aliud est quam *ratio divinae sapientiae, secundum quod est directiva omnium actuum et motionum*" (*ibid.*, q. 93, a. 1). [Italics in original.]

[27] ". . . illa lex quae summa ratio nominatur, cui semper obtemperandum est, et per quam mali miseram, boni beatam vitam merentur, per quam denique illa quam temporalem vocandam diximus, recte fertur, recteque mutatur. . . . Video hanc aeternam esse atque incommutabilem legem. . . . Simul etiam te videre arbitror in illa temporali nihil esse justum atque legitimum, quod non ex hac aeterna sibi homines derivarint . . ." (Augustine, *De Libero Arbitrio*, Lib. I, Cap. VI, Sec. 15; P.L. 32:1229).

[28] ". . . omnis lex est legis aeternae participatio. . . . et participatio quaedam legis aeternae Dei, quae est prima et summa regula . . ." (Bellarminus, *De Laicis*, Cap. XI, p. 467).

[29] "Nam sive quis praevaricetur legem naturalem, sive positivam, sive divinam, sive humanam, semper peccat contra legem aeternam, quia omnis lex est legis aeternae participatio" (*ibid.*). Note that a complete reading of the entire tractate, at least Chapters II-XI, is essential to an understanding of Bellarmine's full position. The citations which follow necessarily only stress the specific point at issue.

[30] "Cum ergo lex aeterna sit ratio gubernationis in supremo gubernante, necesse est quod omnes rationes gubernationis quae sunt in inferioribus gubernantibus, a lege aeterna deriventur.

"Hujusmodi autem rationes inferiorum gubernantium sunt quaecumque aliae leges praeter aeternam. Unde omnes leges, inquantum participant de ratione recta, intantum derivantur a lege aeterna . . ." (Aquinas, *S.T.*, I-II, q. 93, a. 3).

[31] Bellarminus, *De Laicis*, Cap. VI, p. 452.

[32] ". . . et talis participatio legis aeternae in rationali creatura *lex naturalis* dicitur" (Aquinas, *S.T.*, I-II, q. 91, a. 2). [Italics in original.]

[33] ". . . quod omnibus rebus naturaliter insunt quaedam principia quibus non solum operationes proprias efficere possunt, sed quibus etiam eas convenientes fini suo reddant . . . Sicut autem in rebus agentibus ex necessitate naturae sunt principia actionum ipsae formae, a quibus operationes propriae prodeunt convenientes fini; ita in his quae cognitionem participant, principia agendi sunt cognitio et appetitus; unde opportet quod in vi cognoscitiva sit naturalis conceptio, et in vi appetitiva naturalis inclinatio, quibus operatio . . . reddatur competens fini. Sed quia homo inter cetera animalia rationem finis cognoscit, et proportionem operis ad finem; ideo naturalis conceptio ei indita, qua dirigatur ad operandum convenienter, lex naturalis vel jus naturale dicitur. In ceteris autem aestimatio naturalis vocatur. Bruta enim ex vi naturae impelluntur . . . magis quam regulentur quasi proprio arbitrio agentia" (Aquinas, *O.O.*, Vols. VI-VII: *Commentum in IV Libros Sententiarum*, in Lib. IV, d. 33, q. 1, a. 1). The commentary on Lib. I-II is found in Vol. VI. That on Lib. III-IV is found in Vol. VII.

[34] Suarez, *De Legibus*, Lib. II, Cap. VII, Sec. 2.

[35] Bellarminus, *De Laicis*, Cap. V, p. 450.

[36] "Naturale autem est homini ut sit animal sociale et politicum, in multitudine vivens, magis etiam quam omnia alia animalia: quod quidem naturalis necessitas declarat. Aliis enim animalibus natura praeparavit cibum, tegumenta pilorum, defensionem, ut dentes, cornua, ungues, vel saltem velocitatem ad fugam. Homo autem institutus est nullo horum sibi a natura praeparato, sed loco omnium data est ei ratio, per quam sibi haec omnia officio manuum posset praeparare. Ad quae praeparanda unus homo non sufficit: nam unus homo per se sufficienter vitam transigere non posset. Et igitur homini naturale quod in societate multorum vivat" (Aquinas, *O.O.*, Vols. XVI-XVII: *Opuscula Theologica et Philosophica*, Opusculum XVI: *De Regimine Principum ad Regem Cypri*, Lib. I, Cap. I). The various opuscula are contained in the following volumes of Aquinas' *Opera Omnia*: Opusc. I-XXXVII, in Vol. XVI; Opusc. XXXVIII-LXIX, in Vol. XVII. This work is available under the title *On Kingship, to the King of Cyprus*, translated by Gerald

Bernard Phelan, revised with introduction and notes by I. Th. Eschmann, O.P. (Toronto: Pontifical Institute of Mediaeval Studies, 1949).

[37] Bellarminus, *De Laicis*, Cap. VI, p. 452; *et passim.*

[38] "Si ergo naturale est homini quod in societate multorum vivat, necesse est in hominibus esse per quod multitudo regatur. Multis enim existentibus hominibus, et unoquoque id quod est sibi congruum, providente, multitudo in diversa dispergeretur, nisi etiam esset aliquis de eo quod ad bonum multitudinis pertinet, curam habens . . ." (Aquinas, *De Regimine*, Lib. I, Cap. I). For one facet of this obligation to care for the commonweal, see Bayne, *The Duties of a Lawyer to His Profession*, 23 DETROIT LAW 163 (1955); *The Lawyer-Moralist Looks at the Profession*, 8 ST. LOUIS U.L.J. 215 (1963).

[39] Bellarminus, *De Laicis*, Cap. V, p. 450.

[40] Leo XIII, "Humana Libertas," 1888, translated in *Social Wellsprings*, edited by Joseph Husslein, S.J. (2 vols. Milwaukee: Bruce, 1940), I, 123.

[41] Bellarminus, *De Laicis*, Cap. V, p. 450. For reflections on the attitude of the Supreme Court of the United States, see Bayne, 1 DE PAUL L. REV. 216 (1952). For a discussion of the early recognition of this premise, see *An Essay on the Hebrew Civil Code*, 3 CLEV.-MAR. L. REV. 23 (1954).

[42] Bellarminus, *De Laicis*, Cap. V, p. 450.

[43] *Ibid.*, Cap. X, p. 462. For modern illustrations of the natural law in action in the corporate-law field, see Bayne, *Kaiser-Frazer v. Otis: A Legal and Moral Analysis*, 2 DE PAUL L. REV. 131 (1953); Bayne, Mortimer M. Caplin, Frank D. Emerson, Franklin C. Latcham, *Proxy Regulation and the Rule-Making Process: The 1954 Amendments*, 40 VA. L. REV. 387 (1954).

[44] Bellarminus, *De Laicis*, Cap. XI, p. 466; Cap. X, p. 462; Cap. VI, p. 452.

[45] Aquinas, *S.T.*, I-II, q. 95, a. 2.

[46] Leo XIII, *Social Wellsprings*, I, 120.

[47] "Sed sciendum est quod a lege naturali dupliciter potest aliquid derivari . . . alio modo, sicut determinationes quaedam aliquorum communium. . . . secundo vero modo simile est quod in artibus formae communes determinantur ad aliquid speciale; sicut artifex formam communem domus necesse est quod determinet ad hanc vel illam domus figuram. . . . sicut lex naturae habet quod ille qui peccat puniatur; sed quod tali poena vel tali puniatur, hoc est quaedam determinatio legis naturae. Utraque igitur inveniuntur in lege humana posita. . . . Sed ea quae sunt secundi modi, ex sola lege humana vigorem habent" (Aquinas, *S.T.*, I-II, q. 95, a. 2).

[48] Leo XIII, *Social Wellsprings*, I, 121.

[49] ". . . ex intentione legislatoris pendere; an velit revera imperare, et veram legem condere, an vero solum ostendere quid agendum sit, sine alio imperio: sed si velit serio imperare, et veram legem condere, non est in ejus postestate impedire, quin lex obliget ad mortale, aut veniale, pro rei magnitudine" (Bellarminus, *De Laicis*, Cap. XI, p. 471).

[50] ". . . leges positae humanitus vel sunt justae vel injustae. Si quidem justae sint, habent vim obligandi in foro conscientiae a lege aeterna, a qua derivantur, secundum illud Prov. 8, 15: 'Per me reges regnant, et legum conditores justa decernunt'" (Aquinas, *S.T.*, I-II, q. 96, a. 4).

51 Leo XIII, *Social Wellsprings*, I, 121.

52 *Ibid.*

53 "Probatur Primo: vis obligativa est de essentia legis . . . et obligare est effectus necessarius legis, ergo omnis lex et a quocumque; feratur, sive a Deo, sive ab Angelo, sive ab homine, et homine sive Episcopo, sive Rege, sive patre, eodem modo obligat. . . . quia hominis essentia est, rationale esse, et propria passio esse risibilem, omnis homo est rationalis, et risibilis, sive sit creatus a solo Deo, ut Adam, sive a Deo ex alio homine, ut Eva, sive ab hominibus genitus, ut Cain. . . . Ubi notandum est, quod sicut res ceterae, quoad existentiam, pendent ab agente, non quoad essentiam, essentiae enim sunt aeternae . . . ita etiam lex, quoad existentiam, pendet a legislatore; non enim erit lex, nisi dictetur ab eo, qui habet auctoritatem. At quoad essentiam non pendet, quod enim lex obliget est quid aeternum, et immutabile, et participatio quaedam legis aeternae Dei . . . tamen si (per impossibile) esset lex non a Deo, adhuc obligaret ad culpam, sicut si (per impossibile) homo existeret non factus a Deo, adhuc esset rationalis" (Bellarminus, *De Laicis*, Cap. XI, pp. 466-67).

54 *Ibid.*

55 Bayne, 5 DE PAUL L. REV. 165 (1956). [Italics in original.]

56 *Id.* at 166. This summary statement is explained and expanded in considerable detail, *infra*.

57 "In Suarezianis, ponentibus legem opus voluntatis, logica adhuc salvatur, sed in Thomistis, eam dicentibus opus rationis, qui et ponunt finem (seu bonum commune) fundare et ordinare omnia in moralibus: ipsam existentiam societatis, adunationem hominum, auctoritatem, legem et omnia, positio legis pure poenalis est aliquid incomprensibile" (Gonzalez, *Théologie*, Cahiers II-III, p. 323, n. 1).

58 M. S. Gillet, O.P., "Conscience Chrétienne et Justice Sociale," *Revue des Jeunes*, 16 (1922), 141, 241, 452.

59 Davitt, *The Nature of Law*, p. 145.

60 *Ibid., passim.*

61 G. Renard, *La théorie des "Leges mere poenales."*

62 "La loi, en effet, pour saint Thomas, est formellement l'oeuvre de la raison jugeant des exigences d'un fin à atteindre, et exprimant ce que doit être nécessairement l'action pour réaliser cette fin. On comprend dès lors que pour lui l'obligation de la loi dérive de la nécessité de cette fin, et non pas de la volonté du législateur. Le pouvoir législatif est l'analogue, dans l'ordre social, de la conscience dans l'ordre individuel: il traduit pour les membres de la société les exigences du bien commun, comme la conscience exprime pour l'individu les exigences de la fin dernière. Et de même que, en aucune façon, on ne peut dire que la conscience crée ces exigences, de même le pouvoir législatif ne crée pas non plus les exigences du bien commun. Dès lors il ne dépend aucunement du législateur d'imposer l'obligation de la loi ou d'en libérer" (Edmond Brisbois, S.J., "Note de Philosophie morale, A propos des lois purement pénales," *Nouvelle Revue Théologique*, 65 [1938], 1072). Herron also supports this position (*The Binding Force of Civil Laws* [North Miami: Brower Press, 1952], p. 64).

63 "In ordine autem agibilium, primo quidem oportet sumere apprehensionem finis; deinde appetitum finis, deinde consilium de his quae sunt ad finem, deinde appetitum eorum quae sunt ad finem" (Aquinas, *S.T.*, I-II, q. 15, a. 3).

64 "Unde intellectus movet voluntatem per modum quo finis movere dicitur, inquantum scilicet praeconcipit rationem finis, et eam voluntati proponit" (Aquinas, *O.O.*, Vol. IX: *De Veritate*, q. 22, a. 12).

65 Aquinas, *O.O.*, Vol. V: *Contra Gentiles*, Lib. I, Cap. LXXII.

66 Aquinas, *S.T.*, I, q. 79, a. 11, ad 1.

67 "Motus enim voluntatis in finem non dicitur absolute intentio, sed simpliciter velle . . . Qui enim vult sanitatem, dicitur eam simpliciter velle; sed solum eam intendere dicitur, quando aliquid propter sanitatem vult" (Aquinas, *De Veritate*, q. 22, a. 14).

68 Naus, "The Nature of the Practical Intellect According to Saint Thomas Aquinas," *Analecta Gregoriana*, 108 (1959), 174.

69 "Cum autem proponit sibi aliquid sub ratione boni, ad quod alia ordinentur ut ad finem; tunc tendit in illud cum quodam ordine . . ." (Aquinas, *De Veritate*, q. 22, a. 13).

70 Aquinas, *S.T.*, I-II, q. 12, a. 4, ad 3.

71 ". . . intentio est actus voluntatis respectu finis" (*ibid.*, a. 1, ad 4).

72 *Ibid.*, a. 4, ad 3.

73 ". . . et ideo necessaria est inquisitio rationis ante judicium de eligendis. Et haec inquisitio *consilium* vocatur . . ." (*ibid.*, q. 14, a. 1). [Italics in original.]

74 "Unde cum consilium sit quaestio, de fine non est consilium, sed solum de his quae sunt ad finem" (*ibid.*, a. 2).

75 ". . . applicatio appetitivi motus ad determinationem consilii . . ." (*ibid.*, q. 15, a. 3).

76 See, for comments in this specific area, Henri Renard, S.J., "The Functions of Intellect and Will in the Act of Free Choice," *The Modern Schoolman*, 24 (1947), 89.

77 ". . . consequitur sententiam vel judicium, quod est sicut conclusio syllogismi operativi" (Aquinas, *S.T.*, I-II, q. 13, a. 3).

78 Aquinas, *De Veritate*, q. 24, a. 6.

79 This is explained at some length in George Peter Klubertanz, S.J., *The Philosophy of Human Nature* (New York: Appleton, 1953), p. 239.

80 Naus, *Analecta Gregoriana*, 108 (1959), 180.

81 "Imperare autem est quidem essentialiter actus rationis; imperans enim ordinat eum cui imperat, ad aliquid agendum, intimando vel denuntiando . . . et talis intimatio exprimitur per verbum imperativi modi; puta cum alicui dicitur: Fac hoc. . . . Unde relinquitur quod imperare sit actus rationis, praesupposito actu voluntatis, in cujus virtute ratio movet per imperium ad exercitium actus" (Aquinas, *S.T.*, I-II, q. 17, a. 1).

82 Naus, *Analecta Gregoriana*, 108 (1959), 181; citing Aquinas, *S.T.*, I-II, q. 16, aa. 1, 4.

83 H. Renard, *The Modern Schoolman*, 24 (1947), 89.

84 Naus, *Analecta Gregoriana*, 108 (1959), 177.

85 Suarez, *O.O.*, Vol. IV: *Tractatus Quinque ad Primam Secundae D. Thomas*, Tract. II: *De Voluntario et Involuntario*, Disp. IX, Sec. III, para. 4.

[86] "Ce jugement pratique, qu'on peut appeler *praeceptum* ou *imperium*, détermine mon choix, *electio*. Le choix est ainsi un acte véritablement humain, procédant d'une volunté dirigée, cette fois encore, par la raison" (Odon Lottin, O.S.B., *Morale Fondamentale* [Tournai: Desclée de Brouwer, 1954], p. 47). [Italics in original.]

[87] Aquinas, *S.T.*, I-II, q. 11, a. 2.

[88] *Ibid.*, a. 1, ad 3.

[89] H. Renard, *The Modern Schoolman*, 24 (1947), 91.

[90] Naus, *Analecta Gregoriana*, 108 (1959), 175.

[91] H. Renard, *The Modern Schoolman*, 24 (1947), 91.

[92] "Ubi notandum est, quod sicut res ceterae, quoad existentiam, pendent ab agente, non quoad essentiam, essentiae enim sunt aeternae . . . ita etiam lex, quoad existentiam, pendet a legislatore; non enim erit lex, nisi dictetur ab eo, qui habet auctoritatem. At quoad essentiam non pendet, quod enim lex obliget est quid aeternum, et immutabile, et participatio quaedam legis aeternae Dei . . ." (Bellarminus, *De Laicis*, Cap. XI, pp. 466-67).

[93] "His positis haec censeo in re probabiliora. Primum ante electionem antecedere judicium practicum, et non alium actum ab illo distinctum, qui possit dici imperium. Hoc supra dixi et probavi. Secundum post electionem illam, quae abstrahit ab executione ante usum, natura saltem praecedere, et necessarium esse aliud judicium magis practicum in hoc distinctum a judicio, quod praecedit electionem, quia immediatius attingit opus, et omnes determinatas circumstantias necessarias ad operis executionem. Et hinc est quod vehementius etiam movet voluntatem non tam virtute sua, quam virtute electionis jam factae: ratio est, quia ante omnem actum voluntatis debet antecedere judicium intellectus illi consentaneum, a quo dirigatur et illuminetur: sed usus activus est actus voluntatis, quid aliquid addit illi electioni jam factae . . . Et hoc judicium merito dici solet practice practicum, seu omnino practicum . . ." (Suarez, *De Voluntario et Involuntario*, Disp. IX, Sec. III, para. 4).

[94] Raoul de Scorraille, S.J., *François Suarez de la Compagnie de Jésus* (2 vols. Paris: P. Lethielleux, 1912-1913), I, 174.

[95] "Quod autem illi transgressores, per se loquendo, non peccent, probatur . . ." (Suarez, *De Legibus*, Lib. III, Cap. XXII, Sec. 6). See Chapter IV, note 24, *supra*, for the continuation of this quotation.

[96] McGarrigle, *American Ecclesiastical Review*, 127 (1952), 440-41.

[97] Suarez, *De Legibus*, Lib. V, Cap. IV, Sec. 13.

[98] Vermeersch, *Theologia Moralis*, I, 148; Dunn, *Theological Studies*, 18 (1957), 42.

[99] ". . . lex naturae habet quod ille qui peccat puniatur . . ." (Aquinas, *S.T.*, I-II, q. 95, a. 2).

[100] ". . . videtur implicare contradictionem, posse Principes obligare ad poenam, et non ad culpam, siquidem culpa et poena relativa sunt" (Bellarminus, *De Laicis*, Cap. XI, p. 469).

[101] Cooley, editor, Blackstone's *Commentaries*, I, 57-58, n. 12.

[102] McGarrigle, *American Ecclesiastical Review*, 127 (1952), 431.

[103] "Vindicare enim et ulcisci, et supplicium poscere, atque adeo poenam infligere, neutiquam nisi pro culpa fas est" (Soto, *De Justitia et Jure*, Lib. I, Quaest. VI:

De potestate legis humanae, art. 5: Utrum omnis poenalis lex obliget ad culpam, an non, fol. 20a).

[104] Bellarminus, *De Laicis*, Cap. XI, p. 466.

[105] "Omnis autem poena si justa est, peccati poena est, et supplicium nominatur . . ." (Augustine, *De Libero Arbitrio*, Lib. III, Cap. XVIII, Sec. 51; P.L. 32:1296).

[106] "Nam, ut dicitur Deut. 25: *Secundum mensuram delicti erit plagarum modus, et . . .* August . . . *Omnis poena, si justa est, peccati poena est, et supplicium nominatur*; et ideo culpam et poenam correlativa esse dixit Gerson . . . ergo, cum lex poenalis juste puniat, supponit culpam in transgressione ejus. Verumtamen etiam haec ratio non urget; nam, licet poena in quadam significatione rigorosa dicat ordinem ad culpam, tamen latius sumpta pro quocumque supplicio, vel damno aut incommodo potest juste inferri propter justam causam sine culpa. . . . Vel etiam dici potest, licet omnis poena sit propter culpam, non tamen semper esse propter culpam contra Deum, sed interdum sufficere culpam quasi civilem et humanam" (Suarez, *De Legibus*, Lib. V, Cap. III, Sec. 7). [Italics in original.]

[107] Aquinas, *S.T.*, II-II, q. 108, a. 4.

[108] Suarez, *De Legibus*, Lib. V, Cap. III, Sec. 7.

[109] ". . . non debetur nisi peccato . . ." (Aquinas, *S.T.*, II-II, q. 108, a. 4).

[110] See Dunn, *Theological Studies*, 18 (1957), 46.

[111] *Ibid.*

[112] ". . . ad conditionem, sub qua poenam comminatur, in conscientia non obliget, respectu cujus conditionis dicitur pure poenalis, licet respectu ipsius poenae efficaciam habeat obligandi . . ." (Suarez, *De Legibus*, Lib. V, Cap. IV, Sec. 13).

[113] "Mixta vero dicitur, quae simul moralis est et poenalis, et duo praecepta virtute includit, unum, faciendi vel vitandi talem actum; aliud, sustinendi talem poenam si id non fiat . . . Lex autem pure poenalis dicitur, quae solum habet unum praeceptum quasi hypotheticum sustinendi talem poenam, vel incommodum, si hoc vel illud fiat, etiamsi de actu substrato tali conditioni praeceptum non imponatur" (*ibid.*, Sec. 2).

[114] Mo. REV. STAT. § 196.130 (1959).

[115] Mo. REV. STAT. § 196.45 (1959).

[116] See Noonan; in *Proceedings*, p. 267.

[117] "Miram et parum congruam dixerimus voluntatem legislatoris qui parti principali legis, i.e. normae negaret vim obligandi, ut hanc propriam faceret partis secundariae quae est sanctio exterior" (Vermeersch, *Theologia Moralis*, I, 148).

CHAPTER VIII

[1] Dunn, *Theological Studies*, 18 (1957), 48.

[2] *Ibid.*, 47.

[3] Holmes, *The Common Law* (Boston: Little, 1881), p. 38.

[4] Robert J. Kelly, S.J., professor of moral theology, Saint Mary's College, St. Marys, Kansas, in a letter to the author, June 1961.

5 Statement in a letter to the author, August 1961.

6 *Ibid.*

7 For exemplification in the fiduciary duty of corporate control, see Bayne, *The Deep Rock Doctrine Reconsidered,* 19 FORDHAM L. REV. 43 (1950) ; *The Fiduciary Duty of Management: The Concept in the Courts,* 35 U. DET. L.J. 561 (1958) ; *A Philosophy of Corporate Control,* 112 U. PA. L. REV. 22 (1963) ; *Corporate Control as a Strict Trustee,* 53 GEO. L.J., forthcoming (1965) ; *A Definition of Corporate Control,* 9 ST. LOUIS U.L.J., forthcoming (1965) ; *The Sale-of-Control Quandary,* 51 CORNELL L.Q., forthcoming (1965). And the same is true in the matter of shareholder rights in the government of the corporation. See Bayne, *Around and Beyond the SEC—The Disenfranchised Stockholder,* 26 IND. L.J. 207 (1951) ; Bayne, Caplin, Emerson, and Latcham, 40 VA. L. REV. 387 (1954) ; Bayne, *Law, the Proxy and Social Responsibility,* 34 MICH. S.B.J. 36 (1955) ; *The Basic Rationale of "Proper ject,"* 34 U. DET. L.J. 575 (1957) ; Bayne and Emerson, *The Virginia-Carolina Chemical Corporation Proxy Contest: A Case-Study of the SEC's New Rule 240.14a-11 and Schedule 14B,* 57 COLUM. L. REV. 801 (1957).

8 James Barr Ames, *Law and Morals,* 22 HARV. L. REV. 97, 100 (1908).

9 Holmes, *The Common Law,* p. 4.

10 William L. Prosser and Young B. Smith, *Cases and Materials on Torts* (3rd ed. Brooklyn: Foundation Press, 1962), p. 1.

11 In addition to Holmes's work, that of Wigmore and Ames, both highly respected common-law commentators, is most rewarding: John H. Wigmore, *Responsibility for Tortious Acts: Its History,* 7 HARV. L. REV. 315, 383, 441 (1894) ; Ames, 22 HARV. L. REV. 97-100 (1908). See also Nathan Isaacs, *Fault and Liability,* 31 HARV. L. REV. 954, 965 (1918).

12 Hob. 134, 80 Eng. Rep. 284 (K.B. 1617).

13 Prosser and Smith, *Cases and Materials on Torts,* p. 5.

14 *Brown v. Kendall,* 60 Mass. 292 (1850).

15 *Ibid.*

16 256 U.S. 335, 343 (1921).

17 *Randall v. Shelton,* 293 S.W.2d 559, 562 (Ky. Ct. App. 1956).

18 Holmes, *The Common Law,* p. 38.

19 *Ibid.,* p. 37.

20 Wigmore, 7 HARV. L. REV. at 442 (1894).

21 *Id.* at 443.

22 *Id.* at 444.

23 Ames, 22 HARV. L. REV. 99 (1908).

24 Y.B. 7 Edw. IV, f2, pl.2.

25 *Donnelly v. United States,* 228 U.S. 243 (1913).

26 *Id.* at 272.

27 *Id.* at 273.

28 *Id.* at 273-74. The court cited supporting cases from many jurisdictions.

29 Lord Kenyon, C.J., *Rex v. Eriswell,* 3 T.R. 721 (1790).

30 *Donnelly v. United States,* 228 U.S. at 276-77. The quotation is taken from *Mima Queen and Child v. Hepburn,* 7 Cranch 290, 295, 296, 297 (1813). [Excisions in the original by Mr. Justice Pitney.]

[31] See page 143, *supra.*

[32] Holmes, *The Common Law*, p. 38.

[33] *Ibid.*, p. 1.

[34] Kelly. See page 143, *supra.*

[35] *Dougherty v. Stepp*, 18 N.C. 370, 371 (1835).

[36] *Louisville Railway Co. v. Sweeney*, 157 Ky. 620, 163 S.W. 739 (1914).

[37] *Ibid.*

[38] 293 S.W.2d 559 (Ky. Ct. App. 1956).

[39] *Id.* at 560.

[40] *Ibid.*

[41] *Ibid.*

[42] *Id.* at 561.

[43] *Id.* at 562.

[44] *Ibid.*

[45] *Ibid.*

[46] *Kopka v. Bell Telephone Co. of Pennsylvania*, 371 Pa. 444, 91 A.2d 232 (1952).

[47] *Id.* at 235-36.

[48] *Restatement of the Law of Torts* (St. Paul: Am. Law Inst., 1934), § 380, Comment c.

[49] *Restatement of the Law, Second, Torts, Tentative Draft No. 2* (St. Paul: Am. Law Inst., March 1958), p. 1.

[50] Holmes, *The Common Law*, pp. 11-12.

[51] *Vosburg v. Putney*, 80 Wis. 523, 50 N.W. 403 (1891).

[52] *Restatement of the Law, Second, Torts, Tentative Draft No. 1* (St. Paul: Am. Law Inst., April 1957), p. 1.

[53] *Vaughan v. Miller Bros. "101" Ranch Wild West Show*, 109 W. Va. 170, 153 S.E. 289, 290 (1930).

[54] Seymour D. Thompson, *Commentaries on the Law of Negligence* (6 vols. Indianapolis: Bowen, 1901), Vol. I, Sec. 841.

[55] *Rylands v. Fletcher*, in the Exchequer, 3 Hurl. & C. 774 (1865). In the Exchequer Chamber, L.R. 1 Ex. 265 (1866). In the House of Lords, L.R. 3 H.L. 330 (1868).

[56] *Ibid.*

[57] *Ibid.*

[58] 329 Mass. 484, 109 N.E.2d 131 (1952).

[59] [1946] 2 All E.R. 471 (H. of L.).

[60] Prosser and Smith, *Cases and Materials on Torts*, p. 706.

[61] Holmes, *The Common Law*, p. 6.

[62] *Lambert v. Bessey*, T. Raym. 421, 423, 83 Eng. Rep. 220, 221 (1681).

[63] Ames, 22 HARV. L. REV. 99 (1908).

[64] 297 Mass. 323, 8 N.E.2d 769 (1937).

[65] *Id.* at 761.

[66] *Ibid.*

[67] *Id.* at 762.

[68] *Ibid.*

[69] *Ibid.*

[70] *Id.* at 762-63.

[71] *Id.* at 763.

[72] Ames, 22 HARV. L. REV. 99-100 (1908).

[73] *Ryan v. New York Central R.R. Co.,* 35 N.Y. 210 (1866).

[74] *Id.* at 216-17.

[75] *Id.* at 217.

[76] N.Y. CONSERVATION LAW, § 56 ¶ 3.

[77] *Harvey v. Dunlop,* New York Common Law Reports, Hill and Denio, Supplement, 193, 194 (1843).

[78] Ames, 22 HARV. L. REV. 113 (1908).

[79] Holmes, *The Common Law,* p. 38.

## CHAPTER IX

[1] Herron; in *Proceedings,* p. 272; Blackstone, *Commentaries,* I, 95; Dunn, *Theological Studies,* 18 (1957), 49-50.

[2] "Erit autem lex honesta, justa, possibilis, secundum naturam, secundum patriae, consuetudinem, loco, temporique conveniens, necessaria, utilis, manifesta quoque, ne aliquid per obscuritatem in captionem contineat, nullo privato commodo, sed pro communi civium utilitate conscripta" (Isidore of Seville, *Etymologiarum Libri Viginti,* Cap. XXI; P.L. 82:203).

[3] *Zorach v. Clauson,* 343 U.S. 306, 313, 314 (1952).

[4] ". . . dicitur 'honesta,' refertur ad hoc quod religioni congruat . . ." (Aquinas. *S.T.,* I-II, q. 95, a. 3).

[5] 18 PA. STAT. ANN. § 4699.4 (1963).

[6] MASS. GEN. LAWS, ch. 136, § 5 (1958).

[7] 176 F. Supp. 466 (D. Mass. 1959).

[8] 179 F. Supp. 944 (E.D. Pa. 1959).

[9] 362 U.S. 960, 961 (April 25, 1960).

[10] *Crown Kosher Super Market of Mass., Inc. v. Gallagher,* 366 U.S. 617 (1961); *Two Guys from Harrison-Allentown, Inc. v. McGinley,* 366 U.S. 582 (1961).

[11] 220 Md. 117, 151 A.2d 156 (1959).

[12] *Braunfeld v. Gibbons,* 184 F. Supp. 352 (E.D. Pa. 1959), *aff'd sub nom. Braunfeld v. Brown,* 366 U.S. 599 (1961).

[13] *McGowan v. Maryland,* 366 U.S. 420 (1961); *Braunfeld v. Brown,* 366 U.S. 599 (1961).

[14] 314 F2d 89 (2d Cir. 1963).

[15] *Crown Kosher Super Market of Massachusetts, Inc. v. Gallagher,* 176 F. Supp. 466, 475 (D. Mass. 1959).

[16] *McGowan v. Maryland,* 366 U.S. at 568.

[17] *Id.* at 563.

[18] *Braunfeld v. Brown,* 366 U.S. at 613.

[19] *Id.* at 616.

[20] *Sherbert v. Verner,* 374 U.S. 398 (1963). Concurring opinions by Justices Douglas and Stewart. Dissent by Justices Harlan and White.

[21] *Id.* at 404.

[22] *Ibid.*

[23] *Id.*-at 409.

[24] *Id.* at 415. Concurring opinion of Stewart, J.

[25] *Id.* at 415-16.

[26] *Everson v. Board of Education*, 330 U.S. 1, 11 (1947).

[27] *Sherbert v. Verner*, 374 U.S. at 415.

[28] *Id.* at 418.

[29] *Illinois ex rel. McCollum v. Board of Education*, 333 U.S. 203, 210 (1948).

[30] *Ibid.*

[31] *Id.* at 238.

[32] *Zorach v. Clauson*, 343 U.S. 306 (1952). See an excerpt from the opinion on pages 192-93, *supra.*

[33] "Respondeo . . . sicut Augustinus dicit . . . 'non videtur esse lex quae justa non fuerit': Unde inquantum habet de justitia, in tantum habet de virtute legis. In rebus autem humanis dicitur esse aliquid justum ex eo quod est rectum secundum regulam rationis" (Aquinas, *S.T.*, I-II, q. 95, a. 2). Thomas says, commenting on Isidore: "Attenditur enim humana disciplina primum quidem quantum ad ordinem rationis, qui importatur in hoc quod dicitur 'justa'" (*ibid.*, a. 3). ["For human discipline depends first on the order of reason, to which he refers by saying 'just.'"]

[34] Leo XIII, *Social Wellsprings*, I, 123.

[35] Ryan, *American Ecclesiastical Review*, 70 (1924), 409.

[36] Mo. Rev. Stat., § 311.325 (1959); Laws 1959, H.B. No. 248.

[37] *Detroit Free Press*, June 1, 1960, p. 2, col. 1.

[38] Detroit, Mich., Municipal Code, ch. 260, § 24 (1954). Section 36 specified a fine of not more than $100 or sixty days in the Detroit House of Correction or both.

[39] Reference is made to this maxim by Sabetti-Barrett, *Compendium Theologiae Moralis*, p. 92.

[40] Herron; in *Proceedings*, p. 274.

[41] "Secundo, quantum ad facultatem agentium; debet enim esse disciplina conveniens unicuique secundum suam possibilitatem, observata etiam possibilitate naturae. Non enim eadem sunt imponenda pueris, quae imponuntur viris perfectis" (Aquinas, *S.T.*, I-II, q. 95, a. 3).

[42] Arregui, *Summarium Theologiae Moralis*, p. 41.

[43] Davis, *Moral and Pastoral Theology*, II, 193; Vermeersch, *Theologia Moralis*, I, 206 *et seq.*

[44] McGarrigle, *American Ecclesiastical Review*, 127 (1952), 443.

[45] From the form designated "1964 Tangible Personal Property Tax Return of Taxable Values, for State, City and School Taxes (as provided for by Laws of Missouri) City of St. Louis, Mo.," Office of the City Assessor, Room 117, City Hall, St. Louis, Mo.

[46] From a letter to the author, February 15, 1961.

[47] Noldin, *Summa Theologiae Moralis*, I, 234 *et seq.*; Vermeersch, *Theologia Moralis*, I, 135-36.

[48] For a picture of the evil effects of the absence of such knowledge, see Bayne, "Divorcee or Bigamist, Chaos in the Law of Interstate Divorce," *Social Order*, 3 (1953), 387.

[49] INT. REV. CODE of 1954, § 2036(a). For background and history, judicial interpretation and commentary, see *Federal Taxes, Estate and Gift Taxes* (Englewood Cliffs: Prentice-Hall, 1963, permanent edition), paras. 120, 360, *et seq.*; William C. Warren and Stanley S. Surrey, *Federal Estate and Gift Taxation, Cases and Materials* (Brooklyn: Foundation Press, 1956), p. 435 *et seq. et passim.*

[50] Jacob Rabkin and Mark H. Johnson, *Federal Income, Gift and Estate Taxation* (7 vols. Albany: Bender, 1962), Vol. IV, Sec. 57.06.

[51] Warren and Surrey, *Taxation*, p. 435.

[52] *Ibid.*, p. 437.

[53] 281 U.S. 238 (1930).

[54] 283 U.S. 782 (1931), *affirming* 41 F.2d 732 (7th Cir. 1930).

[55] 283 U.S. 783 (1931), *reversing* 44 F.2d 902 (8th Cir. 1930).

[56] 283 U.S. 784 (1931), *reversing* 43 F.2d 277 (7th Cir. 1930).

[57] 74 *Cong. Rec.* 7078 (1931).

[58] 303 U.S. 303 (1938).

[59] 335 U.S. 632 (1949).

[60] 63 Stat. 891, 896 (1949), as amended by 64 Stat. 770 (1950), and 65 Stat. 567 (1951); Reg. 105 §§ 81.18, 81.19, as amended by T.D. 5936 (Oct. 6, 19 ); see *Myron Selznick Estate*, 15 T.C. 716, *aff'd*, 195 F.2d 735 (9th Cir. 1952); *Morristown Trust Co. v. Manning*, 104 F. Supp. 621 (D.N.J. 1951), *aff'd*, 200 F.2d 194 (3d Cir.), *cert. denied*, 345 U.S. 939 (1952).

[61] Int. Rev. Code of 1939, § 811(c)(1), as amended by Technical Changes Act of 1953, 67 Stat. 623 (1953).

[62] INT. REV. CODE of 1954, § 2036(b).

[63] INT. REV. CODE of 1954, § 61.

[64] *LoBue v. Commissioner*, 351 U.S. 243 (1956).

[65] *Commissioner v. LoBue*, 223 F.2d 367 (3d Cir. 1955).

[66] 363 U.S. 278 (1960).

[67] *Id.* at 289.

[68] 363 U.S. 299 (1960).

[69] *Kaiser v. United States*, 262 F.2d 367 (7th Cir. 1958).

[70] *Kaiser v. United States*, 158 F. Supp. 865 (E.D. Wisc. 1958).

[71] 278 U.S. 282 (1929).

[72] 77 F. Supp. 186 (Ct. Cl. 1948).

[73] 255 F.2d 193 (8th Cir. 1958).

[74] "Essentialia legis quatenus est ad bonum commune" (Vermeersch, *Theologia Moralis*, I, 134).

[75] ". . . refertur ad hoc quod expediat saluti: ut necessitas referatur ad remotionem malorum, utilitas ad consecutionem bonorum . . . lex ordinatur ad bonum commune . . ." (Aquinas, *S.T.*, I-II, q. 95, a. 3).

[76] "Injustae autem sunt leges . . . per contrarietatem ad bonum humanum e contrario praedictis: vel ex fine, sicut cum aliquis praesidens leges imponit onerosas subditis, non pertinentes ad utilitatem communem, sed magis ad propriam cupiditatem vel gloriam . . . vel etiam ex forma, puta cum inaequaliter onera multitudini dispensantur, etiamsi ordinentur ad bonum commune. . . . Unde tales leges non obligant in foro conscientiae . . ." (*ibid.*, q. 96, a. 4).

[77] ". . . iusta, seu servet normam aequalitatis et nullius ius laedat . . ." (Vermeersch, *Theologia Moralis*, I, 134 [marginal note]).

[78] "Ad ipsius legis valorem requiritur . . . ut sit justa, i.e. ut, quantum bonum commune permittat, iustitiam distributivam in bonis et oneribus communibus partiendis servet . . ." (*ibid.*).

[79] *Minneapolis and St. L. R. Co. v. Beckwith*, 129 U.S. 26, 28-29 (1889).

[80] *Yick Wo v. Hopkins*, 118 U.S. 356, 373-74 (1886).

[81] SAN FRANCISCO, CALIF., ORDINANCES, Order 1569 (1880).

[82] *Yick Wo v. Hopkins*, 118 U.S. at 359.

[83] *Id.* at 369.

[84] *Id.* at 373.

[85] *Bush v. Orleans Parish School Board*, 187 F. Supp. 42, 43 (E.D. La. 1960).

[86] 13 LA. REV. STAT. §§ 17:337, 17:347-1, and 17:347-2 (1963).

[87] 13 LA. REV. STAT. § 17:347-5 (1963).

[88] La. Acts 1960, Nos. 495 and 542.

[89] 13 LA. REV. STAT. §§ 17:336, 17:337, and 17:341 *et seq.* (1963).

[90] *Brown v. Board of Education*, 347 U.S. 483 (1954).

[91] *Bush v. Orleans Parish School Board*, 187 F. Supp. 42, 44 (E.D. La. 1960).

[92] *Id.* at 43.

[93] *Ibid.*

[94] *Barbier v. Connolly*, 113 U.S. 27, 31 (1885).

[95] G. Renard, *La théorie des "Leges mere poenales,"* pp. 75-76.

[96] "Quare ipse D. [*sic*] Renard, qui leges mere poenales tam absolute excludere videtur, pedibus ire cogitur in sententiam D'Hulst, secundum quam de multis statutis minoribus valet istud: 'De minimis non curat praetor' " (Vermeersch, *Theologia Moralis*, I, 151).

[97] *Swicegood v. Feezell*, 29 Tenn. App. 348, 196 S.W.2d 713, 716, *cert. denied*, October 12, 1946.

[98] *Frank v. Wilson & Co.*, 172 F.2d 712, 715 (7th Cir. 1949).

[99] 28 U.S.C. §§ 201, 216(b), 52 Stat. 1060 (1938).

[100] *Frank v. Wilson & Co.*, 172 F.2d at 715.

[101] *Anderson v. Mt. Clemens Pottery Co.*, 328 U.S. 680 (1946).

[102] *Id.* at 692.

[103] *Frank v. Wilson & Co.*, 172 F.2d at 716.

[104] *Bristol-Myers Co. v. Lit Bros., Inc.*, 336 Pa. 81, 6 A.2d 843 (1939).

[105] Pennsylvania Fair Trade Act, Pa. Laws 1935, No. 266, § 1, 73 PA. STAT. ANN. § 7-8 (1960).

[106] *Bristol-Myers Co. v. Lit Bros., Inc.*, 6 A.2d at 847.

[107] *Id.* at 848.

[108] *Ibid.* See also *Porter v. Rushing*, 65 F. Supp. 759 (W.D. Ark. 1946).

[109] Aquinas, *S.T.*, I-II, q. 96, a. 6; Rodrigo, *Praelectiones*, II, 257-60.

[110] See L. J. Riley, *The History, Nature and Use of* Epikeia *in Moral Theology* (Washington: Catholic Univ. of Am. Press, 1948).

[111] *Ibid.*, p. 137.

[112] "Utrum ei qui subditur legi, liceat praeter verba legis agere" (Aquinas, *S.T.*, I-II, q. 96, a. 6). This entire article with objections and responses to objections should be read for a fuller understanding of the subject of *epikeia*.

[113] "Respondeo . . . quod . . . omnis lex ordinatur ad communem hominum salutem, et intantum obtinet vim et rationem legis; secundum vero quod ab hoc deficit, virtutem obligandi non habet. Unde Jurisperitus dicit . . . quod 'nulla ratio juris aut aequitatis benignitas patitur, ut quae salubriter pro salute hominum introducuntur, ea nos duriori interpretatione contra ipsorum commodum perducamus ad severitatem.' Contingit autem multoties quod aliquid observari communi saluti est utile ut in pluribus, tamen in aliquibus casibus est maxime nocivum. Quia igitur legislator non potest omnes singulares casus intueri, proponit legem secundum ea quae in pluribus accidunt, ferens intentionem suam ad communem utilitatem. Unde si emergat casus in quo observatio talis legis sit damnosa communi saluti, non est observanda; sicut si in civitate obsessa statuatur lex quod portae civitatis maneant clausae, hoc est utile communi saluti ut in pluribus; si tamen contingat casus quod hostes insequantur aliquos cives, per quos civitas conservatur, damnosissimum esset civitati, nisi eis portae aperirentur; et ideo in tali casu essent portae aperiendae, contra verba legis, ut servaretur utilitas communis, quam legislator intendit" (*ibid.*).

[114] See *ibid.*, II-II, q. 120, a. 1.

[115] "Sed tamen hoc est considerandum, quod si observatio legis secundum verba non habet subitum periculum, cui oporteat statim occurri, non pertinet ad quemlibet ut interpretetur quid sit utile civitati et quid inutile civitati; sed hoc solum pertinet ad principes, qui propter hujusmodi casus habent auctoritatem in legibus dispensandi. Si vero sit subitum periculum, non patiens tantam moram ut ad superiorem recurri possit, ipsa necessitas dispensationem habet annexam, quia necessitas non subditur legi" (*ibid.*, I-II, q. 96, a. 6).

[116] *Tedla v. Ellman*, 280 N.Y. 124, 19 N.E.2d 987 (1939).

[117] Vehicle and Traffic Law of 1929, § 85, subd. 6, repealed by L. 1957, c.698, § 5.

[118] *Tedla v. Ellman*, 19 N.E.2d at 989.

[119] *Ibid.*

[120] See Heinrich A. Rommen, *The Natural Law* (St. Louis: Herder, 1949), p. 213. See also Herron; in *Proceedings*, p. 275.

[121] Aristotle, *The Nicomachean Ethics*, Bk. V, Chap. X, translated by J. A. K. Thomson ("The Ethics of Aristotle," London: G. Allen, 1953), pp. 145-47.

[122] ". . . oportet distinguere inter legis interpretationem et propriam epiikiam seu aequitatem: multo enim latius patet interpretatio legis quam epiikia; comparantur enim tanquam superius et inferius: omnis enim epiikia est legis interpretatio: non vero e converso omnis interpretaio legis est epiikia. Notavit distinctionem hanc Cajetanus . . . ait, saepe vel potius semper leges indigere interpretatione propter verborum obscuritatem, vel ambiguitatem, aut aliam similem causam; non tamen omnem hujusmodi interpretationem esse epiikiam, sed illam solum per quam interpretamur legem deficere in aliquo particulari propter universale, id est, quia lex universaliter lata est, et in aliquo particulari ita deficit, ut juste in illo servari non possit" (Suarez, *De Legibus*, Lib. II, Cap. XVI, Sec. 4).

[123] *Tedla v. Ellman*, 19 N.E.2d at 990.

[124] *Id.* at 991.

[125] "Est igitur . . . legis applicatio *secundum aequum et bonum*, secundum quod praesumitur legislatorem nolle legem suam in circumstantiis extraordinariis, quas non praevidit, urgere, eumque exceptionem facturum fuisse, si talis casus ipsius menti observatus fuisset" (Lehmkuhl, *Theologiae Moralis*, I, 147). [Emphasis in original.]

[126] "Interpretation of Statutes," *Restatement of the Law of Torts* (1934), § 286, Comment c.

[127] Herron; in *Proceedings*, p. 271.

[128] Woroniecki, *Angelicum*, 18 (1941), 384.

[129] Noonan; in *Proceedings*, p. 270; Dunn, *Theological Studies*, 18 (1957), 58.

[130] Dunn, *Theological Studies*, 18 (1957), 58.

[131] "Si vero sit subitum periculum, non patiens tantam moram ut ad superiorem recurri possit, ipsa necessitas dispensationem habet annexam, quia necessitas non subditur legi" (Aquinas, *S.T.*, I-II, q. 96, a. 6).


CHAPTER X

[1] GROSSE POINTE, MICH., ORDINANCES, Ordinance No. 74 to amend No. 45, Sec. 8, adopted January 17, 1955.

[2] Heribert Jone, O.F.M.Cap., *Moral Theology* (Westminster: Newman, 1945), p. 49.

[3] Dunn, *Theological Studies*, 18 (1957), 59.

[4] *Ibid.*

SELECT BIBLIOGRAPHY

Ames, James Barr. "Law and Morals," *Harvard Law Review*, 22 (1908), 97-113.

Aquinas, Thomas, O.P., Saint. *Opera Omnia*. 25 vols. Parma: Fiaccadori, 1852-1873. Vol. II: *Summa Theologica*, I-II.

Bayne, David C., S.J. "The Fiduciary Duty of Management: The Concept in the Courts," *University of Detroit Law Journal*, 35 (1958), 561-94.

———— "*Kaiser-Frazer v. Otis*: A Legal and Moral Analysis," *De Paul Law Review*, 2 (1953), 131-93.

———— "The Lawyer-Moralist Looks at the Profession," *Saint Louis University Law Journal*, 8 (1963), 215-31.

———— "The Natural Law for Lawyers—A Primer," *De Paul Law Review*, 5 (1956), 159-215.

———— "The Supreme Court and the Natural Law," *De Paul Law Review*, 1 (1952), 216-42.

Bellarminus, Robertus, S.J., Saint. *Disputationes de Controversiis Christianae Fidei*. 9 vols. Ingolstadt: Sartorius, Vols. I-VI, 1599; Vols. VII-IX, 1593. Vol. III (Liber III): *De Laicis sive Saecularibus*.

Davitt, Thomas E., S.J. *The Nature of Law*. St. Louis: B. Herder Book Co., 1951.

Dunn, Edward T., S.J. "In Defense of the Penal Law," *Theological Studies*, 18 (1957), 41-59.

Ford, John C., S.J. "The Fundamentals of Holmes' Juristic Philosophy," *Fordham Law Review*, 11 (1942), 255-75.

Herron, Matthew, T.O.R. *The Binding Force of Civil Laws*. North Miami: Brower Press, 1952.

Higgins, Frank Bernard, S.J. "The Penal Law Theory of Suarez." Unpublished Master of Arts thesis. Department of philosophy, Saint Louis University, 1957.

263

Isaacs, Nathan. "Fault and Liability," *Harvard Law Review*, 31 (1918), 954-79.

Land, Philip S., S.J. "Evading Taxes—Can't Be Justified in Conscience," *Social Order*, 5 (1955), 121-25.

———— "Tax Obligations According to Natural Law," *Saint Louis University Law Journal*, 4 (1956), 129-46.

Litt, F. "Les Lois Dites Purement Pénales," *Revue Ecclésiastique de Liége*, 30 (1938-1939), 141-56, 359-72.

Lucey, Francis E., S.J. "Natural Law and American Legal Realism: Their Respective Contributions to a Theory of Law in a Democratic Society," *Georgetown Law Journal*, 30 (1942), 493-533.

McGarrigle, Francis J., S.J. "It's All Right, If You Can Get Away with It," *American Ecclesiastical Review*, 127 (1952), 431-49.

Murphy, Kathleen E. *De Laicis; or, The Treatise on Civil Government.* New York: Fordham University Press, 1928.

Naus, John Erwin, S.J. "The Foundation of Obligation in Suarez." Unpublished Master of Arts thesis. Department of philosophy, Saint Louis University, 1949. Pp. 118.

Palmer, Ben W. "Hobbes, Holmes and Hitler," *American Bar Association Journal*, 31 (1945), 569-73.

"The Problem of Penal Law," *Proceedings of the Tenth Annual Convention of the Catholic Theological Society of America.* New York: The Catholic Theological Society of America, 1955. Pp. 259-84. Lawrence J. Riley, pp. 259-63; Michael Noonan, S.M., pp. 263-71; Matthew Herron, T.O.R., pp. 271-82; John J. Lynch, S.J., 'Digest of the Discussion,' pp. 282-84.

Renard, Henri, S.J. "The Functions of Intellect and Will in the Act of Free Choice," *The Modern Schoolman*, 24 (1947), 85-92.

Riley, L. J. *The History, Nature and Use of Epikeia in Moral Theology.* Washington: Catholic University of America Press, 1948.

Rodrigo, Lucius, S.J. *Praelectiones Theologico-Morales Comillenses.* 4 vols. Sal Terrae: Santander, 1944. Vol. II: *Tractatus De Legibus.*

Schuett, John T., S.J. "A Study of the Legal Philosophy of Jerome N. Frank," *University of Detroit Law Journal*, 35 (1957), 28-69.

Suarez, Francis, S.J. *Opera Omnia.* 28 vols. Paris: Vives, 1856-1878. Vols. V-VI: *De Legibus.*

Vangheluwe, Victor. "De Lege Mere Poenali, Inquisitio Historica de Origine Doctrinae Ejusque Evolutione usque ad Medium Saeculum XVIum," *Ephemerides Theologicae Lovanienses*, 16 (1939), 383-429.

Vermeersch, Arthur, S.J. *Theologia Moralis*, fourth edition. 3 vols. Rome: Gregorian University Press, 1947.

Wigmore, John H. "Responsibility for Tortious Acts: Its History," *Harvard Law Review*, 7 (1894), 315-37, 383-405, 441-63.

Infirmities, unavoidable in any human
system of law, 154-63. *See also*
Civil law, necessary infirmities of
Inheritance, nonculpable loss of. *See
Poena* (as hardship)
Initiation fees, excise taxes on, 8-9
Insanity, as bearing upon liability,
*McGuire v. Almy*, 180-83
Integration, in Louisiana schools, 213-15
Intellect
as final cause, 108, 113, 116, 120-21
as formal cause, 112-13, 114, 116, 118-20
as source of law in Thomistic
psychology, 102-07
function in Suarezian psychology,
41-45
functions in Thomistic psychology of
lawmaking process
deliberation on means to end, 110-11
final appraisal, 118
*imperium* (command), 113, 114-18
judgment of feasibility of the end,
109-10
perception of the end, 108-09
practical judgment (*liberum
arbitrium*) in selection of means,
112-15, 116-20
in the young Suarez, 121-22
interaction with will in psychology
of legislation, 105, 106-07, 112-14,
116-17
Intent
as basis of liability, 148-50
definition of, 171-74
in *Restatement of the Law, Second,
of Torts, Tentative Draft No. 1,*
173-74
in *Vosburg v. Putney*, 172-74
to legislate and to oblige, confusion
of, 202, 220
twentieth-century refinement of
notion of, 173-74
*See also* Trespass
Intention
implied, to oblige, alleged *indicia* of,
34-38, 47-48, 62-64
of a parliament, 36

interpretation of, through *epikeia*,
220-25
legislative as determining obligation
(Suarez), 47-49, 53
normally to presume obligation, 58-59
not to legislate, 202, 220
of end, 110
order of, 113-14, 116-17, 118
Inter vivos transfers, 206-08
Interaction of intellect and will, in
lawmaking process, 105, 106-07,
112-14, 116-17. *See also*
Psychology of lawmaking process
Interdict, 50
Interpretation
of a law, *epikeia* as species of, 223-24
statutory
difficulty of, in taxation, 205-10
fundamental rule of, regarding
liability, 205
Inversion of purposes, in purely penal
sanction, 139-40
Iorio, 37-38; 239, nn. 18, 21
Ireland, moral tone of its constitution,
60-61
Irregularity, ecclesiastical, as hardship,
50
Isaacs, 255, n. 11; 264
Isidore of Seville, 191-92; 195; 201;
205; 210-11; 257, n. 2

Janssen, 35; 93; 238, n. 13; 247, n. 5
Jefferson, 61
Johnson, Rabkin and, 206; 259, n. 50
Jone, 230; 262, n. 2
Judgment of intellect in selection of
legislation, 109-21
in young Suarez, 121-22
"Juridic" guilt, 51, 124

Kellogg, 8
Kelly, 143; 157; 163; 165; 243, n. 2;
247, nn. 55, 56, 58; 254, n. 4;
256, n. 34
Kenrick, 8
Kinds of law. *See* Law, kinds of
Klubertanz, 252, n. 79

IMPRIMI POTEST Linus J. Thro, S.J., Provincial of the Missouri Province, September 15, 1964. NIHIL OBSTAT John B. Amberg, S.J., *Censor deputatus*, October 15, 1965. IMPRIMATUR Most Reverend Cletus F. O'Donnell, J.C.D., Vicar General, Archdiocese of Chicago, October 19, 1965. THE NIHIL OBSTAT AND IMPRIMATUR ARE OFFICIAL DECLARATIONS THAT A BOOK IS FREE OF DOCTRINAL OR MORAL ERROR. NO IMPLICATION IS CONTAINED THEREIN THAT THOSE WHO HAVE GRANTED THE NIHIL OBSTAT AND IMPRIMATUR AGREE WITH THE CONTENTS, OPINIONS, OR STATEMENTS EXPRESSED.

*About this book*

*Conscience, Obligation, and the Law* was designed by William Nicoll of EDIT, INC. It was set in the composing room of LOYOLA UNIVERSITY PRESS. The text is 12 on 14 Bodoni Book; the reduced matter, 10 on 12; and the notes, 8 on 10. The display type is Bodoni Book (Mono 875).

It was printed by PHOTOPRESS, INC., on WARREN'S sixty-pound English Finish paper and bound by A. C. ENGDAHL AND COMPANY, INC., in BANCROFT cloth.